Ina Rösing

SHAMANIC TRANCE AND AMNESIA

With the Shamans of the
Changpa Nomads in Ladakhi Changthang

Collaborators:
Sonam Norboo Spurkhapa
Tsultim Kubet
Sonam Wangchok
Thinley Gyurmet

English translation:
Jane Miller

Music transcription:
Jarkko Niemi

Layout and design:
Silvia Gray

Concept Publishing Company, New Delhi

Cataloging in Publication Data—DK
Courtesy: D.K. Agencies (P) Ltd. < docinfo@dkagencies.com >

Rösing, Ina, 1942-
    [Trance, Besessenheit und Amnesie. English]
    Shamanic trance and Amnesia : with the Shamans of the Changpa
nomads in Ladakhi Changthang / Ina Rösing ; collaborators, Sonam
Norboo Spurkhapa ... [et al.] ; English translation, Jane Miller.
            p. cm.
    Translated from German.
    Includes bibliographical references (p.   )
    ISBN 8180692477

    1. Changpa (Indic people)—Rites and ceremonies. 2. Changpa (Indic
people)—Religion. 3. Shamanism—India—Ladakh. 4. Ladakh (India)—
Religious life and customs. 5. Shamanism—Chang Tang Platea (China
and India). I. Miller, Jane. II. Title.

DDC 305.800 954 6   21

Original German Edition:
Trance, Besessenheit und Amnesie.
Bei den Schamanen der Changpa-Nomaden im ladakhischen Changthang,
2003.
Herbert Weishaupt Verlag, A-8342 Gnas
e-mail: verlag@weishaupt.at
ISBN 3-7059-0174-5

English edition is published in India

ISBN-81-8069-247-7

2006

Published and Printed by
Ashok Kumar Mittal
Concept Publishing Company
A/15-16, Commercial Block, Mohan Garden
NEW DELHI-110059 (India)

Phones : 25351460, 25351794
Fax : +91-11-25357103
Email : publishing@conceptpub.com

This book is
dedicated to
Prof. A. Rahman, Delhi,
for his expertise, wisdom and friendship;
for the most important person in India to me

PREFACE

This book focuses on the shamans of the Changpa nomads in the Ladakhi highlands of Changthang. According to their social structure and their religious and ritual tradition (Buddhism and shamanism), the Changpa nomads are culturally Tibetan. Modernity, which has reached even their remote world, is dramatically challenging the very basis of their existence and lifestyle.

It is the traditional healers, the shamans, who see most clearly the "sickness" of modernity. They see this new era in a visionary trance when possessed by a *lha*, a god. If one listens to the chants during their trance – where they speak of so much more violence in our present day ("more blood flows down the valleys") – one recognises their admonitions as remarkably pertinent. (I completed the book shortly after 11 September 2001.) The trance of the Ladakhi shamans is followed by a hermetic amnesia specific to that event. In the present study, I will describe the ways in which one can understand and interpret the shamans – despite their amnesia – and their means of bridging the old and new era, thereby deciphering their message to us.

ACKNOWLEDGEMENTS

Firstly, I would like to thank all Ladakhi shamans who allowed me to share somé of their knowledge by permitting my participation in their healing rituals and through conversations and instructions – above all Lhapa *Sonam Murup* (†) and Lhapa *Thundup*. Many thanks also to everyone else in Ladakh who allowed me to talk to them – every conversation (all of them tape-recorded) has given me more insight into religion and everyday life in Ladakh.

Most especially, thanks are due to my most important Ladakhi collaborators: *Sonam Norboo Spurkhapa*, *Tsultim Kubet* (who tragically died in February 2001) as well as *Sonam Wangchuk* and *Thinley Gyurmet*.

In Germany, first and foremost, I have to thank *Dr. Hans Ulrich Pfeilsticker*, *Prof. Dr. Reinhardt Rüdel* and *Dipl. Ing. Peter Fa Tkaczyk*. Without their support I would not have compiled this book:

(1) It was the digital and editing skills of *Hans Ulrich Pfeilsticker*, who instantly cured me of my "photo-fatigue", induced by 20 years of Andean and 10 years of Himalayan research. Without altering or interfering with the context of the photographs, *Hans-Ulrich Pfeilsticker* improved them considerably.

(2) *Reinhardt Rüdel* has been involved with my Himalayan research from the very beginning. Not only has he read and discussed with me all articles and accounts for my various publications, but he has also tirelessly encouraged me in writing this book which initially was only to be a book of pictures. Without his encouragement this book would never have been produced. Furthermore, *Reinhardt Rüdel* has repeatedly found ways and means to make up financial shortfalls in my Ladakh research, without which I would not have been able to proceed. In particular, it was he who made possible my collaboration with *Hans-Ulrich Pfeilsticker* for one year. For all this I express my deepest gratitude.

(3) Equally, I am most indebted to *Peter Fa Tkaczyk*. I would not have undertaken a second Changthang expedition without a "German" companion, and without the expedition I would not have been able to write this book. I needed to be accompanied not only to be sheltered from the unremitting friendliness and curiosity of the nomads and the thoughtfulness of my Ladakhi collaborators (both consistently hindering me on the first trip to Changthang from protocol writing, which is after all one of the essential field trip tasks) but also to alleviate the excessive workload of documentation and to endeavour to avoid some of the rigours of my first Changthang expedition. Altogether Fa's assistance was invaluable – his presence enabled me to retire alone to write, he took care of the equipment and assisted with the organisation of the work, writing up notes and monitoring the tape recordings. He also endured the same tribulations – including illness. I thank him very much.

I wish to say a particular thank you to a further colleague, *Prof. Dr. Jarkko Niemi* of the Department of Music Anthropology, University of Tamere, Finland: he transcribed for me a few bars of a shamanic song. I am delighted to include this exquisite piece of work in this book (see Appendix D).

A very big thanks also to my wonderful team at the University of Ulm, without whom I could not have taken leave to visit Ladakh, Changthang or any other destinations (they maintain tight control over my small institute), nor could I have completed any other scientific research: *Silvia Gray, Beate Graßdorf-Mendoza, Edith Robinson-Kollmetz* and *Ursula Wolf*.

Many thanks to the institutions that have facilitated this research: the *Land Baden-Württemberg* by means of a highly endowed research award which they bestowed for my research in the Andes and which I used to finance the early years of my Himalayan research; and the *Volkswagen Foundation* for their donation which allowed me to make a number of field trips and supported part of the transcription work.

I also thank the people who were around during my sabbatical in Wintermoos, where the book was written: my friends *Adi* and *Resl Vogl* for their help in many aspects, for their care and protection against distractions and interruptions.

I would also like to express my gratitude to the initial proof-readers of this book: *Prof. Dr. Martin Baumann, Heinz Räther* and *Dr. Frank Seeliger*. I did not follow all of their comments and suggestions; I take responsibility for all remaining shortcomings.

Last but not least: a big thank you to my translator, *Jane Miller* in London – it has been wonderful working with her – competent, charming, humorous and sagacious.

Wintermoos, September 2001
Ina Rösing

CONTENTS

CHAPTER 4: *The enigma of trance and amnesia (157)*

CHAPTER 5: *A key event, an embodied experience and the displacement of the question (187)*

CHAPTER 6: *The great shamanic chant, resolution of the questions* (227)

INDEX OF ILLUSTRATIONS[1]

1 The following illustrations are by Peter F. Tkaczyk: 6, 8, 19 (both illustrations) 31, 40, 41, 42. The other illustrations are by Ina Rösing.

NOTES ON THE ORTHOGRAPHY OF THE TIBETAN TEXTS

In the orthography of the Tibetan texts (transcriptions from tape recordings), I do not follow the usual protocol of established Tibetology and the rules of classic Tibetan, but instead follow the normal practice of scholastic and educated Ladakhis. The transcriptions are the result of work with four Ladakhi collaborators:

SONAM NORBOO SPURKHAPA

Sonam was born to Thinless Dorje (now 87) and Stanzing Dolma (now 84) in a small hamlet called Spurkha Village near Leh, Ladakh (India) to a farmer family on 2nd November, 1949. He has two younger brothers and two younger sisters.

While at school (Gompa Village Primary School, Government High School at Leh) from the age of 7 onwards, his day began at 3:30 a.m. watering the fields with his parents. In those times, there was a shortage of water and the villages got their water on different days. Therefore, on alternate fortnights, Sonam had it relatively easier: he took the family cattle, sheep and goats for grazing at 6:00 a.m. At 8.00 a.m. he brought them back after bathing and washing the face in the stream. Worship was offered at 8:30 a.m.. In between, if there was time, he used to help churning butter – a strenuous physical job in the kitchen. Then after breakfast at 9:00 a.m. he left for school with goats and sheep in tow. After dropping the goats and sheep off at a pasture in care of the shepherd in-charge for the day (duties were by rotation, sometimes Sonam was the shepherd for the day), he walked down to his school. From time to time he had to take leave from school for various duties at home: for ploughing the fields, for shepherding, for harvest and sorting and some *pujas*. When he had half-day or holiday at school, he had other commercial projects: he brought cow-dung, wood blocks and *tsampa* for selling at the main bazaar at Leh, and, at times, he used to perform the role of delivery boy for other people's flour which were ground at his fathers's water-mill. Classes ended at 4:00 p.m. While returning home he picked up the sheep and brought them back to be put in their pens, to collect the grass and fodder from the fields and to assist his mother in milking the animals. After making sure that all animals – sheep, goats, donkeys, cows, *dzos*, yaks – were counted and safe in their pens, the family had their evening worship at the family shrine.

After secondary school Sonam went to Kashmir for further studies at the SP College, Srinagar. He earned his Baccalaureate Degree (B.A.) from D.A.V. College Chandigarh, where he won a three years' scholarship (OISCA International) to study Agriculture at the Tokushima Forest Research Centre in Japan. He became an expert in Mushroom Culture. On his return from Japan in 1975, he worked with the Directorate of Defence. But he was soon tired of government bureaucracy and quit.

Just at that time, Leh was officially opened for tourists. Sonam met a couple from Switzerland and this was the launch of his new career path. From Switzerland this couple kept in touch with Sonam and later appointed him their representative for tour operations in Ladakh. ARTOU India was established in 1976, handling tours for ARTOU (Geneva) from Switzerland. Sonam Norboo was the first Ladakhi travel agent organising trekking, mountaineering, rafting and cultural tours. Later he extended the scope of tours, first to Rajasthan and then to all of India.

In 1977, Sonam underwent a professional Travel Agency Training with ARTOU in Geneva. He visited most of Europe including England, France, the Benelux countries, Italy, Spain etc. He has also visited Japan, China, Thailand, Singapore, Vietnam, South Korea, Philippines, Cambodia, Myanmar, Malaysia.

In 1978, Sonam was the only Japanese-speaking person in Leh. The Koya-san University and Mai Nichi Newspaper who were conducting research on Buddhist Mandala in Ladakh approached him for translation and interpretation – this marked another turning point in his career: research and project assistance and co-ordination for special projects for academics and media. The book resulting from this work was very well appreciated in the academic and intellectual circles in Japan. He was introduced with the Japanese Television Company NTV, with whom he produced a film on *Monks' Life in Monasteries in Leh.*

Introduced by Mr. Takashi Kato, the Mai Nichi newspaper photographer, NHK (Japan Broadcasting Corporation) offered him in 1982 to make a TV documentary called *The Silk Route.* The documentary film has been broadcasted in 35 countries and translated in 35 languages. Sonam has been a much sought after co-ordinator for projects since then, and has been co-ordinating projects for electronic and print media, and universities in Indian, Bhuta, Sikkim and Nepal.

Since 1997, Sonam has been professionally assisting in the German research project on shamanism in Ladakh and Changthang by Ina Rösing.

Sonam Norboo Spurkhapa is married to Mrs. Murup Dolma, a senior bank official working with the State Bank of India. He has two sons, Norboo Wangchuk studying at Delhi University and, Yontan Phuntsok studying at Sanskriti School. They live in Delhi and Leh.

TSULTIM KUBET

Lobsang Rinchen (known as Tsultim) was born on 1st June 1946 in the village of Kubet in Nubra. His parents were farmers. He was the oldest of six children, four boys and two girls. The father wanted him to become a monk and handed him over to the Diskit monastery when he was six. For the next two years, he attended the monastic school. After that he accompanied his lama master to the Lchanglung cave where he completed a meditation period of three years, three months and three days (called *Lho sum kho sum*). Tsultim attended to the everyday needs of the master meditating in the cave (food, drink, blankets). In between the daily meditation periods, he was tutored by this lama in Tibetan writing and Tibetan Buddhism.

He even continued to serve his master for five years after his examinations, and accompanied him on all his monastic engagements. In 1962 at the age of 16, Tsultim then decided to hang up his monk's cloth.

In 1963, he was selected by Bakula Rinpoche as an especially talented student and was sent to Banaras Hindu University, Varanasi. His specialist subjects were History, Social Sciences and English.

Back at his home region, he was then a school teacher for 18 months but did not really enjoy this career. He took the position of manager at the Ladakh Wood Factory and subsequent to that he moved on to be a mountain guide in 1988 when Ladakh had opened up to tourists. He has climbed Stok Kangri 17 times (as well as other peaks in Ladakh) and trekked across Zanskar two dozen times. He was also Vice President of the All Ladakh Buddhist Association for three years. He remained a mountain guide up until his death.

He was married to two sisters and had five children. His son, Kunzang Rigzim, died in the Indo-Pakistan war near Kargil on 19th May 1999 at the age of 20.

Tsultim Kubet visited us in Ulm in the best of health in December 2000, but died in February 2001.

SONAM WANGCHUK

Sonam Wangchuk was born in 1973 in the village of Khardong, in Nubra. He father was a forester. He is the second youngest of six siblings – four boys and two girls. Until his 11th year, Sonam was fully engaged in the family farming business, his main duty being to watch the sheep. Up to that time he had never been to school.

His older brother, however, recognised that he was gifted and arranged for his enrolment at the Central Institute of Buddhist Studies in Choglamsar, near Leh, the capital of Ladakh, from where he graduated at the age of 19. He specialised in Buddhist philosophy and three languages – Tibetan, Hindi and English.

Sonam Wangchuk's family had close ties with Bakula Rinpoche. When the latter was seeking a suitable candidate to receive a scholarship to study Buddhism in Sri Lanka, Sonam Wangchuk was chosen because of his excellent final examination results at the Central Institute. At 19, he travelled to Colombo, the capital of Sri Lanka, and studied Buddhist culture and philosophy (Tibetology) at the Buddhist and Pali University in Colombo. At the age of 24, he completed his studies, receiving a Bachelor of Arts degree (with distinction).

This distinction gave him immediate access to the University of Delhi, where he studied Tibetan language and literature for two years. His outstanding marks throughout the course enabled him to take up his doctorate studies at the Department of Buddhist Studies, Delhi University, at the age of 26 without having to pass a Master of Arts examination. In 2004, he successfully completed his doctorate studies on "Origin and development of the Sakya tradition in the Western Himalaya with special reference to the Matho Monastery in Ladakh". Sonam has been married to Sonam Dolma since 1999 and has a little daughter.

THINLEY GYURMED

Thinley Gyurmed was born in 1973 in the village of Stakna. His parents are farmers. He is the fifth of eleven children – six boys and three girls; two children died. He comes from a polyandrous family: his mother, Yishe Pulit, having married the oldest three of six brothers. The oldest father died when Thinley was 10 years old.

After he had been to primary school for a year, he was handed over to the Stakna monastery at the age of nine.[2] In the monastery, he received primary school education and his first instruction in Buddhism. At the age of 14 – already in a monk's cloth – he progressed to the Central Institute of Buddhist Studies in Choglamsar where he specialised in Buddhist philosophy and in Tibetan and Hindi language. He completed his studies in 1999 with a Master of Arts in Buddhist philosophy.

He was then employed to teach Buddhism at an upper school in Nubra. At the same time, he enrolled for a doctorate course at the Sanskrit University in Varanasi (Benares). His graduation topic in Buddhist philosophy is: "How to clarify the defiled mind". Because he soon realised that work as a teacher and working on a dissertation were incompatible he then decided to give up his teaching duties and devoted his time and energy to his dissertation.

In the ensuing texts, I have taken on the orthography of these four collaborators, the final corrections having been taken on by Sonam Wangchuk and Thinley Gyurmet. It is the simplified Tibetan orthography commonly used in Ladakh.

Even if this means that there are some unavoidable discrepancies from classic Tibetan, I still continue to document the texts in Tibetan script as well – to ensure we have a means by which we can cross-check our translations. In Appendix C, I describe comprehensively where and why these translations are in fact very difficult. But precisely because of this the facility to cross-check must be retained.

---

2 It was, and still is in some places, common practice for a family to hand over one, or even two sons in their early years to the local monastery.

CHAPTER 1

Nomadic life
An introduction and update on research

1. INTRODUCTION

In a black yak-hair woven tent of the Changpa nomads, there is light all day, even when the curtain is drawn across the entrance. Light comes through the vent above the oven and it also filters through the loose weave: the entire inside of the tent – floor and cooker, altar and loom, cooking implements and saddlery, female and male sides of the tent, are bathed in flecks of sunlight, as is the face and body of the shaman, when he conducts healing séances during the day (see Illustration 41). When the shaman rattles his small *da ma ru* hand drum with wild rhythm, it's not only the clappers on the tightly stretched drumskin that dance, but also the spots of sunlight constantly reconfiguring themselves through his rigorous motion.

One soon becomes familiar with everything in such a spacious tent. At least that's what one feels initially. Most things stand or lie on the floor, or can be seen piled up round the edge of the tent – covered, at most, by a blanket. But just what mysteries these tents conceal, what hiding places big and small, just how much history and biography and ways of life are hidden in these tents, only become apparent when one gets close to the family and familiarised with their life; when they start to tell their stories, when faded photographs of Rinpoches and pictures of the Dalai Lama are retrieved from the depths of an old box; when the daughter's first piece of weaving and the most magnificent saddlery is shown...

As with the tent – so it is with the shamans. One quickly becomes acquainted with the procedures at a shamanic séance. Or at least that's what one feels at first. The fundamental structure of the séance remains the same, many ritual procedures are repeated, many prayers will soon sound very familiar (especially if one already knows them from the routine daily Buddhist practice of every Ladakhi, or from the pilgrims' prayers in the monasteries). But then when the shaman, attending to his patient, is carried away in a wild trance then suddenly everything seems new and unfamiliar, frequently also alarming and, above all, often dark and mysterious.

In my research on the shamans of the Changpa nomads, it was my aim to throw the light of the black tent into the shaman's trance chants. I consciously choose this picture and I consciously apply this analogy. For I do not claim to bring daylight, and the light of the remote Changthang's open country into the shaman chants – my life as a researcher is insufficient for that. But, by means of the small areas covered by my research work, I can nevertheless cast speckles of sunlight onto these chants and, by deciphering fragments, gain some insight into the shamans' religious world and their political depths.

However, before I embark on this task of deciphering, I feel it is important, first of all, to portray a concrete picture of the living conditions and way of life of nomadic people in general and that of the Changpa nomads in particular. Without being acquainted with their everyday life one will not understand any shamanic chant. This portrayal will be given in the current chapter. In the following section (Part 2: Shepherd Nomadism and the Ecosystem) I shall firstly illustrate the inseparable connection between the extremes of the environment, on the one hand, and the nomadic way of life, on the other. In the next two sections, drawing on research to date, I will then present what is known specifically on the Ladakhi and Tibetan Changpa nomads (Parts 3 & 4). This review of existing research does, however, reveal blank pages (as I will show in Part 5), part of which will be filled in the ensuing chapters of this book.

2. SHEPHERD NOMADISM AND THE ECOSYSTEM

By nomads we mean people who "handle animals primarily or exclusively to secure their existence, constantly compelled to change location in order to seek fresh pastures, and whose material culture corresponds to this mobile lifestyle" (SCHOLZ 1994, p. 72).

Similar, too, are other definitions of nomads: According to GALVIN (1996), nomadism is a way of life, in which men secure their living by animal husbandry and, without a permanent home, constantly wander through the landscape with their herds, according to season, in search of food and new pastureland. For Rada and Neville DYSON-HUDSON (1980), nomads are "people who are primarily dependent on livestock, who live in environments with marked seasonality and who choose as their basic strategy for providing year-round food for their herds the movement of livestock to pastures rather than bringing of the fodder to herds" (p.18).

The first-cited definition (SCHOLZ 1994) is, in comparison to the other two, both broader and more precise. According to this definition, nomadism is not simply a specific economic system under certain ecological conditions, but also implies a particular cultural pattern. Here Scholz is cautious and confines his definition to material culture. I think one can go a step further and also include culturally conditioned social patterns. Not only the tent, but perhaps even marriage patterns, may be viewed as a correlate of ecology and economic strategy, as I shall discuss with the Changpa nomads.

The four key defining factors of shepherd nomadism as a survival system, i. e. as an economic strategy, are as follows: (1) animal husbandry, (2) seasonal, resource-dictated changes of pasture land and domicile (moving all belongings, above all the herds), (3) accommodation in tents or other portable housing, and (4) the structuring of social relationships in a way best suited to these economic conditions.

Pure nomadism is rare on earth. A nomadic life is frequently combined with phases of a settled existence, or encompasses a population that in part is temporarily settled and making a living from arable farming. Wherever the ecosystem allows it, even if only limited arable farming is possible, people live as semi-nomads.

Pure nomadism exists only in extremely barren environments.[1] It is a way of life that is suitable for such extreme environmental conditions. The study of nomadism allows one to understand, like no other way of life, the adaptation of CULTURE to NATURE, that is, a cultural lifestyle with its manifold customs and habits to the realities of an ecosystem. It illustrates the influence of the environment on the cultural inventions of man.

Firstly, just a few remarks on research on nomadism in general. Many scientists have already attempted to come up with an all-encompassing theory regarding nomadism[2], and this extreme form of survival strategy certainly tempts one to theorise. But attempts at a general theory on nomadism are no longer being taken seriously today, and a coherent theory has also never arisen from these attempts.

Indeed, comparative empirical studies on nomadism in the world reveal an enormous breadth of variation in this way of life, to which an overall theory, in its nature designed to simplify, cannot do justice.

However, in trying to understand nomadism the theory of cultural ecology is still pertinent. It examines the complex relationships of ecological conditions, on the one hand, and man's cultural patterns, primarily the social structure, on the other. Currently, the cultural-ecological approach is also discussed with respect to polyandry (the marriage of one woman to several men) in nomadic communities (see Chapter 2).

Thus, the cultural-ecological approach is, up to now, still in vogue.[3] But the critique of this approach, as formulated by Rada

1 The decline of nomadism seems inevitable to many nomad researchers, see e.g. SCHOLZ (1991, 1994) or MERKLE (2000).
2 See e.g. AL-WARDI (1972), ASAD (1979), GOLDSCHMIDT (1971, 1979), PLANHOL (1979), POHLHAUSEN (1954), SALZMAN (1979, 1980), SPOONER (1971, 1973), VAJDA (1968); also see HOFFMANN (1998).
3 See ANDERSON (1973), DYSON-HUDSON & SMITH (1978), FRAKE (1962), GUILLET (1983), MILTON (1997), MORAN (2000), STEWARD (1968); for the application of cultural-ecological approaches to Ladakh see MANN (1978b, 1985, 1990).

Illustration 1: The desert-like high altitude plains of the Ladakhi Changthang (Rupshu) at twilight

and Neville DYSON-HUDSON as early as 1980, is also still valid: Cultural-ecological approaches tend to overlook certain perspectives. With respect to the nomadic life, these are above all a perspective on CHANGE, e.g. towards semi-nomadic hybrid lifestyles, on the interaction of nomads with the "outside" world, on the role of the state, colonial and post-colonial conditions on nomadic life.

The cited work by Rada and Neville Dyson-Hudson is still worth reading today. It ties together a decade of research into nomadism (1970-1980). Of the 161 books and articles on nomadism they cite, only two, indeed rather old articles, relate to Central Asia (BACON 1954 and PATAI 1951) – and not one single article (including Bacon and Patai) relate to Tibetan nomadic culture.

A comprehensive and detailed discourse on the fundamentals of nomadism is provided in the book *Nomadismus. Theorie und Wandel einer sozio-ökologischen Kulturweise* (Nomadism. Theory and Transformation of a Socio-ecological Way of Life) by Fred SCHOLZ (1995).[4] In this volume, one can find one's way not only through the manifold variations of nomadism, but also through the full spectrum of theories which anthropologists, geographers and other specialists have put forward in order to understand this form of survival strategy.

Several more recent volumes (from 1990) compare models of nomadic survival in various parts of the world, and – balancing the early critique by Rada and Neville Dyson-Hudson – focus particularly on the question of change under conditions brought about by political and economic development (modernisation), as discussed, for example, in the book *The World of Pastoralism: Herding Systems in Comparative Perspective*, edited by GALATY

---

4 See also his bibliography on nomadism (SCHOLZ 1992) and the earlier book published by him *Nomaden: Mobile Tierhaltung. Zur gegenwärtigen Lage von Nomaden und zu den Problemen und Chancen mobiler Tierhaltung* (Nomads: Roaming Herd Ownership. On the current position of nomads and the problems and opportunities arising from roaming herd ownership) (SCHOLZ 1991).

Illustration 2: Changpa nomads transferring to new pastures

and JOHNSON (1990) (see also BARFIELD 1993a), or that by GINAT and KHAZANOV (1998) *Changing Nomads in a Changing World*. In the latter publication Tibetan nomadism is, however, not at all discussed. Even in the chapter that summarises the book (KHAZANOV 1998) all research on Tibetan culture is neglected, in spite of this chapter concentrating on the questions of politically- and economically-dictated changes and even though the situation for Tibetan nomads subject to Chinese politics offers, precisely in this area, a particularly impressive field of study.[5]

After this brief and general introduction on nomadism, I shall next discuss the state of the art of research on the Changpa nomads. They live on the distant high plateau of Changthang in former Tibet (today China) and in today's Ladakh (India).

Changthang is a Tibetan word. *Chang* means north and *thang*, or *tang*, plain or plateau. The Tibetan Changthang plateau – that constitutes approximately 70 per cent of Tibet on the political map, and also stretches to Ladakh, northern India – is by far the largest and highest plateau in the world. The whole Changthang region lies, on the average, at over 4,500 metres above the sea level and covers from 600,000 to 800,000 square kilometres.

---

5 In passing, I would like to mention another category of literature that is particularly entertaining to read if one has to become acquainted with "real" nomads: the usage of the term "nomads" in the sociological literature on post-modernism, see, first of all, Zygmunt BAUMAN (1996), but also MAFFESOLI (1997) and then the biting and cynical critique of the inflationary use of the nomad "metaphor" by Dick PELS (1999) (see also the critique of that critique by BRAIDOTTI 1999).

3. THE LADAKHI CHANGPA NOMADS: UPDATE ON RESEARCH

In the research to date information on Ladakhi Changthang nomads is very scarce. In 1995, Prem Singh Jina summed up the situation regarding research as follows:

> There is an absolute dearth of scientific information, data and literature of socio-economic and environmental conditions of the people of these pasture belts. So far my knowledge goes, for Chang-Thang area this is the first attempt in the history of Ladakh when a research work on pasturelands is carried out...
> (JINA 1995, p. 11)

This description of the research situation from 1995 – "absolute dearth" – still holds true even today, and indeed not only with respect to the socio-economic and ecological conditions, but also in relation to all ways of life of the Changpa nomads.

There is evidently only one scientifically serious ethnological study on Ladakhi Changthang, the study of Monisha Ahmed (1999) (see below). Somewhat better is the research situation in relation to the Tibetan (today Chinese) Changthang. I shall briefly summarise both strands of research:

The work of Prem Singh Jina, from whom I quoted above, constitutes in fact the first monograph on Ladakhi Changthang (JINA 1995; see also the two articles JINA 1990 and JINA 1999). One year later, a further monograph appeared, *Transhumants of Himalaya* (1996), in which the author, Veena Bhasin, compares the Changthang nomads, the nomadic Gaddis of Himachal Pradesh and the Bhutias from Sikkim. As regards Ladakh, her presentation is so similar to that of P.S. Jina, that one of the two must have copied up pages of text from the other (without any acknowledgement). Therefore, Jina and Bhasin cannot reliably be considered as being two different sources.

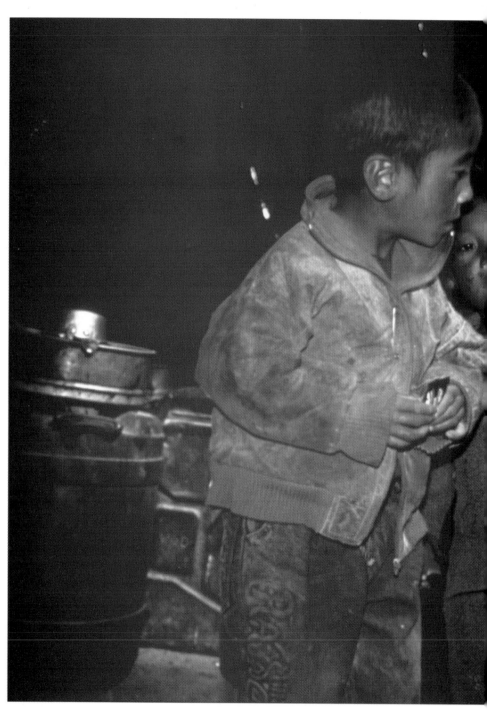

Illustration 3: Nomadic woman with her children

Regarding Bhasin, it must also be noted that her book is character-ised not only by a series of omissions and errors,[6] but also by the inclusion of appraisals and valuations for which there should be no place in scientific writing. Here we have her verdict on the Changpa nomads:

> Among Changpas, the whole families are crowded promiscuously in tents which are always too close and sleep in greasy beds eaten up with vermin, in an atmosphere tainted with smoke. Neither the men nor the women take any care of their persons. They wear their clothes very long without changing, brushing or shaking them, keep them on even at night and take them off only when they drop off of themselves. They never wash their bodies and rarely wash their hands and faces. However, to protect themselves against the bites of the wind, they cover themselves with most rancid butter (BHASIN 1996, p. 52-53).

One does not feel much better when JINA (1995) cites "earlier" valued judgements on the Changpa (those of HEBER & HEBER 1903/1976) in order to reassure us that the nomads today, how-ever, wash and comb their hair "decently":

> People of Chang-Thang have rather a projecting chin, their eyes are typically Mongolian, their noses large and firmly flattened. Long hair, which surely has not made the acquaintance of brush and comb for years if ever, and which ends in a pigtail, surmount faces unaccustomed to washing, but well-acquainted with smoky fires (HEBER & HEBER 1976). Today many people are educated and Jammu and Kashmir Government has opened many schools in Chang-Thang with the result, they live like other Ladakhis. Their living condition and living style has been changed. They wash their hair properly and comb them (JINA 1995, p. 77).

6 False statements include, for example, the assertion that only men work as shepherds; (no: girls must also take the herds to graze, at least until they are married) and that only the women weave; (no: the men weave too). The division of the tent into right-hand side male and left-hand side female halves has also been overlooked by BHASIN (1996) as has the marked retreat of polyandry.

36

Illustration 4: Nomadic girl peeps into the tent

An excellent and hitherto the only scientific ethnography of Changthang is the dissertation by Monisha Ahmed (1996) (also see AHMED 1999).[7] Certainly her focus is specific to the subject of weaving of the Changthang nomads, but as she examines how "fibres, weaving, and textiles are constructed, symbolised, understood, enacted, and experienced" (p.2) her studies encompass all areas, from economy and technology, social structure and religion, through play and politics. As a result of precisely this broad span, some omissions become all the more apparent. There is no discussion in her study (nor in the aforementioned books) of concepts of health, illness, and of traditions of healing. There is not a single mentioning of the Changpa shamans in these monographs.[8]

4. THE TIBETAN CHANGPA NOMADS: UPDATE ON RESEARCH

Somewhat better than the research situation regarding Ladakhi Changthang is that regarding Tibetan (today Chinese) Changthang and the Tibetan nomads in general.

From traditional Tibet (pre-1950) R.B. Ekvall and M. Hermanns have presented important studies on Tibetan nomads. Between 1926 and 1941 EKVALL (1939, 1968/1983; see also EKVALL 1961, 1964b, 1964c, 1974 and DOWNS & EKVALL 1965) spent in total eight years with the Samtsa nomads in northeastern Tibet. Ekvall was primarily a missionary but subsequently also studied and qualified as an anthropologist through the Department of Anthro-

---

7 Also DOLLFUS (1999) makes a very important contribution; this article, however, is confined to religion and is not a comprehensive ethnography of the Changthang. I shall go into his study in Chapter 2.

8 A visual impression of Ladakhi Changthang (focusing on beauty and not information) – including three pictures from shamanic séances – can be enjoyed in the picture volume *Les Bergers d L'Hiver* by Olivier and Danielle FÖLLMI (1999). However with this, and the three authors mentioned, Jina, Bhasin and Ahmed, the ethnography of this region is exhausted.

Illustration 5: Nomadic woman

pology at the University of Chicago. His education facilitated his precise descriptions while his career conditioned his value judgements and appraisals. It is particularly in the field of religion – see also his book on Tibetan Buddhism (EKVALL 1964a) – that the value judgements become apparent. Buddhism in Tibet – and more so that of the nomads – is – according to him – a rather "corrupted" form of Buddhism, in which "completely incompatible" and mutually exclusive beliefs and practices of the animistic and shamanic pre-Buddhist Bön-religion are mingled with Buddhism (EKVALL 1939, p.10-11).

M. Hermanns was also a missionary. He spent many years with the Amdo nomads of Tibet and declared repeatedly that he had won their trust. In his book *Die Nomaden von Tibet (The Nomads of Tibet)* (HERMANNS 1949; see also KUSSMAUL 1952/1953), he focuses on the nomads' economy, on animal rearing, bartering, on material culture and property rules and regulations. His book *Die Familie der A mdo-Tibeter (The A mdo-Tibetan Family)* (HERMANNS 1959) deals with the establishment of a family (search for a partner, marriage customs, etc), the safeguarding of a family (role of the husband and wife, raising children, etc) and the disintegration of the family (separation, death) of Amdo nomads. In his book *Mythen und Mysterien, Magie und Religion der Tibeter (Myths and Mysteries, Magic and Religion of the Tibetans)* (HERMANNS 1956), religion and ritual are explored, focusing on the Buddhist religion and also on many pre-Buddhist customs. However, we learn very little about the shamans; Hermanns tends to subsume the Tibetan shamans under Siberian shamanism, cites research on Siberian shamans, thus characterising the Tibetan shamans in a highly generalised (and often incorrect) way. Nevertheless, he correctly describes their external appearance (clothes/costume, crown, drum etc) and correctly mentions that they perform their healing while in trance.

As to more recent research on Tibetan nomads there are – apart from smaller studies (see e.g. BARFIELD 1993a, 1993b; TOPGYAL et al. 1998) and pure economic-geographic orientated studies (e.g.

MANDERSCHEID 1998, 1999a, 1999b) – primarily two experts to mention: firstly the Tibetologist and cultural anthropologist Melvin C. Goldstein, and secondly the physical anthropologist Cynthia M. Beall. Their work is based on a total of 20 months' fieldwork (1986, 1987, 1990) in the autonomous region of Tibet, China, 14 months of which were spent with the Phala nomads of the Tibetan Changthang.[9]

Their main work is the monograph *Nomads of Western Tibet: The Survival of a Way of Life* (1990) (see also GOLDSTEIN & BEALL 1989a). One of the focal points of their research is the dramatic transformation in the nomadic system through China's changing political policy towards Tibet – firstly as a result of the Chinese cultural revolution (forced permanent settlement of the nomads, suppression of their cultural tradition and religious practices) and then, following the death of Mao Tse Tung, through the liberalisation of Chinese political policy towards some cultural autonomy of Tibet.[10]

Following such an extended period of Chinese oppression and "re-education", the nomads' return to their traditional values and customs, and the rebirth of many forms of Buddhist and shamanic religious expression, is an impressive testimony to the survival rigour of their cultural traditions.[11]

Besides these politically dictated changes in the life of the Tibetan nomads, the authors have also focused particularly on the changes in the social structure that have arisen from it, and especially on the traditional form of Tibetan marriage – fraternal polyandry, – i. e. the marriage of several brothers to one wife (see GOLDSTEIN 1981, GOLDSTEIN & KELLY 1987, GOLDSTEIN & TSARONG 1987). They have also discussed what the demise of this tradition

---

9   For a short description of their research see GOLDSTEIN & BEALL (1987).
10 For a comprehensive account see GOLDSTEIN, BEALL & CINCOTTA (1990). Important works about the influence of Chinese political policy on the nomadic economy are also CLARKE (1988, 1992, 1998) and LEVINE (1998); on LEVINE (1998) see also GELEK (1998).
11 Using the same focus, these authors then turned to study the Mongolian nomads. See GOLDSTEIN & BEALL (1994) and also MÜLLER (1994).

Illustration 6: Mother and child

means in demographic, economic and cultural terms to this population development.[12]

5. CHANGPA SHAMANS: A BLANK PAGE

What is the situation now with the shamans in this research on Tibetan Changthang and on the nomads in other Tibetan regions? As was the case regarding research on Ladakhi Changthang, similarly here obvious omissions must be mentioned.

In HERMANNS (1949) nothing at all is said about the shamans. Ekvall, who even in his principal work on the Samta nomads, (1968/1983) only devotes four pages to religion, mentions them in one single sentence only: These "divinely-possessed" people, who speak in trance with God's voice, were sought advice by the nomads in problems of deciding about propitious ways of acting (EKVALL 1968/1983, p.83).

In GOLDSTEIN's & BEALL's key study (1990) and in most of their numerous articles (1989a, 1991 etc.), the shamans are not mentioned: This is all the more striking, as these authors examined with particular interest the return of the nomads to many of their traditional ways of life after the death of Mao Tse Tung. They also admit that in no other areas are these changes more apparent than in· religion – and in spite of this focus, only a few lines on prayer flags, pilgrimages, Mani-walls and monasteries turn up in the text (see GOLDSTEIN & BEALL 1991).

---

12 The research works of Goldstein and Beall on the Tibetan nomads of Changthang have not been without their critics. They come from various quarters, mostly from cultural anthropology (e. g. NEWELL 1994), where the authors' popular portrayal of the nomads at the cost of professional substance is mostly being criticised, and from the politically motivated Tibet-Movement (see COX 1987 and 1991 and GOLDSTEIN's responses 1988 and 1992).

Only in one place in their work (1989b) do we find the following description of a shaman emerging from obscurity following prolonged Chinese oppression:

> The extent of the changes under the new policy is especially notable in the practice of religion. During the period of our field work in Phala, the nomads, for whom religion had again become an important part of life, were free to pursue the cycle of religious rites that typified the traditional society. Most households had small altars in their tents and flew prayer flags from their tent poles and guylines. Nomads no longer feared open displays of religion, and a number even wore Dalai Lama buttons and displayed his photograph openly. Individuals turning prayer wheels, counting rosaries, and doing prostrations were common sights. Even government functions such as the summer horse-race fairs at the district headquarters included unofficial, but open, religious components, for example, monks reading prayers in special "monastery" tents...

> These traditional practices did not reappear all at once or in an orderly fashion. At first, the nomads feared that the new policy was a devious trick launched to expose pockets of "rightist" thinking, and individuals were reluctant to take the lead and risk being singled out. Change occurred only gradually as individual nomads took specific actions that, in effect, tested the general policy. When no protest or punishment came from the district officials above them – all of whom are ethnic Tibetans – a desirable practice spread, and this process is still going on. The reemergence of nomad "mediums" (individuals whom deities possess and speak through) exemplifies this...

> ... it reappeared in Phala in the winter of 1987 when an adult in one camp took ill and was in great pain for days before he dies. A man from the same encampment went into trance spontaneously during the illness and was possessed by a deity who gave a prognosis and explanation of the disease. When no official criticism of this event occurred in the ensuing weeks and months, he and others fashioned the traditional costume worn by mediums, and he is

now sought by others in Phala in cases of illness (GOLDSTEIN & BEALL 1989b, p. 626-627).

This passage is precisely all we learn on the shamans of Tibetan nomads. There is nothing on shamans in either Ladakhi or Tibetan Changthang. (For information on Ladakhi shamans OUTSIDE Changthang, however, see Chapter 3.)

6. OVERVIEW OF THE PRESENT BOOK

If, in the research to date, this sketching mention of a re-emerging shaman is the only description of the Changpa-nomad shamans in Ladakhi and Tibetan Changthang, then one must indeed also describe the research position in this section as an "absolute dearth" of information (JINA 1995). This book attempts to fill that gap.

In the next chapter, Chapter 2, I want first of all to describe in greater detail the environment and way of life of the Ladakhi Changpa nomads: firstly their environment, i. e. the extreme living conditions; then aspects of their economy (animal rearing, pasture rotation and trade); and finally aspects of their social structure and religion.

In the third chapter, I provide a thorough account of the Ladakhi shamans – drawn first and foremost from my own research findings. Indeed, as I mentioned earlier, in the research to date the Changpa shamans (certainly the Ladakhi, but also Tibetan ones) have been almost completely overlooked – but not the shamans of other Ladakhi regions. Ladakh as a whole has an economic structure altogether different from Changthang; traditionally it is primarily a farming community. But the shamans of other regions of Ladakh – here one can draw on an abundance of research findings – teach us some very important things about the shamans in Changthang.

In Chapter 3, I shall deal briefly with the village and the monastic shamans. Most importantly, I shall explore "madness" as the

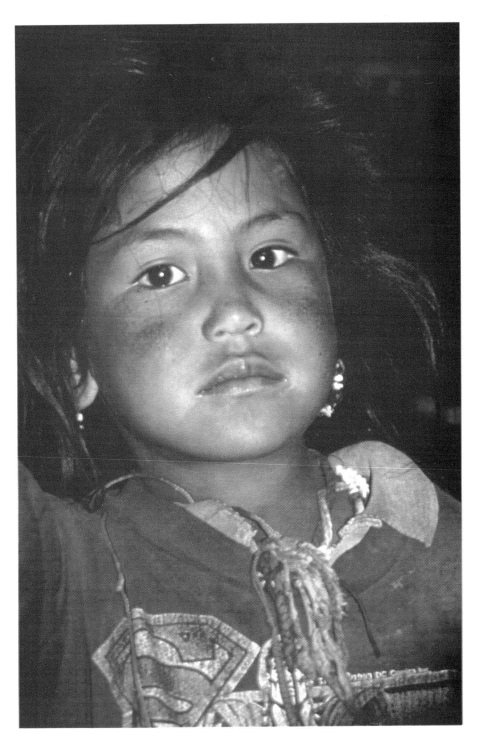

Illustration 7: Nomadic child

starting point of their calling and I shall demonstrate how this "madness" is then transformed into an induced, controlled trance at a healing ritual. I shall also describe a shamanic séance and examine the reputation and the esteem in which they are held in the Ladakhi community – primarily amongst the Buddhist clergy.

Chapter 4 then penetrates to the core of Ladakhi shamanism – the mystery of trance and amnesia. This is where my own personal research story begins. Not only did I doubt the authenticity of the shamanic trance, but I also almost failed in my research when confronted with the hermetic shamanic post-trance amnesia.

But doubts and problems aside, I also wanted, of course, to give the shamans a fair hearing. Therefore, in this chapter, I document what the shamans THEMSELVES say about trance and amnesia. Only then do I ask, from an "external" perspective, the question whether the shamanic trance is perhaps good THEATRE – though indeed quite possibly an entirely effective means of healing – and whether my suspicion that the alleged amnesia is in fact a particular defence strategy to counter the ever-growing numbers of western researchers filing past the Ladakhi shamans.

If a shaman remembers nothing at all following trance, then of course he cannot explain how he heals – and further research is blocked. The answer to the question of the authenticity of trance and amnesia, appeared to me to lie in remote Changthang: up until then researchers had not reached as far as the Changthang shamans. This is the beginning of my own voyage of discovery into the mystery of shamanic trance and amnesia, and the starting point of my expeditions into Changthang.

I begin my story in Chapter 5 at the point where I had managed to trace the shamans with astonishing ease among the roaming nomads on the remote high plateau of Changthang. The first encounter was with the shaman Lhapa Thundup. I will cite his life story, and he also gets his full say in describing the trance. I also document the first of his séances in which I participated. In the following séance of this shaman Lhapa Thundup – something happened that for me would be the "key experience" in relation to

Illustration 8: Nomadic boy

the question of trance and amnesia. I describe this key experience and I demonstrate how this, in the personal account of my shamanic research, suddenly and quite fundamentally displaces the original questions. But the old questions: trance as theatre, amnesia as a defence strategy? – as well as the new question: what had happened to the shaman during that trance which became my key experience? – are answered in the final chapter.

In the sixth and final chapter, we become acquainted with the other two shamans of the Changthang nomads, and familiarise ourselves with their life stories as well as their healing practice. (The consensus of opinion among the nomads is that there are no more than three shamans, though this excludes the town, Nyoma).

The question of amnesia as a defence strategy is settled when I met the second shaman, Lhapa Ngawang. In order to solve the mystery of what happened during the "key experience", however, much more long and arduous research work was necessary. To achieve this, it was necessary to decipher a long chant of Lhapa Thundup. For days on end I sat on the floor in the nomads' tents with my co-workers and worked on this long shamanic chant with Sonam Tashi, assistant to Lhapa Thundup.

This song, these few deciphered pages, are the most important part of my research. The song bridges in a most fascinating way the divide not only between shamanic and Buddhist religion, but also between the old and new era. It is specifically the admonitions relating to the new era with all its adverse tendencies and value changes which could indicate to us that the shamans of remote Changthang may well have a message for us.

CHAPTER 2

The world of the Changpa nomads

Overview

1. CHANGTHANG: THE ENVIRONMENT

Ladakhi Changthang – an area of approximately 21,000 km² (JINA 1995, 1999; BHASIN 1996) is situated at an average height of 4,500 metres above the sea level. It is inhabited by nomads and semi-nomads. Besides roaming animal ownership, the semi-nomads also make a living from farmland and, on their farmland – besides the tents in which they move around – they also have modest accommodation with one or two rooms (on this subject see JINA 1999).

This raw and arid, cold and high, most inhospitable and extreme region – that of Rupshu, Korzok, and Kharnak[1] – is the world inhabited by the only nomads of Changthang (see map).

This region covers approximately 8,000 km² (JINA 1999). Only a very small number of the nomads have permanent occupancy at the foot of the monastery of Korzok overlooking Lake Tsomoriri. Until the seventeenth century the feudal ruler of Changthang had his seat in Korzok, and early travellers of the eighteenth century counted ten small houses in which the old and the ill remained. Today in Korzok (see Illustration 9), there are 70 dwellings, though most are used for storage (BHATTACHARJI 1993). The inhabitants of Korzok make a small part of their living from agriculture – and this at over 4,500 metres! With careful irrigation, a small crop of barley can sometimes thrive and be harvested once a year. However, it is not uncommon for the crop to fail to ripen, in which case the hulks are harvested while still green and serve as winter fodder for the cattle (RIZVI 1996, p.38-39). However, settled Changpa people are in the minority. This book focuses on the majority – the nomads who move on all year round with their herds of sheep and goats and their stock of yaks and horses.

---

1 Korzok and Kharnak are regions and also settlements. Rupshu is the area near Lake Tsomoriri. AHMED (1996) conducted her research there.

Climatically, the land they roam in is extraordinarily hard. Changthang is hemmed in by enormous mountain ranges – including the Himalayas as well as the Kunlun, Altun, Qilian and Hengduan ranges, with absolute minimal rainfall. According to information from SCHALLER (1997), precipitation is less than 25mm per year; BHASIN (1996) suggests approximately 10 cm; JINA (1995) three inches, i.e. barely 8 cms. Whatever the precise amount, Changthang is certainly very dry, and virtual desert conditions prevail (see Illustration 1).

Sketch outlining the position of Ladakhi Changthang (adopted from DOLLFUS 1996)[2].

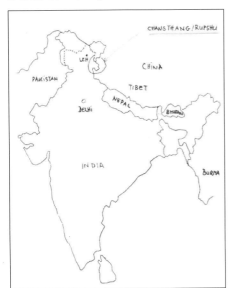 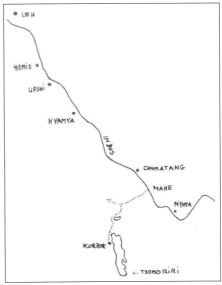

The temperatures are likewise extreme. In summer, the temperature can rise to 30°C by day, but can fall to minus 5°C at night. The fluctuations between day and night are thus very great. In winter, the

2 It is astonishing that one cannot find any decent maps of the Changthang area – even AHMED (1996) leaves us in the dark here. The map above at least gives some idea of the position of Ladakh in Northern India. Ladakhi Changthang lies to the far east of Ladakh, on the border to China. The dotted lines indicate the disputed borders.

temperature can plummet to minus 40 degrees. EVERDING (1993) records an average annual temperature of between -5 and +6 degrees. Bitter winds sweep across the high plains almost constantly.[3]

Under these climatic conditions, farming is very difficult; there is no woodland and the vegetation is extremely scant. Changthang does have many lakes but they have no outlets and are either salty or have brackish water which will not sustain fish. Drinking water is, therefore, also very scarce. The prime sources of drinking water are the glaciers on the surrounding mountain peaks. Consequently, there are insufficient numbers of wild animals for man to survive by hunting.

In an environment that excludes hunting, fishing and farming as the basic means of acquiring food, there remains only stock raising. But since the available food for maintaining herds is also extremely scant, the Changpa have to keep moving on through the land. Once the meagre vegetation has been grazed to its roots and the grazing land further afield from the settlement cannot be reached by foot within a few hours, then it is time to move on (see Illustration 2) – a move involving all livestock and belongings.

Altogether, the environmental conditions in Changthang are so exacting, bringing man and beast so close to the brink, that any slight deterioration in the weather beyond the norm – e.g. the snowstorm in the winter of 1985 – can immediately reduce the number of ani-

---

3 On studying all the statistics recorded, there are discrepancies regarding the size, climate and population density of Changthang. MA LIHUA (1993) and EVERDING (1993) report the area as being 600,000 km², SCHALLER (1997) 750,000 km², and QUIERS (1998) 800,000 km². The following average heights above sea level are given: EVERDING (1993): 5,000 m, MA LIHUA (1993): over 4,500 m, QUIERS (1998) average 4,500 m, SCHALLER (1997): over 4,000 m. MA LIHUA records a population density of 1 inhabitant per km² while EVERDING (1993) states 1 inhabitant per 10 km². As for Korzok RIZVI (1996) reports the average height above sea level as being 4,500 m or 4,600m. BHATTACHARJI (1993) reports Korzok at 4,570 m and 4,604 m, and Lake Tsomoriri 4,512 m and 4,581m.

Illustration 9: Korzok, monastery and settlement

mals, whether wild[4] or shepherded by man by 50 per cent (SCHALLER 1997). The nomads have many tales of catastrophe relating to the extreme winters with so much snow that blights Changthang, when the livestock cannot find sufficient food and die off in great numbers.

Humans, however, are most inventive. If livestock is their only means of survival, they make full use of the animal, using pelt, hide, bones, tendons and dung to make tents and clothes, tools and jewellery, saddlery and containers, ropes and fuel. And of course, they gain sustenance from the meat and milk.

However, it is extremely hard to achieve a balanced diet on animal products alone, and in the long-term it is unhealthy.. Shepherd nomadism as an economic system and as a survival strategy is, therefore, mostly combined with some form of trading. By bartering products with people from other economic regions their own dietary needs and their material culture are balanced.

In the following sections, I shall describe more precisely the life of the Changpa nomads: livestock and pasture rotation (Part 2), the black and the white tent as their housing (Part 3), past and present-day bartering (Part 4), polyandry (Part 5) and also their Buddhist-shamanic blend of religious traditions (Part 6).

2. LIVESTOCK AND PASTURE ROTATION

The nomads of Changthang primarily keep sheep, goats (see Illustrations 10 and 11), yaks and horses.

---

4 There is an attractive picture volume by G. B. SCHALLER (1997), *Tibet's Hidden Wilderness. Wildlife and Nomads of the Chang Tang Reserve* that illustrates the wild livestock in Changthang. See also his article *Tibet's remote Chang Tang* (1993).

Sheep provide meat (for their own consumption or for trading), wool (likewise for their own needs or to sell) as well as milk for three months of the year (mainly for their own consumption: for immediate consumption as a drink and as a basic ingredient for the production of yoghurt, butter and cheese). Sheep are also used to carry burdens and they can carry up to 10 kg for a distance of 12 km per day.

Of equal importance to the Changpa nomads are goats. The most valuable product that the Changthang goats provide for the people – apart from the hide (pelt), meat and milk – is the *pashmina* wool. The nomads use this purely for trading: they do not keep any for themselves. The *chang ra* (northern goats) are a special breed of goat which are found only in this region (and in the ecologically comparable regions in Mongolia): in the extreme cold of winter a sort of under layer of the finest wool grows, called *pashmina*. This *pashmina* wool is combed out, cleaned and sold.

Pashmina wool is handled by intermediate traders and brought mainly to Kashmir, where it is processed to create the legendary *pashmina* shawls, which, at a size of 2 x 1 m can fetch over one thousand US Dollars. The nomads receive only a small percentage of this from this *pashmina* trade (for more information on the economics of the *pashmina* trade see AHMED 1996, Chapter 9.3; RIZVI 1999 and ALTMANN & RABOUAN 1999, RABOUAN 2001), but nevertheless it makes a substantial contribution to their wealth in relative terms. Since the closing of the borders with Tibet, from where most of the *pashmina* wool previously originated and was considered to be the best, Ladakhi Changthang nomads have greatly benefited: now it is THEIR *pashmina* wool which is in demand. Correspondingly, the profile of the nomads' livestock has altered – the number of goats has increased many times over.

The mighty yak is also an indispensable animal for the nomads (BONNEMAIRE 1976; EPSTEIN 1974). The female yak (*dri*) produces milk all year round, and yaks are the principal animal for facilitating

Illustration 10: Sheep in the pastures

transportation of tents and all worldly possessions for the ten or so moves per year that the nomads have to make. Two yaks alone are needed to transport both halves of the heavy black nomad tent, weighing some 120 kg, to the next grazing area.

Horses are also used to transport goods from time to time, but most of all they are used for riding (Illustration 12). For the nomad, they are always a status symbol.

Illustration 11: Pashmina goats. Here: facing each other, horns locked, to enable milking undisturbed from behind, in two rows

If we examine these very high regions of Ladakhi Changthang, those of Rupshu, Korzok and Kharnak, the region where we find real nomads in the true sense of the word, then it becomes clear that the animal population greatly outnumbers the human population. Unfortunately there are huge discrepancies in the statistics relating to the population densities of both – but certain average values give some indication. JINA (1995) believes that approximately 4000 people live in this region; BHASIN (1996) speaks of 2,900; JINA states in a later publication (1999) of 320 tents – in each of which an extended family of 7-14 members live. In any event, these different figures are nevertheless consistent in showing that the population in this region is extremely sparse. And most of the data given allows for the fact that a certain number will drift away to the capital of Ladakh, Leh. · For example, DOLLFUS (1999) cites a population count of 363 people in the Kharnak region, but mentions at the same time that since the count 25 "tents" (families) have moved away from this region.

For the region of Rupshu, AHMED (1996) quotes the results of the population count in 1981 which recorded 499 inhabitants, but in 1990 there were only 399 in a total of 73 tents. Here again, it is the migration to Leh which has reduced the number.

Now in Ladakhi Changthang, there are not only Ladakhi nomads but also Tibetans. Since the Dalai Lama fled from Tibet, over 10,000 Tibetan refugees have come to Ladakh, many of whom are nomads from the Tibetan part of Changthang. There was no frontier before – the nomads moved freely from one pasture to the next, beyond the inconsequential political border on the high land. But in 1962, China occupied substantial areas of Ladakhi Changthang; the border was closed and since then both sides have been constantly guarded by military presence.

The situation in Ladakhi Changthang has changed dramatically as a result of this political event. The greatest change has been that of the population density. There are no figures for the number of Tibetan nomads who now live in Ladakhi Changthang. AHMED (1996) quotes for their region under examination, Rupshu, an estimate of 130 people, practically one-third of the number in Ladakhi Changpa.

Independent of the fluctuations in the population density (migration of Ladakhi nomads and the arrival of nomadic Tibetan refugees), the size of the herds has increased substantially and very noticeably. For 1985/86, JINA (1995) records 190,000 sheep and goats; by

Illustration 12: En route to the neighbouring encampment

1993/94, that number had virtually doubled (300,000 sheep and goats) – both statistics are based on the official figures of the District Husbandry Department in Leh. Monisha Ahmed (1996) believes, however, that these numbers are far too low – no nomad would be ready to reveal the number of animals he owned particularly as the taxes levied by the Indian state, however small, are set according to the number of animals owned.

A nomad owning 300 sheep and goats, 30-35 yaks and 4 horses is viewed as being rich in Changthang. A moderately wealthy nomad would have 100 to 150 sheep and goats, 10-20 yaks and one or two horses. Nomads considered poor have only 30-40 sheep and goats, one yak and one horse (AHMED 1996).

The entire life of a nomad is determined by the simple fact that their animals have to be led to graze every single day of the year – 365 days a year, no holiday and no days off.

It is the children (girls and boys from the age of 6) and men who are responsible for the shepherding. Milking the animals is the women's job. Another job for the children is to collect fuel for fire. For this they go off for the whole day – always in pairs (see Illustration 13). That means two trips daily into the surrounding pastures, walking for 2-4 hours. Sheep and goats graze together, whilst yaks and also horses graze separately. Often the occupants of several tents go to the pastures together – of course one shepherd with sled and dog cannot keep more than 200 sheep and goats together. The less wealthy nomads offer their services as shepherds and earn around 500 to 550 rupees per month (AHMED 1996). In 1995, a horse – to give some comparison – cost around 10,000-12,000 rupees. So a shepherd would have to work for 18-24 months without spending one single rupee before he could afford a horse for himself.

The grazing areas are for each family very precisely identified and circumscribed. They are divided up and allocated by the *go ba*, a chief selected by the whole nomadic community of a particular

Illustration 13: Nomadic children after gathering material for fuel: product of a day's work

region (*yul*). Any person overstepping his allocated area must pay a penalty to the *go ba*. And the penalty is not insignificant: one animal for every ten animal violations of the boundary. If a shepherd with his herd of 200 sheep and goats then ventures outside the grazing land allocated to him (and it does happen) he would have to forfeit 20 sheep to the *go ba*. From the sale of these sheep the expenses of the *yul* are financed: the cost of festivals as well as the expenses involved when government representatives visit etc.

The seasonal cycle of migration of a tent group – five to ten tents – involves six (BHASIN 1996) seven (JINA 1995) or ten (AHMED 1996) different areas of pasture, in a very precisely-defined sequence depending on the season. Within each seasonal grazing zone the individual pasture areas are divided up anew every three years so that each family in turn comes to hold all the land, good or poor. The size of the apportioned areas is measured according to the size of each family's livestock.

The herds of the two Changthang monasteries, those of Thugju and Korzok, receive special treatment. Each year three families are selected by the *go ba* to take over these herds, in addition to their own, without payment. No one objects to being a monastic shepherd since it is primarily considered to by an act of piety which is certain to be rewarded in the next world, and secondly the monasteries get the best grazing land, from which the families' herd also benefits. Additionally, one family is selected to put to graze the horses of the whole region, a demanding task which is paid.

The move from one grazing region to the next usually takes place in two stages – simply because most families do not have enough yaks to load all their belongings onto them in one go. So one party goes ahead first; the yaks are lead back and then the second stage of the move begins. The most difficult item to transport is the nomads' accommodation – the black tent. It is divided into two parts, and, as previously mentioned, is transported as two 60 kg halves. Only yaks can tolerate this weight. This black tent – and these days often an additional, or alternatively, a white one – tells us a great deal about the life of the nomads.

3. THE "BIG BLACK SPIDER" AND THE WHITE TENT

Following the detailed study by FEILBERG (1944), the black tent has doubtlessly gained a certain anthropological fame (see also FAEGRE 1979, Chapter 1). They are widespread over Africa and Asia – they can be found among the nomads of Mauritania and Morocco, in Algeria and Iran, in Afghanistan and Beluchistan and also in Tibetan and in Ladakhi Changthang.

In Changthang, it is only the men who weave the tent from the yak hair. Women also weave (see Illustration 14) but never the tent. In contrast to the rest of Ladakh where it is only the men who weave, weaving in Changthang – where it also plays a much greater role – is something undertaken by women AND men. Sewing, however, is a man's job. The men in general weave the "male" items: saddle blankets, saddlebags etc. However, where the men are not available, the women are permitted to undertake this work too. However, women must NOT weave the tent – they are prohibited from laying a finger on it.

The tent (re bo) made from yak hair[5] is constructed from single lengths of weave stitched together (see Illustrations 15 and 16). These strips are 23-30 cm wide (the width depends on the size of the portable weaving loom and is 10-12 metres long. It is woven loosely so that light can penetrate and smoke can escape. These individual

5 In the description of the black tent I look primarily to the studies of AHMED (1996) in Rupshu (Changthang), MANDERSCHEID (1999a) on the Tibetan nomads in Dzangthang and likewise JONES (1996).

strips are sewn together to form two trapezoid halves, each half comprising 32 strips.

Although it lets in light, this tent is rainproof. It is firstly "impregnated" with the natural lanolin content of the yak wool, and then receives constant re-impregnation from the fatty smoke of the butter lamps and from the animal dung which is used as fuel. In addition to this the woven fabric of the tent swells when it rains and thus becomes denser.

The black tent is essentially a suspension construction, and thus minimises the requirement for wooden tent poles – after all there is no wood in Changthang.

Inside, the tent rests on two strong posts, forked at the top, a crossbeam running from one to the other. There are no other posts inside. Guy ropes are attached to the upper and outer stitching of the tent, and these lead to six or eight external posts (also forked at the top) a small distance away from the tent, and are tightened and secured to the ground with stones. All the tents that I came to know in Changthang provided an internal space of some 6 x 6 m or greater.[6]

The tent is always erected over an area of ground dug out to a depth of 80-100cm and lined with stones so that the inhabitants are protected from the wind when sitting on the ground. Within this wall there is also a stone shelf where, for example, one can store butter, keeping it cool whilst outside a 30°C of sun is beating down on the black roof of the tent.

In the middle, opposite the entrance to the tent, there is the oven, also built of stone. The stone enclosure and oven construction remain on this very same site and strictly belongs to one family. When the

---

6 MANDERSCHEID (1999a) records tent sizes varying from 5x5 to 10x10 metres. The tent which can be found in the National Museum of Denmark measures 8.75m x 3.75m (JONES 1996). BHASIN (1996) records a size of 4 x 3 m and JINA (1999) 41 square feet.

Illustration 14: Weaving in tent

family then returns to this spot they once again adopt this oven as "their own" (see Illustration 17).

The most frequently-cited descriptions of the Tibetan black tent originate from Father Régis-Evariste Huc, who travelled through China, Tibet and Mongolia in the middle of the 20th Century (HUC 1931 quoted by JONES 1996). He writes:

> With all this strange complication of sticks and strings, the black tent of the Tibetan nomads bears no slight resemblance to a great spider standing motionless on its long lanky legs, but so that its great stomach is resting on the ground. The black tents are by no means comparable with the tents of the Mongols; they are not a whit warmer or more solid than ordinary travelling tents. They are very cold, on the contrary, and a strong wind knocks them down without the least difficulty ... When they have selected an encampment, they are accustomed to erect around it, a wall of four to five feet high, and within their tents they construct furnaces, which are destitute neither of taste nor of solidity" (HUC 1931 quoted by JONES 1996, p. 94).

Father Huc, as we see here, does not avoid expressing valued judgements: for him the black tent is an ugly spider that blows down easily in the wind, and whose interior is likewise unstable and unattractive. Also subsequent authors do not speak highly of the black tent. To DUNCAN (1933, p. 72), the tent is a "huge spider with a hundred legs". HERMANNS (1949, p.48) views the black tent as "unconvivial housing"; and MANDERSCHEID (1999a) concludes her discussion of the tent by saying that it may well make sense in hot regions, but not under Tibetan weather conditions that prevail in Changthang – here the people in these tents are largely unprotected from the influences of the weather. Anyone who has ever spent a few hours in such a black tent in 30 degrees of heat next to permanently bubbling cooking pots and continuously being supplied with hot butter tea, or alternatively has experienced days of icy wind, will not be able to dispute the justification of these assertions.

Illustration 15: The black tent

Nevertheless, their black tent means a great deal to the nomads, though certainly today there are alternatives. One can buy material cheaply and sew together a white tent (gur) (see Illustration 18). It has the advantage that it is very much lighter (weighing just one third of the black tent), so consequently one can also make them bigger, and in summer it does not get so hot inside. On the other hand, however, it only lasts 3-4 years (the black tent will last for 10-12) and in winter it is much colder than the black tent. Today one can see both types of tents among the Changpa nomads, and those who can afford it will even have both, a re bo and a gur, a black and a white tent.

The interior of the tent – whether black or white – is divided into male and female space (see Illustration 19). On entering the tent, the left-hand side is the women's side. It is here the woman works, busies herself with various tasks and sits; it is here the children play, it is here the food stocks are kept, it is the woman's domain. On the right side is the men's space, where at the edge of the tent all the men's possessions are stacked up: riding blankets, saddles, saddlebags, etc. It is also on the right that the religious artefacts are kept, and it is only on the right that a Lama prays or a shaman goes into his trance.

As regards the seating order in the tent, the family, as well as guests, are divided according to gender (the smaller children sit on the female side, see Illustration 3). It is also hierarchical. Directly opposite the entrance over the oven there is a Buddhist altar with a shrine, offering cups, pictures often of Rinpoches, and particularly frequently the Dalai Lama. The seat next to the altar, on the female side as well as on the male side, is the seat with the highest status, occupied by the male head of the family on the right, and the female head on the left, or by the highest ranking guest. There is no doubt that I momentarily irritated my hosts, the shamans Ngawang and Sonam Lathar in their black tent in Thugu, when I, a woman with my three male colleagues, wanted to – and did – sit on the RIGHT (because of the tape recorder, photography and the possibility of being able to whisper to my colleagues), and, therefore, when a monk joined us later, he had no other place to sit except on the female side (see Illustration 40).

4. BARTERING: PAST AND PRESENT

One cannot discuss the nomadic economy in Changthang without also mentioning trade. Changthang, uncommonly barren, offers too little to enable even its most frugal population to be self-sufficient. There is a dire lack of wood, tea, barley and sugar.

Illustration 16: The material of the black tent: woven Yak hair

In the past Changthang was – and particularly in the purely nomadic region of Rupshu – a very important passage and stopping point for central Asiatic trading. Tea traders from Lhasa, and other traders from the Punjab, and from Kinnaur, Lahul and Kulu would pass through Rupshu on the border with Tibet (JINA 1995, p.52). Some goods were traded in Rupshu, and some further on in Leh. From Leh goods moved in the opposite direction.

By offering meat and wool, the nomads were tied into this trading and their most needed goods were tea and barley. The most important commodity, which came along with tea from Tibet to Rupshu and to Leh, was salt; and one of the most important commodities which came from Tibet via Leh and on to Kashmir was the much-desired *pashmina* wool.

Following the Indo-Chinese conflict in 1962, however, as mentioned above, the borders between India and China (i.e. also that of Tibet annexed by China) were closed. There are military guards on either side. The Indian military presence is visible all through Changthang. As a politically highly sensitive area, Changthang was accordingly out of bounds to all visitors. In 1993, however, Changthang was opened to Indian visitors and tourists, and in 1996, also to foreigners.

Nevertheless, the visiting restrictions for Changthang are to date still considerable: as a foreigner one can only travel with official written authorisation accompanying one's passport. The official procedure can take days. Furthermore, one is not permitted to travel alone; there must be a minimum of four foreign visitors. One's stay is limited to seven days (though with special permission can be extended), and the routes are stipulated.[7]

Since 1962, trading for the nomads of Changthang has changed fundamentally. Suddenly, with the closing of the borders to Tibet, all Tibetan *pashmina* exports foundered, as did all salt exports from Tibet. As regards *pashmina*, this was a great blessing for the Changthang nomads, for suddenly it was THEIR *pashmina* wool that was in demand, which previously had been of less value. This doubtlessly led to an economic upturn in

7 With special authorisation these restrictions can sometimes be partly lifted.

Changthang. Today *pashmina* is by far the most important trading commodity for the nomads. And its cost has increased tenfold since the border closing (though certainly this is also partly due to inflation).

There are today (primarily Muslim) traders from Leh and Manali, who buy the *pashmina* in Changthang and – at a considerably inflated price – sell it on to Kashmir, where even today still, most *pashmina* is processed. Joining this trade in increasing numbers, however, are also the emigrated Changpa nomads, and above all the Tibetan nomads who came to Changthang as refugees.

Tibetans are regarded as being extremely business-minded and in comparison with the Ladakhis they certainly are. Recently, Tibetans have been buying *pashmina* in great quantities, and a considerable amount is believed to be going over the border to China these days. The Kashmiri traders are already most concerned. And prices are rising.

Things are very different when it comes to salt. The salt caravans have completely disappeared from the central Asiatic region. Who needs salt any more from the salt lakes of Tibet? Ladakh brings sea salt in plastic bags, and that at minimal cost. And the Changpa nomads acquire their own salt for their personal needs. The salt required for their livestock (approximately 1kg per animal per year) is acquired from their own salt lake, Tso kar, to which they travel once a year with a large caravan of sheep to extract the salt (AHMED 1999).

Of the products sold by the nomads today *pashmina* is the primary commodity – in economic terms – followed by wool and meat and to a lesser extent butter and cheese. The commodities they lack and for which they trade or must buy are tea and barley and in more recent years other food products such as rice and lentils. Of particular importance for them is wood (above all for the tent posts) and metal artefacts like knives and kitchen equipment including pots and containers. Lately, there has been a significant increase in demand for cheap Chinese goods – primarily clothes, and also torches, kerosene ovens, thermos flasks and radios. It has been the Tibetan refugees

Illustration 17: Abandoned site which the family will return to at the appropriate time the following year. Clearly visible: the protective peripheral wall with the oven in the middle

driven out of China who in recent years have clearly been very active in promoting this "Chinese trade". As a result of this, one can find a happy mix of things ancient and new alongside each other in many nomads' tents today.

BHATTACHARJI (1993), who visited Rupshu for the first time in 1983, notes that ten years later, a considerable number of Changpa nomads own transistor radios, soap and pressure cookers, and handle bundles of banknotes. And regarding trade with China (Tibet), he says: "Trade with Tibet is quite common here but kept under wraps. Everybody participates, and everybody denies it, too"(p.131).

Totally in the dark lies an area of bartering which offers extraordinary money-making opportunities: smuggling *shahtoosh* wool of the wild antelope *chi ru*. The animal is an internationally protected species. Its winter "undercoat" is even finer than that of the Changra goat, but in comparison with the Changra goat yields only one-fifth to a third per year in amount of wool. Portraying Chinese Changthang today, SCHALLER (1993, 1997) has described most impressively the extent of this unbridled illicit trading and smuggling of *shahtoosh* wool. As regards the *chi ru* population in Ladakhi Changthang, however, no information is available; and any questions put to the nomads concerning the *chi ru* are only greeted with silence. However, Monisha Ahmed (1996) certainly found out a few things about it. She talks about 1994 and a "thriving business". At that time one kilo of *pashmina* could fetch 1,300 to 1,500 rupees, but for *shahtoosh* it was 22,000 – 32,000!

Tourism is certainly still not a regular, nor a much-pursued option for making money for the nomads, although a few Changpa have embarked on it, by opening "tea-shops", though mainly close to India and not in the remote, cold region around Rupshu, Korzok and Kharnak, building accommodation (in Korzok there is a tourists' campsite and a guesthouse for Indian officials) and earn money by hiring out horses and working as trekkers' guides. Even though this

Illustration 18: The white tent

may not be in full swing, it has nevertheless already made a great impact on the salary considered appropriate by nomads in Changthang. If a Changpa today hires out his services to tend sheep, he will certainly no longer be content with 550 rupees per month (12 US Dollars), and the man who is selected each year to take all the horses in the region to graze will likewise demand his earlier pay many times over.

Understandably, the demand for money in Changthang has increased overall. The conflict with China brought roads and bridle paths to Changthang. Military goods are carried along these routes, and also more recently lorries (heavy goods vehicles) belonging to traders. A Changpa nomad no longer leads his herds to Leh to barter and buy. Now they are transported in lorries and, starting from the valley of the Indus also buses. There is now also a growing trend for a number of families to get together (and pool their resources) to move all their belongings from one camping area to another by lorry. The money is there: *pashmina* has empowered them.

5. SOCIAL STRUCTURE: POLYANDRY, THE MULTIPLE-MALE MARRIAGE

In different regions man on earth has thought out many different forms of marriage. The most frequently encountered form is monogamy (two partners) and polygamy (several partners). With polygamy there are two distinguishable forms: polygyny (several women, one man) and polyandry (several men, one woman)[8] – the latter being much rarer throughout the world.

---

8 The terminology comes from the Greek *polys* = many, *gamia* = marriage, *gyne* = woman. *Polygynie* – many-women-marriage. *Andro* = man. *Polyandry* = many-man-marriage.

Illustration 19: The female and the male side of the tent; cooking implements and butter-tea container on the left, saddle bags and travelling bags on the right

An area in which polyandry has been explored in particular depth is in the Himalayas.[9] But polyandry in these regions is not the general rule, not the norm, – as monogamy is in the western industrialised countries – but one of several different options. The polyandry practised here is in most cases the so-called fraternal polyandry in which a woman marries several brothers.

I have only to observe the forms of marriage agreement in the families of some of my most important Ladakhi collaborators who have helped me with my Changthang research. One comes from a polyandrous family – two brothers are the fathers. The younger one, who in a polyandrous marriage is always in a subordinate position, is – rather defensively – today called "uncle".

Another collaborator has three "fathers" i.e. his mother has three brothers for husbands. The youngest is no older than the mother's oldest son, so for this collaborator a "father" and a brother are the same age. In this big family, there are many small children. A three-year-old boy is likewise a brother of my collaborator (son of the youngest "father", i.e. the youngest husband of the mother). Another

9 See AHMED-SHIRALI & SAIN (1994), BEALL & GOLDSTEIN (1981), BERREMAN (1960, 1962, 1968, 1975, 1978, 1980), BHATT (1991, 1997) CASSIDY & LEE (1989), CHANDRA (1972, 1973, 1987), CROOK (1994) CROOK & CROOK (1988), CROOK & SHAKYA (1994), FAHLÉN (2000), FERNANDEZ (1981), GOLDSTEIN (1971, 1976, 1977, 1978, 1981), GOLDSTEIN & KELLY (1987), GOLDSTEIN & TSARONG (1987), GUPTA (1985), HADDIX (1998), HERMANNS (1953), JAHODA (1994), KAWAKITA (1966-1967), LE CALLOC'H (1987), LEACH (1955), LEVINE (1977, 1980, 1988), LEVINE & SANGREE (1980), LEVINE & SILK (1997) MAJUMDAR (1954-1955, 1960-1963), MAJUMDAR & ANAND (1956-1957), MANN (1978a), NANDI (1977), PANT, RAWAT & SAMAL (1997), PARMAR (1975), PETER PRINCE OF GREECE AND DENMARK (1948, 1955a, 1955b, 1963, 1965, 1980), PHYLACTOU (1989), PITTARD (1900), Polyandry (1980), RAHA (1991), RAHA & COOMAR (1987), RIZVI (1987), SAKSENA (1962), SAMAL, CHAUHAN & FERNANDO (1996), SAMAL, FARBER & FAROOQUEE (1996), SARKAR (1973), SCHULER (1978, 1983, 1987), SHARMA (1987), SISHAUDIA (1987), SMITH (1998), STULPNAGEL (1955), TREVITHICK (1997), UJFALVY (1884).

three-year-old boy is a nephew, son of the oldest brother. The small nephew is also "uncle" to the youngest father....

My third collaborator comes from a polygynous family and chose this form of marriage for himself: he has two wives.

In the Tibetan culture the rules regarding polyandry are very simple. Two, three or even more brothers marry ONE woman. The oldest brother has clear priority and is also head of the family. Apart from the oldest brother having pride of place, the woman is expected to treat her husbands equally. Which child is from which father is of no great importance.

As a rule this arrangement works excellently. Otherwise, it would not have survived over the centuries. But, as with all forms of alliance, problems do of course arise. Problems arise, for instance, from envy and jealousy. Even if equal treatment is EXPECTED from the wife, (such as one would expect a mother to love all her children equally), preferences do arise and that can naturally lead to jealousy and tension.

The problem becomes more acute if the age difference between the brothers is great. Let us assume the oldest brother at the age of 22 marries a young woman of 20, and has two more brothers aged 18 and 15. The wife is then married to a 22-year-old, an 18-year-old and a 15-year-old man. And why shouldn't there be perhaps a further youngster, a boy of 4? He, too, may be included as a husband to this woman. And if, in the parents' marriage, further sons are born to the brothers, then these sons could also be husbands of the woman (GOLDSTEIN & KELLY 1987).

What solutions are there in the event of there being some jealousy and a large difference in age? The first solution would be a dissolution of the polyandrous marriage arrangement.

It is, however, not easy for a man to break from a polyandrous marriage. On paper in Tibetan culture each son is entitled to an equal share of the inheritance; but because the polyandrous marriage has been sealed in order to preserve the inheritance, a brother breaking from the marriage would not find it easy to reclaim his share (GOLDSTEIN 1978). And there are virtually no financial alternatives. That means: if only for economic reasons the brothers must try and resolve their differences – and that is in fact a formidable counterbalance for jealousy and other problems.

That men – particularly the younger brothers – WOULD indeed break away from a polyandric arrangement if they had economic alternatives, can be demonstrated in the case of the Tibetans in the Limi valley in North-West Nepal. After the defeat of Tibet by China, many Tibetans fled. They began trading in their new region and they brought their animals with them, which they sold very cheaply so they could move on. In this region of the Limi valley there were, therefore, suddenly two further economic alternatives – the trade of the Tibetans in exile and the opportunity to acquire livestock for oneself very cheaply. Many brothers from a polyandrous marriage took advantage of this. Since the Tibetans fled from their country, the number of "breaks" out of polyandrous marriages in Limi has increased noticeably (GOLDSTEIN 1977, 1978; see also PARMAR 1975 on the effects of education and economic change on polyandry).

However, under normal circumstances, breaking away is not an easy option. There is, nevertheless, another way out, and this course of action has also been taken within polyandrous arrangements – polygyandry.

Thus what sometimes happens is that the polyandrous arrangement is then extended to include two or three women, and so we do NOT have a polyandrous constellation any more, but a multi-female marriage (polygyny) and at the same time a multi-male marriage (polyandry). This arrangement is known as polygyandry.

If polygyandry is not sought as a solution, and a brother does break away from the polyandrous marriage, let us say one of the brothers who was sexually active, then the question of paternity regarding the children does become an issue. How are these children

84

split up, who gets which one? In many regions all children quite simply belong to the oldest brother. In other regions the woman – who otherwise does not refer to calculations regarding date of conception – designates the father. Or the children are divided quite simply, the oldest child belonging to the oldest brother, the second-oldest child to the second-oldest brother, etc. Alternatively, a die is thrown. Sometimes also the woman will allocate her favourite child to her favourite husband. All these different means are employed to resolve the situation.

Now there are still more marriage options for men in Tibetan culture:

There are, of course, families in which there is only one son – or none at all. If there is only one son, he will have simply a monogamous marriage. However, it is not forbidden, when marrying a woman, to also marry her sister or sisters, or even to take another woman in addition to the sisters. Thus we find in Tibetan culture also monogamy and polygyny, a many-woman marriage (see the case of my above-mentioned collaborator).

The other marriage possibility for men is marriage into the woman's household. If a family has only daughters, the daughter chooses a man, who – contrary to the common rules, which is patrilocal (i.e. the woman moves into the man's home) – moves into the woman's home (*mag pa* marriage as opposed to *bag ma* marriage, PETER PRINCE OF GREECE AND DENMARK 1948, 1963). With this move, however, the man has no rights to her property which remains in her hands. He must also adopt the name of his new family. If there are several sisters in the home, they share the man – a polygynous constellation, or they bring more men in to form a polygyandrous constellation once more.

Western researchers have puzzled long and hard as to why people enter into a polyandrous marital arrangement. PETER PRINCE OF GREECE AND DENMARK (1963), a polyandrous researcher schooled in psychoanalysis, believed that it was to do with suppressed latent male homosexuality, upheld by a reactionary psychological defence mechanism...

When researchers question the parties of a polyandrous arrangement as to their reasons, instead of speculating about Oedipus etc, they generally get an answer which is clearly linked to economics: with a brother-polyandrous marriage, property and belongings are retained and this alone enables them to enjoy a higher standard of living.

The nomads of Changthang are also familiar with polyandry – and in years gone by such arrangements constituted 40 per cent of marital agreements. If a father had 100 sheep and goats and three sons, and each wanted to have an equal share, this would result in three small, economically unsustainable herds and none of the three families would live comfortably.

Other reasons are also given: Every nomad had to supplement his living by trading, and furthermore go on exceptionally long journeys with part of his livestock – perhaps for months – so it was in the past. And if there is only one man, the woman is left alone with children to take the rest of the livestock out to graze all day and every day. In a polyandrous arrangement other husbands are still around to take over the normally male shepherding duties. In a polyandrous marriage the burden of work that falls to each man is also lighter than in a monogamous marriage.

One consequence of polyandry is that the population (growth) remains relatively stable. Of course, it does mean too that many women remain unmarried. However, these women can certainly still have children; it is not taboo and nobody looks on and asks who has fathered these children. A relatively consistent population size is particularly critical for survival in such an extremely barren environment such as Changthang, where natural resources – the grassland – is so scarce.

As much as polyandry might make sense in view of the economic basis and use of resources in such a barren environment as seen in

Changthang, so it is also certain that, primarily as a result of the influence of external contact, it is now in steady decline.

That "polyandry" is a source of amusement to "modern" man, is probably nowhere near as important as the change in values and attitudes through contact with the open market and the capitalist economic structures (see the study by FAHLÉN 2000 particular to Ladakh). With capitalist economic structures, the value of the INDIVIDUAL profit making inevitably goes hand in hand. The polyandrous marriage, on the other hand, is based on the value of COLLECTIVE profit making.

For the Tibetan culture in the Himalayan regions the earlier-mentioned nomad researcher, M.C. Goldstein, has presented some impressive demographic calculations that signify the erosion of polyandry in extreme environments like that of Changthang (GOLDSTEIN 1981, GOLDSTEIN & TSARONG 1987).

He terms such environments as "encapsulated". Encapsulation is, according to Goldstein, a situation in which, as a result of the prevailing – i.e. extremely restrictive environmental conditions, the possibility of any kind of planned increase in earnings is nil and the existing economic base and social structure (e.g. polyandry) is dictated by it.

The Changthang nomads cannot increase their income by increasing their livestock: there is insufficient grassland. They cannot farm more land: crop farming is almost impossible at such heights, in such a cold, windswept, and arid environment which is only free of frost for a short time. Substantially, increasing bartering would also be of little use because the products (consumer goods, property, wealth) are not fully compatible with a nomadic way of life.

Goldstein uses the term "encapsulation" when this system – e.g. as a result of a dramatic increase in population (instead of sharing one woman and having six children, each of the three brothers has one wife each, and each of those has six children) or as a result of a completely new source of income such as tourism – is shattered.

In the present context, however, it is not necessary to summarise the entire polyandry discussion – there are only two important elements I would like to point out:

1. What do aridity, wind and cold – the environmental conditions – have to do with marital arrangements? I hope I have clarified that under extreme environmental conditions, such as those described in Changthang, certain social structures – in this case polyandrous marriage – may have been thought up by man for a particularly good reason.

2. Following on from this, one can see that polyandry must not merely be viewed as an isolated and exotic curiosity of this culture, but more importantly as an ecologically-conditioned social and economic structure.

Nevertheless, a cultural-ecological perspective is in no way sufficient to fully "explain" polyandry; one must also take into account many other historical and cultural circumstances. The nomads of Amdo in Tibet live in conditions no less difficult than the Changpa nomads. And despite this HERMANNS (1959) failed to find one single case of polyandry in that region.

6. THE RELIGIOUS TRADITION: BLENDS OF BUDDHISM AND SHAMANISM

All nomads in Ladakhi Changthang are Tibetan Buddhists belonging to the Kargyad sect. For the nomad researcher and missionary EKVALL (1968/1983), Tibetan Buddhism is a "composite of abstruse philosophy, formalised doctrine and an extensive pantheon" of gods and spirits (p.80). On this pantheon he expands:

> The pantheon seems virtually limitless: Buddhas and Bodhisattvas perpetually releasing emanations, borrowings from the Hindu pan-

theon of numerous gods and demons, and the even more numerous spirit beings of every category taken over from the earlier pre-Buddhist folk religion of Tibet. Among those of the latter class there is a continuing, perceptible, increase. In the goblin class, for example, ghosts of the newly dead, having strayed from the round of rebirth, become additions to the fluctuating population. Gods also may have two aspects, the wrathful – which has given rise to some terrifying iconography – and the mild.

To these concepts of the supernatural and its myriad denizens, the Tibetans respond with a depth of devotion, shown in allocation of effort, time, and wealth, that has made Tibetan society and culture the classic example of religion-oriented living (EKVALL 1968/1983, p.80).

Similarly BRAUEN (1982):

The multiplicity of deities, gods and spirits is, including all local sub-categories, almost never-ending... What we have here is a most complex pantheon (BRAUEN 1982, p.247) (Translation J.M.).

The nomads, however, do not seem perturbed by this complex pantheon, and as far as Tibetan Buddhism is concerned, they are even less concerned about an "abstruse philosophy", or a rigid dogma. They have their own way of taking Buddhism seriously (alongside their deities and the abundance of spirits in their folk religion).

There are two monasteries in Changthang – the monastery at Korzok (see Illustration 20) and the Thugje monastery. At the annual five-day monastic festivals, the nomads participate with wholehearted devotion; they take a share in the preparations in many different ways: assistants are selected by the go ba as helpers in the monastic festival. Contributions – butter, cheese, tea and also pashmina (used to buy any additional item required) – are donated by everyone, animals are consecrated in the monastery, butter lamps are lit, people

Illustration 20: Courtyard of the monastery at Korzok

make prostrations and the monks are all honoured. Each nomad also has in his tent a Buddhist altar (see Illustration 21). This is located opposite the entrance to the tent, erected on the back wall, and it consists of a shrine with relics, icons of Tibetan Rinpoches – often of the Dalai Lama – and the seven offering cups. They also contribute to Buddhism in that each family offers a son to the monastery. In the past this was the norm, and families still do this frequently even to-day.

Further evidence of the nomads' commitment to Buddhism and the high esteem in which they hold it can be seen in their attitudes towards killing animals. According to the teachings of Buddhism, the killing or even just the injuring of every form of life – be it even an insect – should where possible be avoided[10] as it has an adverse effect on the cycle of rebirths. This puts the nomads into a paradoxical situation. After all, they MUST castrate (injure) their animals, they MUST kill animals in order to eat, and to protect themselves from the notorious cold of winter. In winter they wear sheepskins: woollen clothes would never be adequate. The injuring and killing of animals is, therefore, unavoidable. The nomads have a great number of "precautionary measures", to mitigate the adverse consequences of these necessary practices: when castrating animals, people are usually hired from outside, and before killing an animal they pray to it for forgiveness (AHMED 1996 for more details and examples).

More important to the nomads than Buddhism, however, are certainly the aspects of their religious traditions stemming from pre-Buddhist times – their belief in countless numbers of gods and spirits that are often place bound and are worshipped in that place: moun-

---

10 Nevertheless in 1983 the ethnologist Peter Prince of Greece and Denmark – much to his horror – watched a bloody animal sacrifice in Korzok/Changthang (PETER PRINCE OF GREECE AND DENMARK 1974/1975).

tains, river sources, lakes, passes.[11] To the nomads these gods and spirits are indeed very real: "The Changpa live in the midst of formidable swarm of gods (*Lha*) and demons (*Deh*), whose rustling they hear, whose breath they feel, of whose vague forms they catch glimpses in the darkness" (BHASIN 1996, p.80).

Also much of everyday life, everyday space and everyday business is interwoven with these divine spiritual beings. One can best describe these if one studies the interior of the tent.

In the middle of the tent – dividing the female and male sides – is the oven. The oven is a holy place. It is inhabited by an oven deity (*thab lha*). One must, therefore, ensure particular cleanliness at the oven. No litter of any sort may be thrown into the ashes, and also no food must overboil. If this does occur, the oven spirit must be appeased with offerings. Before each meal, a small offering is brought to the spirit of the oven.

Apart from the middle of the tent – the oven space, the place of the Buddhist altar – is also the right-hand area, the male area of the room, associated with religion. As mentioned earlier, all religious objects are kept on the right-hand side. Another holy place, however, is – for no reason that a Changpa could ever begin to explain – the left-hand area of the tent: the seat of the *pha spun* god (*phug lha*). *Pha spun* is an ancestral group (following the male line); they worship a common god or spirit and they help each other at special stages in the life cycle – primarily in the event of a death. The *phug lha* sits right at the very top of the tent and is honoured by the head of the family every morning with incense and a butter lamp.

The interior of the tent is not only divided horizontally into sacred and non-sacred areas, but also vertically:

11 In this summary I follow – as far as it also applies to Ladakhi Changthang – the description of HERMANNS (1949, p. 47-51), and then above all AHMED (1996, p. 93-106). See also KAPLANIAN (1995).

Illustration 21: The interior of a black tent: the Buddhist altar above the oven (with, amongst other things, an image of the Dalai Lama)

94

The Changpa nomads' world is divided into three. The "Upper World" is occupied by the gods, the *lha*. It is called *lha yul*, domain of the gods and is associated with the colour white. The top part of the tent, where the god *pha spun* resides, belongs to this world.

The "Earth World" (*bar tsan*) is inhabited by man and the spirits of *tsan*. Viewed from the front the *tsan* are beautiful female figures, but from behind their body is open and one sees all the guts. The "Earth World" is associated with the colour red. The more central space, the middle layer of the tent's interior, as it were, is *tsan* space.

The "Lower World" (*yog lu*) is the realm of the *lu* spirits that reside in water and under the earth; their colour is blue. The floor of the tent and everything under it is the *lu* area.

Of the two interior tent posts, the one at the back – next to the seat of the *pha spun* god by the altar – is considered the connecting line, a channel of communication linking these three worlds (AHMED 1996).

All these spiritual beings, gods and demons have a very specific character: they are sensitive, rather demanding, easily irritated, but nevertheless are basically well-meaning. They do not give anything for free. They constantly require respect and sacrifices and they are also appeased prophylactically in many ways by the nomads (daily gestures to demonstrate their deference, small offerings) or alternatively by "retrospective" appeasement – when "something has already happened", some harm has been caused, perhaps a man or an animal has become ill – by means of grand, dramatic shamanic rituals (see Chapters 4 and 5).

The most important gifts the Changpa nomads bestow upon the gods and spiritual beings of all three worlds are sheep. Each family selects five (always male) sheep from their herd, which are dedicated to, or consecrated in the name of the deities and spirits.

The ram presented to the gods (*lha*) in the white (*kar po*) world is called the "white sheep of the gods" (*lha lug kar po*). The sheep dedicated for the *tsan* is the "red tsan sheep" (*tsan lug kro po*) and the one for the world *lu* is the "blue *lu* sheep" (*lu lug ngon po*).

Additionally (at least in Rupshu), a sheep is dedicated to the deity Genpo and another one specially selected to protect against a curse – curse in both senses: cursing meaning angry words and thoughts of other people, and also a curse that may bring misfortune in life. With incense and prayers for this sheep, one can be assured that all evil spells of this type are banished (AHMED 1996).

Also the others, the white, red and blue sheep as well as the Genpo sheep are consecrated every morning with incense. Further more, these animals are never slaughtered or sold. When one dies, a little wool from its coat is tied into the coat of its successor, the next "god-ordained" sheep.

(Male) horses and yaks are likewise dedicated to the gods and spirits of the three worlds and to Genpo, but not from every single family – they do not usually have sufficient horses and yaks to meet the needs of the white, red and blue world – but from the monastery instead. As I mentioned earlier, the monastery also owns herds that are cared for by the Changpa in turn. The monastery, too, has its white *lha*, its red *tsan* and its blue *lu* sheep. At the big monastic festival in July all these animals are brought into the monastery yard and are decorated by the Rinpoche with a *kha tak* (ceremonial scarf) and honoured with incense and prayer.

In earlier times, goats played no part in religion and ritual. Goats were seen in a more negative light. Shepherds in particular do not like them since they are so much faster than sheep and keep the herdsmen running about, swearing and cursing endlessly. It is only a recent development that goats too have been dedicated to the gods, spirits and to Genpo. Earlier, when goats were economically far less significant than they are today (with the price of *pashmina* having risen by a large factor making the goats more valuable than sheep) there were no white, red, blue or Genpo goats. But today most families also consecrate goats for the deities in the same way. That goats have also been drawn into religious ritual life demonstrates how economic factors can influence religious practice.

97

In addition to those already mentioned, there is one other class of animal dedicated to the gods. They are called *tshe thar*, literally: life-saving. *Tshe thar* can be any animal, horses, yaks, goats, sheep (though not dogs) and indeed of either gender. Such animals are mainly associated with a particular person when they are in need. The animal's gender must match that of the person. Let us assume a child becomes ill: a *tshe thar* is chosen for him or her. The animal is chosen by throwing a rosary high into the air and observing which animal it lands on. This selection must, however, be legitimised with a blessing by a Rinpoche (a prominent Buddhist dignitary). In this way, the animal gains its special power to protect this person. *Tshe thar* animals are given highly preferential treatment: *tshe thar* horses may not be ridden, *tshe thar* yaks may not be used to carry loads. Furthermore, these animals may not be killed. When a *tshe thar* dies, long after the child has recovered from his or her health crisis, a new *tshe thar* is not necessarily designated.

Yaks play a special role in man's tributes to the gods. An especially fine looking specimen is sought: it must be of noble stature, completely black, with beautifully shaped horns. This selected yak (male or female) can be laden, though only with "pure" burdens. Impure burdens would be, for example, the woman's clothing; a pure burden would be the tent's Buddhist altar. These chosen animals, which should honour and appease the gods, are treated in a special way at New Year: butter is smeared onto their horns and hooves, and they are adorned with prayer flags.

Up to this point, we have examined nomadic religion inside the tent and then outside in the herds, but now we follow on – primarily with DOLLFUS (1999)[12] – with an examination of the wider landscape. As Rupshu was the main region under examination for AHMED (1996), so Kharnak is for DOLLFUS (1999), and a comparison shows that there are considerable regional variations in religious practices.

12 See also MA LIHUA (1993) for Tibetan Changthang.

Indeed all REGIONS (*yul*) have their special deities (*lha*) – the *yul lha*. Most of them reside in the mountains, and most particularly in the impressive (awesome) or craggy mountains. Their palaces are up there, on high. These palaces are inaccessibly enthroned above the snow and glaciers. At the foot of the mountain, the mountain gods have, so to speak, their second homes *lha tho* (the seat of *lha*), a holy place constructed mainly of stones stacked up, and decorated with an abundance of prayer flags (see Illustration 22). This is where man comes to worship them.

The mountain deities of a religion vary in importance; they each have their position in a hierarchy – according to the power allocated to them. In the region (*yul*) of Kharnak the highest (*chen po* = great) deity (*lha*) i.e. the *yul lha chen po*, [who is] the Ka la bu skyong, whose name indicates the most important power he has – to give sons. His palace is a particularly beautiful mountain, at the foot of which, at 4,150m, stands his *lha tho*, his home in the valley.

There, at the *lha tho* of the greatest mountain god, a ritual takes place every year. During this ritual, he is honoured with offerings and approached with uncountable requests.

This *yul lha chen po* ritual takes place within the five-day religious monastic festival and is performed by a monk, a Lama belonging to the monastery. It is not only for the monastic festival but also for this ritual that the assistants, called up by the *go ba*, gather gifts, which serve as offerings, from all the inhabitants.

The *lha tho* of the supreme mountain god is one hour away from the monastery. Having arrived there, the Lama will, first of all, re-adorn the *lha tho* – with new yak horns, with prayer flags, with *kha tak* – and then perform libations with *chang* beer and lay down offerings.

These offerings are designated for, *inter alia* Padmasambhava (a very important figure in Tibetan Buddhism) and for the "God of this place", i.e. for Ka la bu skyong (the mountain deity here is not specified by name, thus it must be a pre-Buddhist deity), and so both are peacefully united in this ritual performed by a Buddhist monk.

One of the highlights of the ritual is the recital of prayer texts. In preparation for this the monk removes his sheepskin coat and puts on the Buddhist red stole around his neck and shoulders.

Also in prayers Buddhist and non-Buddhist elements are mixed. One pleas to this mountain deity, above all, for protection against all misfortune that can befall man or animal:

> Reduce to a speck of dust within a minute
> and whatever they are the obstacles
> who harm the Buddha's Doctrine and the Community
> Raise their conscious mind to the unborn dharmādhatu,
> Dismiss on enemies the ma mo and all kinds of diseases and
>   epidemics
> Dismiss on enemies the 404 kinds of illness
> Dismiss on enemies the 360 bdon (gdon) demons
> Dismiss on enemies the 80,000 obstacle-creating demons dgegs
>   (bgegs)
> Dismiss on enemies the 81 bad omens (ltas ngan)
> Dismiss on enemies all the terrible accidents.
> May the wishes of the yogi be fulfilled...
> (DOLLFUS 1999, p.107)

As we shall see, this Buddhist monk's prayer could be spoken just as easily by a shaman. In the next chapter, I shall describe the Ladakhi shamans and their methods of healing, their healing rituals and healing techniques.

Illustration 22: A latho on the pass to Changthang

CHAPTER 3

The shamans in central Ladakh

1. SHAMANS, MEDICINE MEN, HEALERS: DEFINITION AND DIFFERENTIATION

Shamans and medicine men are traditional healers. They are viewed by their culture as experts in traditional healing methods. They have specialised knowledge on the concepts of health, illness and healing specific to their particular culture.

Different cultures have varied ideas about health, illness and healing. What, in western culture, might not be considered a "proper illness" – "burn out", chronic fatigue syndrome or stress reactions – is in other cultures a much-discussed syndrome called "soul loss", which, once diagnosed, leads to a series of formal healing approaches and treatment (RÖSING 2002b).

Traditional healers – be they shamans or medicine men – always become officially recognised through vocational experience and through education and initiation into the occupational group. In all cultures, they are subject to a certain "quality control", which enables one to distinguish between traditional healers who are experts on the therapeutic management of illness, and charlatans who merely purport to be experts.

The difference between shamans and medicine men can be defined by their way of healing. It is important to remember this difference and not to simply call all traditional healers "shamans", as often happens in everyday conversation (and in the commercially well-established scene of "plastic shaman".) Out of five criteria, the first and most important distinguishing feature of a shaman (TOWNSEND 1997) is his healing practice in a state of altered consciousness.

1. Medicine men heal in a state of everyday consciousness. In contrast, shamans go into a state of extraordinary consciousness. The technical term is ASC – altered state of consciousness. This is the central criterion for the difference between the two types of traditional healers.

There are two sorts of shamanic altered states of consciousness and with it also two types of shamans: one being a "flying trance", in which a shaman, in this state of consciousness, travels into the transpersonal world of gods and spirits; and the other being the "possession trance" or "embodiment trance", in which the transpersonal beings – gods or spirits – come to the shaman and "possess" him.

The altered state of consciousness of the shamans in Tibetan culture, to whom we are referring here – whether in the former Tibet or in Ladakh – belongs to the possession-type trance. In the following pages I shall just use the term "trance" but this refers throughout to the possession-trance.

The altered state of consciousness, during which the shamans heal, is, however, not the only factor that defines a shaman. If this were the case, one would not be able to distinguish him from a "madman" imagining he is possessed by an other-worldly being that has given him special healing powers.

In addition to the altered state of consciousness, the minimum number of additional defining factors of a shaman that must be taken into consideration are the following four:

2. Shamans are mediators between two worlds, man's world and the transpersonal world.

3. In their mediation between these two worlds, their attention is directed to the human world, as shamans go into a trance in order to help and heal the people of THIS world.

4. Shamans have control over their extraordinary state of consciousness during which they heal; i.e. they can choose to go into this state of mind, and also to come out of it (which distinguishes them from the above-mentioned "madmen").

5. This state of extraordinary consciousness is only applied in a specially sanctioned, institutional, i.e. in culturally well-defined ritual contexts.

According to this minimum definition comprising five distinguishing features, no person who is prone to uncontrolled episodes of altered consciousness or persons who go on personal "consciousness trips", or who heal in a non-institutional context, or under conditions of normal consciousness, can be termed a shaman. Let us summarise the five elements into a concise definition of a shaman:

Shamans are traditional healers who, under a controlled state of altered consciousness, mediate between the human and the transpersonal world, are focused on this world, and, in the context of sanctioned and institutional rituals, help, prophesise and heal.

2. RESEARCH UPDATE

Shamans in Tibetan culture – including Ladakh – belong to the genre of possession-shamanism. Various aspects of shamanism in Ladakh have been explored by AHMED (1990), BRAUEN (1980), DAY (1989,1990), FRANK (1983), GOLOMB (1995), GUTSCHOW (1997), KALWEIT (1987), KAPLANIAN (1981, 1984, 1985), KAPLANIAN, RAAB & RABOUAN (1992), KRESSING & RÖSING (2001b), KUHN (1988), RÖSING (1997), SCHENK (1990, 1993, 1994, 1996), VOLF (1994) and YAMADA (1991/1993).[1]

The nomadic shamans of Changthang, however, are not featured in any of these works – a vast Ladakhi region has to date been neglected. As I pointed out in Chapter 1, this omission is also true of Tibetan Changthang.

This volume addresses precisely that gaping hole in research: the shamans in Changthang. After I had already completed 15 research trips to India, eight being field trips to Ladakh and seven to

---

1 See also the Collected Work of Isabella Krause (1991) on "The Phenomenon of Possession in Tibet and Ladakh", which, in connection with Ladakh, does not cite Kaplanian, Frank, Kalweit, Kuhn, Day or Schenk.

Delhi and Benares to pore over the translation of the terribly difficult shaman texts, I undertook field trips in 2000 and 2001 to the
nomadic shamans in Changthang.

Certainly, the research into the shamans in Ladakh including
my own – though excluding Changthang – gives a good account
which describes some of the general aspects of shamanic healing
in this region. I will treat this healing tradition in five parts:

- Monastic and village shamans;
- "Madness", the shaman's calling;
- The transformation of "madness";
- The shamanic séance; and
- Popular perceptions and attitudes towards the shamans.

3. MONASTIC AND VILLAGE SHAMANS, OR THE DANCE AT THE PRECIPICE

In Ladakh, the shamans are called *lha pa* or *lha mo*. *Lha* means
deity -*pa* being the masculine ending, and -*mo* the feminine ending. The English word "oracle" is also used for shamans in Ladakh.
This label is derived from one of their activities: making predic-
tions about the future, unravelling secrets, identifying thieves, lo-
cating missing belongings.

In Ladakh, there are two different types of oracles; the monastic
oracles and the village shamanic healers. During the big annual
festival of some of the Buddhist monasteries in Ladakh, the performance of oracles is part of their tradition. Through lengthy
meditation, they move into a deep trance, then perform in trance,
display extraordinary behaviour, predict the future and answer
questions for anyone who can get near them.

As an example, I would like to mention the oracle of the monastery at Thiksey. In November 1995, I took part in the two-day
monastic festival. On the first afternoon the monastic oracle, known

in everyday life as Lobsang Chotrak, performed for the first time. After a very long wait, by which time the excitement and anticipation among the audience had risen to fever pitch, he stormed up from the inner monastery in his dramatic shamanic disguise and onto the highest roof terrace where countless numbers of spectators had gathered. He raged about wildly, lashing out with his sword at one group of spectators, then at another one. Horrified, they backed away from his weapon. Sweat was pouring from his contorted face. He leaped up effortlessly onto the boundary wall enclosing this highest terrace, and danced up and down as though he were being chased from one end of the scene to the other, wildly gesticulating with his requisitions (see Illustration 23). This wall is barely 40 cm wide and very uneven with pieces broken off in a number of places. On the side overlooking the central courtyard of the monastery, there is a 10 or 20 metre vertical drop.

Everyone caught their breath.

A few ventured closer to him and asked him questions. In the huge general excitement, in the great crowding, the many shrieks from the audience, the loud panting and groans of the oracle and the resounding music which the monks were playing from another terrace, I could make out neither the questions nor the answers. After five or ten minutes drama was over.

Two days later, I had the opportunity to talk to Lobsang Chotrak in his house. He was, of course, not in trance.

As a small boy his parents handed him over to the monastery at Thiksey. As I mentioned, it had been the Ladakhi tradition (and it still is in part today) that each family gives a son to the monastery. During the fifth year of his life, Lobsang started to wear a monk's red cloth.

But he does not wear it now. He renounced it as a young man, left the monastery, lived in Leh for two years and then got married. However, he then returned as a layman and took up certain monastic duties as a monastic administrator (chag dzod).

The traditional monastic oracle – so Lobsang said – was not available, and another oracle had to be selected before the big festival plays. This is done by using a divination technique known as *tag ril* and is usually only carried out in monasteries. Despite the absence of his monk's cloth, Lobsang was called in to join this divination. This was not a chance happening. For, one day during the monastic plays, when he was participating – without his cloth – he fell into an involuntary trance – indication of a possible calling to *lha* possession (see below). And so it was that he joined a number of candidates, one of whom would be selected as an oracle. Lobsang describes the *tag ril* experience as follows (HI-20):

དེ་ནེ་དགེ་འདུན་འདུ་ཁང་དེ་ནང་ང་རྟགས་རིལ་གཏང་གག་ལེ། དེ་ནེ་
རྟགས་རིལ་བཏང་སྟེ་ནང་མེ་གོ་གསུམ་གྲུ་བ་གསུམ་ཡ་ལེ་བྱིང་གག
དེ་ནེ་དེ་གྲུ་བ་
གསུམ་མའི་ནང་ནེ་ཡང་གཅིག་གཅིག་ག་རྟགས་དཔྱད་བཙོས་པ་དེ་
ནེ་དེ་གསུམ་བེ་ནང་ན་དེ་ང་བྱིང་གག།

རྟགས་རིལ་པོ་འདུ་ཁང་ང་འབྱེར་དེ་ནང་ན་ཆོས་སྐྱོང་མ་དུན་ལ་
གསོར་སྐྱེམ་ཕུལ་དེ་དེ་ནེ་རང་རང་དེ་མེང་བྱིས་དེ་ཁོ་ལག་གོ་ནང་ང་
བཏང་སྟེ་དེ་ནེ་རིལ་རིལ་བཙོས་དེ་ནང་གར་ཡོལ་ཅིག་གེ་ནང་ང་
བཏང་སྟེ་བརྫོར་ར་རོག། དེབརྫོར་ར་ནང་མཉམ་པོ་དེ་ཆང་མེ་ཁྲོན་
གཅིག་གཅིག་ཤག་བྱིངས་སྟེ་ཚ་རོག། དེ་ནེ་དེ་ཁོ་ལག་པོ་གསེད་དེ་
བསྒྲས་པ་སྤུའི་མེང་འདུག་ལུ་རོག། གསུམ་པོ་ལ་བཏང་པ་སང་ན་
གཅིག་གཅིག་བྱིང་གག། གཅིག་གཅིག་པོ་དེ་མེང་པོ་ཡོད་གག།

Translation:

Then the monks performed the *tag ril* divination in the prayer hall. When this was completed three monks emerged as candidates.

Illustration 23: Lobsang Chotrak, the monastic oracle of Thiksey, dancing at the precipice (Cham-plays 1995)

And from the three monks they then selected one. From those three they chose me.

Tag ril proceeds as follows: the monks come into the prayer hall and prepare the offerings (*ser kyem*) of the guardian deities. The candidates' names are written (on small pieces of paper) and these bits of paper are pressed into *tsam pa* pastry from which round balls are made and placed in a container. The container is shaken and suddenly one ball rolls out. The *tsam pa* pastry ball is opened and the name inspected. Following the divination for the three names, one name came out, and that was mine.

The chosen one must then spend one month and eight days in complete solitary confinement in a retreat (*tshams*), meditating and practising tantric exercises as prescribed by Paldan Lhamo (*tene palden lha moe nyan pa tang gos sa nok*) and on the day of the festival the signs of being possessed by a guardian deity will be recognised (*tene srung ma skyod shes si rtags po bi nga nok le*).

"And what", I asked Lobsang Chotrak, "do the people ask the oracle while he is in trance?" Lobsang answers: "I don't remember..." (HI-20):

དེ་པོ་མ་ན་ང་པ་ཏུ་ཡོང་ང་མ་ནོག་ཡ། ང་གཉིད་ལ་སོང་མཁན་ཚོག་
ཡིན་ནོག །དེ་ཟ་ན་ལྷ་པོས་གསུང་གཏང་སྟེ་ཡིན་ནོག །ལྷ་པོ་ང་དང་ང་
སྙིང་ང་ནང་ང་འཐིམ་པ་སང་ན་ང་ཏེ་དེ་པོ་མ་ན་ཉུས་སྟེ་མེད་ཁན་ཞིག
ཚ་ཡོད་གག། མ་ན་མེད་མཁན་ཚ་ནོག།

Translation:

I don't know, I can't remember anything at all. It's as though I'm in a deep sleep. At that stage it's only the god speaking, the deity engulfs our whole heart; we lose consciousness; it just goes away, that's what happens; it completely disappears.

A monastic oracle goes into trance only once a year – at the time of the monastic festival plays. At no other time does he go into trance. There are also monastic oracles at other monasteries including Shey, Mato, Stok, Traktok, Likir, Gya.

Among the spectators watching the oracle at the monastic festival plays at Thiksey in 1995 was also Sonam Murup, one of the best-known shamans of central Ladakh. I learnt the most from him, and it was he who confronted me most dramatically with the problem of amnesia (RÖSING 1997) which Lobsang Chotrak manifested so clearly. Sonam Murup died in 1999 at well over 90 years of age.

Sonam Murup belongs to the second category of oracles in Ladakh, the village shamans – those who HEAL and go into trance at every healing séance. These shamans are there for the ill, the unfortunate and those who seek divination.

No-one can say exactly how many shamans of Sonam Murup's kind there are in Ladakh. Estimates in the past are: perhaps eight? maybe ten? possibly even 20?

Certainly today all shamans without exception (and also all non-shamans) agree about one most noteworthy phenomenon regarding the "demography" of Ladakhi shamans: they all say that in the last ten years or so there has been a huge proliferation in the number of shamanic callings, and that the number has increased three or even four-fold. What is also most striking is that it is predominantly women who are now becoming shamans. Annoyed, disgruntled and moody (uncharacteristic for Sonam Murup) he said to me that he no longer felt inclined to take on female shamanic candidates; he simply wanted to instruct a MAN once more... (HI-24).

Together with a collaborator, I have investigated this phenomenon regarding the increase of shamanism in Ladakh in a research project (KRESSING & RÖSING 2001b). There is much to indicate that this proliferation is a result of social tensions which has arisen from the diverse influences of modernisation and contact with the outside world. This theory is backed up by the fact that in remote nomadic Changthang there has been no such increase in the number of shamans (see HI-37, HI-38, HI-43), as the Changthang shamans I met and many other testimonies maintain.

4. "MADNESS" AS THE SHAMANIC CALLING

The narratives of the Ladakh shamans' paths to their vocation, though varying in detail, nevertheless, all have common elements. The calling always begins with a mental problem. The problem is described primarily as a kind of "madness" (tsha ba tshu ba, nyon pa song are the most commonly used terms for it), manifesting as erratic roaming around, various aches and pains, vivid dreams, confused visions and hallucinations, or perhaps indecent or nonsensical behaviour and running away. Initially, these people are always looked upon as being "mad", until gradually it becomes clear that they are not suffering from a non-descript "normal madness" but from a shamanic illness. The problem is caused by a dramatic struggle between a lha, a god, that wants to possess the body, and the de, the demons.

I would like to give four examples of those narratives of "madness" as an expression of shamanic vocation. Firstly, I want to describe it as I witnessed it in a young man, Deldan – who had already been diagnosed as having a "shamanic illness" during two shamanic séances (HH-7 and HH-8) – and secondly how he describes the condition himself (HI-18).

Then for my second example Sonam Murup – whose healing techniques and ways of thinking I had come to know particularly well through the many healing séances, teachings and conversations – reports on the course and development of his vocation as a shaman. Finally, two female shamans then tell of their calling.[2]

---

2 With the exception of Sonam Murup, who explicitly gave me permission to mention him by name, I have given the shamanic men and women pseudonyms to protect their identity.

(1) Deldan

I am at a shamanic séance (HH-8). There are about 30 people in the room – all patients, seeking help. Two female shamans are conducting the séance. (See below for proceedings.) By singing, drumming and ringing bells, they move deeper and deeper into trance. They have a shamanic assistant, Deldan. Prior to the session, he prepared the altar and made all the other necessary preparations, and was highly focused in carrying out this task. He caught my attention very quickly because he was constantly muttering to himself and somehow seemed breathless. Whilst the shaman women sang and drummed he swayed along rhythmically and is also sounding a bell.

All of a sudden, he lets out a great cry towards everybody, hunches himself up, face contorted as though in extreme pain, stares towards the window as though utterly horrified, hunches himself up anew in acute "pain", rips off his coat, thrusts his arms into the air, immediately draws them back in as if in panic, groans loudly, grinds his teeth, grunts to himself, and begins to dance on his knees, curls up again, cries out ... the whole outburst was incredibly dramatic.

Everyone present watched the drama, absolutely fascinated and spellbound, eyes wide open – and completely without embarrassment. Sometimes, everyone winced (myself included) when he let out a piercing shriek, or shuffled back for fear of perhaps getting hit in the face during his wild gesticulating.

For a long time, the two women shamans continued undeterred, the singing, drumming and ringing forever intensifying. But then – it had come to a point where one had to fear that the shamanic assistant would physically collapse (from hyperventilation) – the leading shaman quite calmly puts aside her drum and bell (though continues to sing uninterrupted), approaches the shamanic assistant kneeling on the floor, gently leans his upper body forward, lets her right hand rest on the man's neck as though soothing him and then sprinkles a little water on his neck with the other hand.

This continues for some time. The man remains crouched forward, motionless onto the floor. Finally, the shaman picks up her drum and bell once more and the proceedings continue.

Deldan, however, had calmed down entirely – that is what she had achieved – and stepped out of his role as shamanic assistant. He then sat normally and quietly – just like all the other participants – and later carried out menial non-sacral errands for the acting women shamans.

I have had long talks with Deldan (HI-18) as I had with other shamans and shamanic apprentices. His story is dramatic. Time and again, he has gone "mad". Once he even injured himself. He showed me the terrible scars:

Deldan:

ང་དམ་ན་སྐྱོན་པ་ཚིག་སོང་ཉེ་རང་ང་མ་ན་སྐྱོས་ལོ་ག་ཚིག་གཉིས༑

A woman shaman, his mentor, joins in the conversation:

མགོ་ཚང་མ་བ་འག་ཌོག་ཎེ་ཚང་མ་མེན་བདུག་སེ་ཡིན་ཉོག་ཡ༑

Deldan:

ཉེ་རང་ང་ནོ་འདི་ལུ་སྐྱོན་ཡོངས་མེ་ཡོད་ཉེ་རང་ང་། པད་འདི་སག་མེ་
བདུག་མེ་ཉེ་རང་ང་། འདི་སག་མེའི་ཌེས་ཡིན་ཉེ་རང་ང་འདི་བོན་
གཟིགས་སང་། མེས་བདུག་པའི་ཌེས་ཡིན་ཉེ་རང་ང་།
དེ་ནེ་འདི་ཌ་ཡོད་ཕེན་ཉེ་རང་ང་འདི་ག་ཡང་ང་ཅི་ཌེ་ར་ཡོད་པ་ལེ༑
ནོ་འདི་ག་མ་ན་པད་ཞག་ག་ཚིག་མཆན་ལ་མ་ནེ་དུས་ཕེང་འཁྱེར་
སོག་ཉེ་རང་ང་། དུས་མ་ན་སྐྱར་ཚིག་ཡ་ལེ། དེ་ནེ་ཡང་ཕོབ་སེ་
འཁྱོང་སེ་ཡང་རེན་པོ་ཚེན་འཁྱེར་སོག་ཡ་ལེ། དེ་ནེ་རེན་པོ་ཚེན་
འཁྱེར་པ་འདི་ནེ་ལྷ་སྐྱོན་ཡིན་ཚུག་མོལ་པ་སང་རེན་པོ་ཚེན་ཡང་འག༑
ཌེས་སལ་ལེ་ཡིན་ཚུག༑ སྐྱོན་པ་ཚིག་ཚེན་འདུག་ཀྱུག༑

116

Translation:

Deldan:
It is as if I have gone mad. For one or two years I was mad.

A woman shaman, his mentor, joins in the conversation:
He cut his head and then inflicted all these burns on himself.

Deldan:
It was the *lha* illness that afflicted me. Suddenly, I was driven to burn myself in these places on my body. You can see the scars here. Look at this! They're burn scars.

After that we rented a room here in Leh. There, however, it (the madness) drove me out at night. I completely disappeared. When I was found I was brought to the Rinpoche. The Rinpoche declared that I was afflicted with the *lha* sickness and he gave me a letter (for an experienced shaman, who would take over the separation of *lha* and *de*). But I have remained mad up to this day.

That means *lha* and *de* are still within him, unseparated. And when at the start of a séance he senses the faintest hint of trance coming on, the *de* breaks out – so he explained to me – and it was then that all the dramatic events of that séance unfolded.

(2) Sonam Murup

Sonam Murup (see Illustration 24) had instructed many younger shamans, who are now all practising independently (I myself know at least a dozen of his erstwhile students). He was also an intriguing instructor for many western researchers, myself included.

This man was extremely kind and loving, indeed tender, but also wild and hot-tempered and uncouth. His face was covered with hundreds of wrinkles, he was as old as the hills, as thin as a rake and a bundle of energy during his séances – from his booming voice over his springily agility, to the power-packed gestures of his uncommonly long, narrow hands. I have learnt most of what I know about him from his shamanic seances (HH-3, HH-4, HH-10, HH-12, HH-13) and from my many conversations with him (see primarily HI-8, HI-11, HI-24 and also HI-23, HI-27).

Let us see what he has to say about his vocation and his life story. I cite it from Amélie SCHENK (1994, pages 39, 50-51). Sonam reports:

> When it began, no-one was bothered about me. I behaved as though I was mad (*nyon pa*), and whether it was *de, shin de, son de, tsan* or *lha*, nobody was interested...

> Before I became a shaman, I roamed and flitted around everywhere. Sometimes, the *lha* carried me off for several days, they led me to unknown spots in areas I was unfamiliar with. No-one could find me there, even when they were specifically looking for me. I frequently just disappeared. If ever I saw a horse I would jump up onto it and gallop away – I did not remember any of that afterwards but subsequently people told me about it. I rode everywhere. I could control the horses and managed to cover long distances at great speed. Even then people said of me: the *lha* is coming to him! When the *lha* came the first few times he rode to all kinds of *gon pa* with me. All this happened at a wild gallop right until the destination. I received many ritual ablutions (*chab-thus*), seven times alone from Bakula Rinpoche, but mostly from Stakna Rinpoche and from our own monks up in the monastery.

> It happened that I suddenly stopped doing whatever it was that I was doing, and fell into a deep, deep sleep. My consciousness was then, as it were, carried away. Also, sometimes, I would be out and about and I would suddenly get lost or no longer know where I was. Then everybody would come looking for me, my parents, all my relatives. They would look everywhere for me, and for a long time.

Illustration 24: Sonam Murup

Because of my own experiences, I know how important it is to help the new *lha* straight away. As soon as I realise that a *lha* is coming to a person, I get that person to a Rinpoche as quickly as possible. Usually that is to the Rinpoches in Stakna and Spituk. Then, as soon as they have seen for themselves that a *lha* is manifesting itself, they appoint me to adopt that person as an apprentice and to train him as quickly as possible. If it takes too much time it can become difficult. Now that I am older, however, I have more stamina for the training.

For three years, I did not know what was wrong with me and during this time *lha* and *de* were in continuous conflict and plagued me. For three years I was helpless. It was difficult at that time to find a Lama who was experienced in these things as there were only a few of them. All Rinpoches were still very young, including Stakna Rinpoche. For three years, the *lha* tormented me and declared: I am a *lha*. I don't care whether you believe me or not, sooner or later I shall do just what I please with this *luyar* (receptacle body for a *lha*).

The inhabitants of Thiksey were entirely on my side. They looked after me and always kept an eye on me, regardless of what I tried to get up to or where I went. When a prayer was offered for me on the tenth day of the month in a house, the *lha* within me would drive me, and I would run so that I could take part. Whenever there were celebrations going on somewhere in someone's house, the *lha* within would drive me every time and I would run directly to the house in question.

In those days, it often took me off in the middle of the night, I simply ran out of the house. Once my family were searching for me all night long and only discovered me towards dawn – in a small cave in the mountains. It was not easy to find me there as the cave was well concealed.

On another occasion, I was torn from my home and had been away for several days when a shepherd from our vicinity discovered me. It was early morning and he turned up in the Arzu valley with his herd of goats. They had already gone a good distance when suddenly the herd took fright, started to bustle and prepared to take flight. The shepherd thought it was a wolf and started yelling out. He attempted to hold the herd together and ran this way and that. But of course there was no wolf. What he found was me. I must have looked a terrible sight: shabby, pale and weak. The man grabbed me and pulled me out of my hiding place. Presumably it (the *lha*) would otherwise have sent me off further afield. As he seized me so tightly I struggled and yelled out all hell for leather. But it was no good; he brought me home.

Before *lha* and *de* were separated, I had to go through a lot. Compared with my students today I had to endure a protracted ordeal. I ensure that my students, in contrast, endure no more pain after four or five months.

In those days, I received the *lha* mainly in the presence of a Rinpoche; the same applies to my students too. When, at that time, I used to burst head over heals out of the house, the monks and the village inhabitants instantly saw that I was a *lha* and not a *de*.

Really, everything that was possible happened to me. Once I was nearly arrested. A policeman accosted me. Luckily a Tibetan intervened and took me along with him and thus rescued me.

To start with I did not know what had happened to me. Only three years later did I sense that a *lha* wanted to enter my body. However, my father Tsering was not convinced and was suspicious of the whole business. He had great doubts and finally brought me to a very high-ranking monk at the monastery in Thiksey. He was to bless me, take care of me and elucidate the causes of my difficulties. He recognised that a *lha* was entering me. So he blessed me once more and recommended I seek a mentor.

I had the same mentor as my brother. He came from Sakti and lived there too. He blessed me first and then showed me how I had to do good things to people, to heal them. Then he taught me to heal animals and preserve all life. Since then thirty years have passed.

I now feel I have been released and unburdened. My body feels good. I am content. Back then, when the *lha* came to me, I was very concerned as to whether or not it really was a *lha*. Every time it took over me and drove me mad, I wanted to die; I also thought I had to die. But that's all over now. My family life is good, everyone is healthy and my children and grandchildren are all well. To begin with I had to be very strict with myself. I could never drink out of another person's cup. Now I am old and much has changed. An old *lha* is allowed to do some things that a young one must not. Now I drink from other people's cups.

Today I can say: to be a *lhapa* is not an easy undertaking, it does not make life any easier; on the contrary, it makes it more difficult and creates many *problems*, bringing unrest into life. As I personally view it, it's a strenuous life, the life of a *lhapa* (SCHENK (1994: 39, 50-51; Übersetzung J.M.).

(3) Dechen

No less dramatic was the start of events leading to Dechen's shamanic vocation (HI-16).

She speaks enthusiastically and with great intensity about the time when this condition came over her. It was very unsettling and caused her continuous unease. *Lha* and *de* had still not been separated (*nyis ka lha ang zhuks, de ang zhuks te le*). She was out walking and wanted to pick some flowers, and when she picked them – something remarkable came over her. She became more and more deranged (*nyon pa*) and after that she could not remember anything; she no longer felt herself. She was always behaving nonsensically: for example, in a bus she would just sit in reverse direction on her seat or she would hop around on one leg... Often she was unable to remember what had happened;

once someone poured water on her head in an attempt to bring her to her senses but she could not remember where she was ... She once came to a *lha tho* (a *lha*'s dwelling place) and suddenly lost her mind and ran from it so quickly that no one could catch her and bring her in. (At this point in our editing of the transcript my collaborator Tsultim tells me that his daughter, also a shaman, would also regularly go into trance at the sight of a *lha tho*...) And at night there was something in the room; the others also noticed it, but they were unable to see it; only she could see it. On another occasion she saw the figure in shaman's clothing; no-one else could see it, only her. Then she saw butter lamps lighting up. But nobody else saw it. She ate nothing all day long and was most ill at ease... She went to Bakula Rinpoche and then to Stakna Rinpoche, and they confirmed that it was a *lha*, and Stakna Rinpoche said that she should go to Ayu Lhamo, a woman shaman, or to Sonam Murup, and have *lha* and *de* separated and seek instruction.

(4) Kunzes

The path to shamanism for Kunzes was not so dramatic (HI-18), possibly due to the fact that a *lha* possession was by no means unfamiliar to her family. Her father was a shaman, her brother was a shaman. And then – having had four children – the *lha* came to her.

She describes earlier minor peculiarities, her feeling of unease and inner unrest (*tsha ba tshu ba*), her semi-conscious roaming around, her nonsensical behaviour in everyday life, e.g. while cooking, and her provocative behaviour particularly towards her parents. (At this point during our transcript work, again Tsultim, drawing from personal experience with his daughter, mentioned that when the *lha* manifested itself, her aggressive and defiant behaviour towards her parents was particularly pronounced.)

Their first step as parents was to bring her to Abi Lhamo (i.e.Ayu Lhamo from Sabu) for healing – treating it as a "normal madness", which would naturally fall within the healing expertise of a shaman.

But the shaman soon recognised that this was a "genuine" *lha* (*lha ngos*), and she was taken to Stakna Rinpoche. Clearly, the parents wanted Stakna Rinpoche to STOP the *lha*. However, the Rinpoche said that such action would risk their daughter's life; this *lha* was already far too deep within her. And he gave her a letter to take to Abi Lhamo, for her to then separate *lha* and *de*.

With great deference the parents and daughter went to Abi Lhamo with the letter from the Rinpoche. And she separated *lha* and *de*.

But still the *de* remained. The path of suffering continued – she was still not able to apply her powers to benefit the patients. The uncle first had to perform many *thus* (cleansing with pure water and many prayers) – and this would evidently help the *lha* to break through. And now it is anchored so deeply within her that it would be impossible to stop it:

དག་གུ་བཞི་སྐྱེས་སྟེ་ནེ་ནེ་ང་ཡོངས་པ། སྲན་ལ་ད་ཁ་བ་ཡོང་གྱག་ལོ། ཨ་བེ་ཀ་ན་དམ་བཅའ་བཙོས་གྱག་སྲག་སྟེ་རེན་པོ་ཆེ་སོ། དེ་ཀ་ནེ་ཨ་བེ་དམ་བཅའ་བཙོ་ཡིན་ཞིག་དང་མིང་བོ་ལ་ཡོངས་ལོ། མིང་བོན་ཡོངས་སྟེ་མིང་བོའི་དམ་བཅའ་བཙོས་འབུག་ཆེན་རེན་པོ་ཆེ་སོ་མཛད་གྱག། དེ་ཀ་ནེ་རྟེང་བོ་ན་ནེ་ནོ་རྣག་གེ་ང་རང་ང་ཡོངས་སྟེ་དམ་ནེ་པད་ཆབ་ཚོབ་བ་ཀ་ཏོན་སོང་བཏང་ཀ་ཏོན་སོང་བཏང་ང་མེད།

མར་ནག་བགལ་ལེ་ཡོན་ན་མར་ནག་བགལ་ཀན་བོ་ཁོ་རང་མ་སྲག། ག་ཙོང་མ་ནེ་མ་བཏང་ང་རེས་ག་རེག་ཙོང་མ་ནེ་མ་བཏང་ང་ཁར་ཞི་བཙོས་སྟེ་ཡོང་འདུག། རེས་འགན་རེག་མ་ནེ་རྒགས་པོ་མ་ནེ་པ་ད་མེད་པ་འགྱལ་བཏང་སྟེ་ཡིན་ནོག་པ་ལོ། མ་ནེ་ང་རང་མ་ནེ་སེམས་པ

བར་ཞིག་ག་མ་ནེ་ཨ་བ་ཨ་མ་གུན་ལའང་ལན་མ་ནེ་ནི་ནི་ཡར་
ཡར་ལོག་འདུག། ཡ་པད་འཁྲབ་བྱེས་གཅོག་པོ་ཡོང་ང་རག་པ།
ད་པད་འཛིང་མོ་བཏང་བྱེས་སེ་ཅན་ཞིག་མ་ནེ་ནི་རྩག་མ་ནེ་ནི་རྩག་
ཅི་ཏོང་ཟེ་རེན་མ་ནེ་བསམ་མ་མེ་རག་ཡ་ལེ། ད་ག་ནེ་ལོ་དེ་རྩག་པད་
འཁྲབ་བྱེས་པོ་ཡོང་ང་ཅིག་དང་ད་ནེ་མ་ནེ་ལོ་དེ་གརྲགས་པོ་པ་ད་
མེད་གན་ཅོག་ཞིག།

དེ་རྟིང་ནེ་ད་ནེ་ལོ་དེ་ཨ་བི་ལྷ་མོའི་ག་སྟེབས་པ་ད་ནེ་ལོ་རྩག་གི་ད་ནེ་
ཁོ་རང་དུས་བཟང་ཞིག་ག་འདུག་དེ་ཡོད་པེན་ཡ་ང་ན་རང་ཅང་མ་
ནང་ང་ལེ། ཡོད་པ་སང་པད་ཆབ་ཆུབ་ཡོང་བཏང་ཏོག་མ་ནེ། ཆབ་
ཆུབ་ཡོང་བཏང་པ་སང་མ་ནེ་ལོ་རྩག་གི་གཅིག་གཅིག་ག་ཆང་བཏང་
ངེན་འདུག་སྟེ་ཡོད་པེན་ཡ་ལེ། ད་ནེ་ང་ལྷ་ཡིན་ཟེར་རེན་པད་ཆང་ལོ་
ཁོ་རེ་མགོའི་ག་རྟོན་བཏང་ཏོག།

ད་ག་ན་ནེ་ལྷ་དངོས་རྟོགས་ད་ད་ནེ་རེན་པོ་ཆེ་མཆལ་ལ་སོང་སྟེ་ད་ནེ་
རེན་པོ་ཆེ་རྩག་སྲུ་མཆལ་ལ་སོང་སྟེ། རྩག་སྲུའི་རེན་པོ་ཆེས་ད་མ་ནེ་
མགོན་པོ་རང་ཅི་བསམ་ཏེ་ཡིན་ཁྲི་འདུག་གུའི་སྲོག་ག་བར་ཆད་
དགོས་ས་ད། ད་ནེ་བར་ཆད་དགོས་ཤེས་ཡོད་ན་ནེ་ད་ནེ་ཡོང་མ་
བཅུག། ཁོ་ལྷ་སྲིང་ང་འཁྱིལ་ཆར་རེ་ཡིན་ནོག།

རྩག་སྲུ་ནེ་འབག་དམ་བཏང་སྟེ་ཨ་བི་ལྷ་མོའི་འབག་དམ་བཏང་ལེ། ད་ནེ་
ལྷ་དང་འདྲེ་པེས་མོ་ལེན་ཞིག་དང་། གཉེར་མཆོད་བེར་མཆོད་བསྙིག་
སྟེ་ཨ་བི་ལེ་ད་འབག་མཆལ་དར་ཕུལ་ཏེ་འབག་དམ་བོ་སལ་འདུ་འདུ་ང

ནམ་ནེ་ཕྱུགས་རྟེ་མཛོད་དེ་ང་མིན་འདོད་ཆུག་ཟེར་ཏེ། དེ་ནེ་ཁོང་ལ་
འཆུ་ཟེར་ཏེ་དེ་ནེ་ལྷ་སྲུང་ན་ནེ་ཁོ་རང་གུན་ནེ་ཅི་མོ་ལ་རང་མོ་ལད་ཀུག།

དེ་ནེ་ཡ་བ་ཨ་མ་གུན་ཆང་མ་མོང་སྟེ་འཆུ་བག་སྲིས་དེ་དག་གུན་ནེ་
རྲུག་མཐོང་ཏག་ཡིན་མཐོང་འདུག། ནི་རྲུག་བརྒག་མཐོང་འདུག།
འཆུ་འཆུ་ཏེ་རང་གུན་ནེ་ཅི་མཛད་ནའང་ཕྱུགས་རྟེ་མཛད་དེ་མཛད་
ཟེར་ཏེ་ལྷུང་ནང་ཞུས་ཀུག་ཡ་ལེ། མིའང་ཞུས་ཀུག། དེ་ནེ་ལྷ་དང་འདྲེ་
པོན་མཛད་དེ་ཡིན་ཀུག་ད་ཁོང་དེ།

དེ་ནེ་ནོ་དེ་ག་ནེ་ཕ་ལ་ནེ་དེ་ནེ་ལྷ་དངོས་རྟོགས་དེ་བསྐྱོད་ཡིན་ནོག་ཡ་
ལེ། སེམས་ཅན་ནེ་འགྲོ་དོན་ཞིག་གང་སྒྲུབ་མ་ཕུབ། ད་ཅ་བ་ཁྱེས་
པོ་ཁོ་རང་ཆོ་ཞིག་སལ་ཡ་གུ་ལེ་གུན་ནེ། པད་ཁྱུས་སལ་ལེ་སལ་
ལེ་ཁྱུ་རང་དེ་ལྷ་དག་གཅང་ཡིན་ནོག་ཟེར་རེ་ཡ་གུ་ཞེས་མ་ནེ་ཏན་
ཏན་མཛད་དེ་དེ་རྲུག་བཅས་སེ་མ་ནེ་དག་ས་འདྲུག་ཆེན་རིན་པོ་ཆེ་
དམ་མ་ད་རིན་པོ་ཆེ་གང་སོང་ཆང་མ་ཁྲེ་རེ་དམ་བཅའ་བཅས་མོ་ལེ་
མ་ནེ་བཅོ་མ་ཉན། ད་ཁོ་མ་ན་སེམས་ཅན་ནེ་འགྲོ་དོན་སྒྲུབ་སེ་ཡིན་
ནོག། སྙིང་ང་ཆུད་ཆར་པ་ན་ཅང་ཉན་བྱེ་མེད།

ལྷ་དང་འདྲེ་ཡ་བི་ལེས་པོན་མཛད། ཡ་ཡུ་ལྷ་མོའི་རྟེང་ན་ཁབ་ལྷུང་
པོ་དང་འཇིབ་ལྷུང་པོ་དར་ཅིད་མ་ལྷ་མོ་དར་ཅིད་མ་ལྷ་མོའི་ཀ་སལ་
ཡིན་ལེ། དེ་རྟེང་ནེ་དེ་ནེ་འ་རྟེང་ན་དེ་ན་ལོ་གཅིག་དང་རྲ་བཞི་རྟེང་ནེ་
ཞིན་ན་ང་རང་ནེ་ནང་ང་དེང་ཞུས་ཡིན།

Translation:

It came over me after my fourth child was born. For sure the *lha* came to my father first. And my father took his vows (*dam cha*) before Stakna Rinpoche. After my father had made his vows, the *lha* came to my brother. He also took his vows, before Dugchen Rinpoche. And after that the *lha* came to me. It caused me great unrest (*chhab chhob ba* or *tshab tshub*), and I no longer knew what I was doing or not doing.

Sometimes I would put onions in the mustard oil without heating it up and sometimes I would cook without adding any onion at all. Other times, I would rush around, unaware of my physical body. And because I had *no* control over my mind (*sem pa*) I behaved rebelliously towards my parents. I would suddenly start to argue vehemently. I would suddenly start with an outburst and could not do anything about it. And then such a feeling would come over me and I would no longer have any idea of what was going on.

And then we went to the old woman shaman, Abi Lhamo. It was a propitious day. As we sat next to her, a feeling of great unrest (*tshab tshub*) came over me again. We sat there and somebody was offered *chang* (local beer) as this unease overtook me. And I said at once: I am a *lha* and took the beer and poured it over his head.

When finally it became clear, that it was a real (*ngos*) *lha*, I went to the Rinpoche. We went to Stakna Rinpoche (and my father asked him to stop the *lha*).

Stakna Rinpoche said to my father – Mr. Gonpo, do you want to risk your daughter's life? It would put her life at risk to stop the *lha*. The *lha* is already deep in her heart (*syning*).

Stakna Rinpoche then gave me a letter to take to Abi Lhamo, which read as follows: Please separate *lha* and *de* for her! (So we went to her once more.) Once we had prepared the offerings, we gave her the *kha tak* and bowed down before her and gave her the letter and begged the favour of her (to separate *lha* and *de*), so that I could become a normal person again. That is what I asked of her. In trance, the *lha* then said whatever he felt like saying.

My father and mother also turned to her and asked in all respect: our daughter has so many difficulties (*dag lib*) – please (try and resolve them). And they asked the shaman to do some good – whatever it was – and most of all they asked for help. And then *de* and *lha* were finally separated by the shaman.

So that was done, and then the real (*ngos*) *lha* came to me. But I was not yet able to help people through healing. My uncle then arranged a great number of *thus* for me (cleansing with pure water and prayer), and after he had performed so many *thus* for me, he said – now you are a pure *lha*. He performed everything with the greatest care and also instructed me to go to Dugchen Rinpoche and other Rinpoches, wherever they might be, to make my vows (*dam cha*). We would be unable to proceed until this had been done.

Now, however, all the necessary requirements to help all people have been met. The *lha* is anchored deep in my heart and nothing can stop it.

So *lha* and *de* were separated by the shaman Abi Lhamo, and then I received instruction from the woman shaman from Tarchid on how to remove needles from the body (*khab lung*). After one year and four months, I started practising here in my house.

On examining these four accounts of "madness" as the starting point of the shamanic calling – alongside the other published reports (SCHENK 1994) and the many accounts documented by me – one can identify three common themes that keep manifesting themselves:

1. In the life stories and professional development of the Tibetan/Ladakh shamans, "madness" plays such a funda-

mental role at the outset on the path towards a vocation in shamanism, that in every case one can say that these shamans are called to duty through this "madness", brought on by a *lha* (DAY 1990, p.208).

If a person behaves as described above, people in Ladakh certainly do not automatically suspect it might be a shamanic calling. In the Tibetan teachings on illness there are many different forms of "madness", distinguished in part by the degree of "madness", as it were slight or severe "madness"; and in part by the cause of the "madness" – e.g. the sort of possession (witches, souls of the dead, *de*....)

2. Secondly, as a general rule, healing is first approached by using Tibetan medicine, though in many different ways: by means of food and herbs etc. on the one hand, but also by means of religion, the Buddhists' way – pilgrimages, prostrations, reciting mantras, on the other.

3. If there is no improvement over months or even years, one resorts to comprehensive Buddhist house rituals. And if that does not help, there is only one final course of action: a Rinpoche must be consulted. And only at this stage in the illness do the family and village people gradually come round to contemplating the prospect of a *lha-de* possession.

The Rinpoche now has the difficult task of ascertaining whether the madness in question is simply "normal madness" or whether it is caused by a *lha-de* struggle within the body of the afflicted person.

The Rinpoche examines the case with all his books to hand: is it a case of the body being occupied by a *lha*, a god (even if it is in combat against evil spirits) – in which case this is the (afflicted) person's call to shamanism? Or is it a *de* – a normal, common madness? Without confirmation of there being a *lha*, i.e. a divine possession, no candidate in the whole of Ladakh can ever begin education into shamanism or become a shaman.

The Rinpoches, the highest dignitaries of Tibetan Buddhism, are thus the critical key figure on the path to becoming a shaman. They must give their *ka*, their command, their sanction, which is given in writing. The candidate diagnosed with a *lha* receives a letter from the Rinpoche. The letter is directed to a prominent shaman, usually specifically named, who is asked to separate *lha* and *de*, and to begin with the task of instruction and training.

In my conversations with all the shamans I have spoken to, they have all stressed how absolutely essential it is to have the formal sanction of a Rinpoche (here, e.g. HI-18).

Deldan:

རིན་པོ་ཆེའི་བཀའ་མེད་པ་ནི་ཅང་ཐབས་མེད་ཀྱག་ཡ།

Kunzes:

རིན་པོ་ཆེའི་བཀའ་མེད་པ་ནི་ཚོ་ལའི་མ་ནེ་སྱཉང་མ་བཅོན་ཡིན་ རོག།

Dechen:

མ་ནེ་མ་ཉན་བ་ཡིན་རོག།

Translation:

Deldan:
There is no possibility of becoming a shaman without the sanction of the Rinpoche.

Kunzes:
Without the Rinpoche's sanction a shaman cannot help anyone.

Dechen:
It's completely out of the question.

5. THE TRANSFORMATION FROM "MADNESS" TO CONTROLLED LHA POSSESSION

Whenever a Ladakhi is presented to a Rinpoche in a state of *tsha ba tshu ba* ("madness"), and is then diagnosed by him as being possessed by a *lha*, there are still various powers – divine (*lha*) and evil (*de*) – in conflict. What is then required is the "separation of *lha* and *de*": that is the universal explanation given by all shamans.

One can perhaps clarify the task that now needs to be undertaken by rephrasing it (admittedly in non-shamanic terms) as follows. *De* represents the negative aspect of the altered state of consciousness, which represents the point of origin of the shamanic calling. Aimlessness and absence of control are the essence of this negativity – of the *de*.

A person called to shamanism cannot consciously decide when he goes into his special state of consciousness, nor can he decide how he will behave while in that state – he has no control over "When" or "How". The "madness" simply happens to him and his behaviour is erratic and aimless.

It is now a question of linking this experience – this altered state of consciousness into which one is thrown powerlessly – with certain signs, and a plan of action, so that exclusively this constellation of signs triggers the altered state of consciousness in which focused action (i.e. healing) is possible. It is a formidable task of transformation! This is precisely what happens in shamanic instruction.

It is very difficult to describe exactly the nature of this tuition. Neither master nor student can describe it – since during instruction both are, without fail, in trance. If the student is not in trance then nothing can be taught. Sonam Murup mercilessly flogged his students and subjected them to "psychoterror" until they really did in fact become "mad" (a tendency which they certainly brought with them), i.e. put them in a state of altered consciousness. Once the state of trance has set in (i.e the *lha* state is established) the student has total amnesia. Nothing more can be remembered about this process.

Fortunately, a great number of young shamans do know at least something about how the tuition proceeds. I also had the opportunity to observe a number of tuition sessions. The shaman apprentices do, however, go to great lengths to make it clear that they do not remember anything personally, and that they have been told by other people. This is plausible. For often a student – as Sonam Murup and others told me – has an assistant present, who mediates between the instructor in trance and the student who is possibly not yet in a state of trance – and who, for example, "translates" for the student, telling him what the instructor under trance has asked him to do.

The instruction comprises a number of distinguishable tasks. Naturally, the candidate learns the rules of purification, the preparatory tasks that must precede a séance: washing hands and perhaps also face and neck, rinsing out one's mouth.

Another integral part of every shamanic séance is the preparation of the Buddhist offering (*nyer shod*). This is the very first thing the pupil must learn. He must pray and sing, and recite mantras. The *da ma ru* drum must be beaten and the bells sounded. The master does it incessantly, the student must simply follow him in this process. He must also learn to burn incense and how to put on the shamanic costume.

All this must first be mastered perfectly. It must be commanded in a state of trance – in altered consciousness, during *lha* possession – tied in with an abundance of sensory, visual and acoustic signals. It is like a process of conditioning. It will be the sensory experiences – as reported by the shamans (see Chapter 4) that enable the shaman to slide into trance.

Only then are specific healing practises learnt. One of the most important healing practises of the shamans from central Ladakh is the extraction of *dib* – liquid pollution, dirt, bewitchment, *jadu* (destructive magic) – or even of solid objects of the same origin. These tasks are always practised in the first stage of the learning process in connection with healing. Fortune telling and learning to cope with such difficult spiritual beings as *ti mo, ti po, shin de, son de*, are reserved for later stages of learning.

All reports on shamanic instruction – whether from the shamanic masters about the contents of their tuition or from shamanic apprentices about their newly-gained knowledge – concentrate always on the remarkable and elaborate experience of an examination ritual, testifying to the completion of the *lha-de* separation. It is a dramatic test, and, at least for foreign researchers, is full of "irrationality". The candidate is introduced to one perplexing conundrum scenario after another, and only when everything is solved and is correct is he a full-fledged *lha*. In order to clarify shamanic tuition and this challenging test, I would like to document what two young women shamans themselves have to say. First, I shall summarise what Dechen (HI-16) explained to me in great length and detail. She went to Sonam Murup for her instruction. We learn how Murup teaches and tests. Then I give Palzes' account. She received her tuition from the shaman, Kunzes.

(1) Dechen

First of all, the master teaches *ser kyem* for four weeks: the preparation of offerings and recital of prayers – this is how the *lha* is invoked. Then follows a significant testing scenario which probes the authenticity and strength of the *lha*. There is a big gathering for that: the family must be present, as well as a monk, and also neighbours and of course the examining shaman. The *lha* is invoked through prayers and singing: Sonam Murup goes into trance, and she (Dechen), too, falls into trance. But she cannot remember anything; she was told what happened:

Sonam Murup hid mustard grains somewhere under the carpet and she had to step across the carpet. A *lha* will not step over mustard grains and she chose exactly the way to avoid them.

Next, a black and a white stone were placed in an opaque fluid, and she picked out the correct stone – or so people told her; she herself did not remember. The *de* would have taken out the wrong stone.

She was also led into another room where certain objects had been hidden: her *lha* would have to find the hidden objects straight away. Her *lha* had evidently achieved this. There were (she says) always correct and false objects. A *de* would pick the wrong ones. But she was told she did not make a single mistake.

And once the test has been passed, the tuition, *la pok*, continues. It is only the *lha* that teaches (Sonam Murup only instructs when in trance). First comes *dip lung* (*dip* = pollution, lung = instruction), then *khab lung* (*khab* = needle).

This means: firstly the apprentice is taught how to suck out some poisonous fluid, and then how to remove solid objects from a patient's body. Her *lha* swallowed everything that she had removed. Her *lha* had been very strong. Today her *lha* would spit it out.

And *khab lung* proceeds as follows. In trance, Sonam Murup is given a glass of milk containing a needle with a five-coloured thread on it. He drinks up the milk, needle included. She (Dechen) is in deep trance (*lha zhug ste nanga*), and the instructing *lha* asks: "Where in my body have I hidden the needle? Suck it out!" And indeed, she sucked it out. But she herself again remembers nothing. She only knows from others.

She was given a great deal of instruction in *la pok* – but by no means learnt about all of it. She can suck *jadu* and *dib* from the body of the patient, but she is still rather unfamiliar with *ti mo, ti po, shin de, son de*.

(2) Palzes

I would like to quote the description by shaman Palzes verbatim (HI-18/4), not least because it nicely illustrates the shamanic-Buddhist amalgamation relating to shamanic training and the shamanic "examination":

དེ་བོ་དངྷྱེ་དགར་ནག་ཁྱོངས་ཏེ་ཁོ་གན་མ་ནེ་མདུན་ལ་འདུག་མ་
བཅུག་པ། དེ་ནེ་ཆུའི་ནང་ད་རྟོག་བིག་གོ་ནང་ད་རྒྱ་བཏང་སྟེ། དེ་ནེ་
ཡང་ནོན་པོ་འཁྱོང་ནའང་ཡ་བླམ་འཁྱོང་ནའང་ཡང་ཁོང་གན་ལ་
སྐྱེ་འདྲེན་ཚོག་ཤིག་ཕྱུལ་ལེ་རོག། དེ་ནེ་ནོ་དེ་རྣ་ད་ཅེ་ཏོང་བི་ཏོང་
རིག་སྣས་པ། སྐུ་ཡིན་ན་དེ་གན་ལེན་བྱེས་འབྲེན་བྱེས་ཅབ་ཅབ་
འབྱོང་བྱེས་ལེ། འར་རྟོ་རྟེ་སེམས་པ། ཕྱོ་རིན་ཆེན་འབྱུང་གནས། བྱ་
ང་ནོན་ཡོད་གྱུག། རྣབ་སྣང་བ་མཐའ་ཡས། དགྱེས་རྡུམ་པར་སྣང་
མཛད་པོ་ཆང་ག་མང་ད་རིག་ཅེ་ག་བཙའན་ནོག་པ་ཡ་ལེ། དེ་ནེ་དེ་ཕྱུ་
རྟེ་ཕྱིང་བྱེས་ལེ། དེ་ནེ་དེ་ད་འི་རྣུག་གོ་ཁོའི་ཁོ་རང་རྟེན་འགྲེལ་ཞིག་
ཡོང་ངད་གྱུག་པ།

དེ་འོ་རྣུག་གོ་ཕྱུ་སྐྱེ་བཙོ་རྣུག་པ་མེ་མེ་ལེ་གན་ནེ། མ་ན་འི་རྣུག་གོ་
ཁོ་རང་དྲང་པོའ་འགྱོར་འདུག་ཡ་ལེ་ཡོས་པ་ན་འགྱོར་བྱེས། ཡང་
མགོ་ལོག་ཅེ་ག་མ་ནེ་ཕྱུ་འི་རྣུག་གོ་ཅེ་ག་འདྲེ་མང་ད་རིག་ཡོད་གན་
བོ་ལ། འི་རྣུག་གོ་མ་ན་ཅེ་ག་ཁོ་རང་དྲུལ་ལེ་ཀོ་རེ་ནང་ན་ཆུའི་ནང་
ན་འ་བོ་མགོ་ལོག་ག་འགྱོར་འདུག་པ་ལེ། དེ་ནེ་ནོ་རྣུག་བཙོས་མེ་ནོ་
དེ་ཆང་མ་བཙོས་མེ་ཁྲིག་བཙོས་མེ་ནང་ནེ་དེ་ནེ་དགོན་མཆོག་གོ་
མཐུན་ག་རྣུག་གོ་ཕོ་འད། འར་རྟོ་རྟེ་སེམས་པའི་ག་ཡིན་རོག། ཕྱོ་

135

རིན་ཆེན་འབྱུང་གནས་ཀ་ཡིན་ནོག །བྱང་དོར་ཡོད་སྐྱབ་པའི་ཀ་
ཡིན་ནོག །ནུབ་སྐྱང་བ་མཐའན་ཡས་ཀ་ཡིན་ནོག །དབུས་རྣམ་པར་
སྣང་མཛད་ཀུན་ནེ་ཀ་ཡིན་ནོག །

ཟེར་རིན་ཞིག་དང་རེ་རེ་དང་རེ་རེ་ལག་པའི་ཀ་ལེན་བཅུག་སྟེ་དེ་ནེ་
སྐྲན་ལ་འིན་ན་ཏུ་ཐུངས་ཀར་གཏང་འདུག་པ་ལེ་ཡོག་ག། དེ་ནེ་འདེ་
ཐང་ང་འཁྱི་རིན་ཞིག་དང་དེ་ནེ་ཕོ་དེ་ད་དར་ཚང་མ་པོ་སེ་དེ་ནེ་མི་གུན་
ལ་བདུག་རྣས་བྱི་མོ་གུན་ལ་ཁ་བཏག་བཀལ་ལེ་དེ་ནེ།

དེ་ཕོ་བཅལ་བཅུག་བྱེས། དེ་ནེ་ལག་པའི་འེང་བ་ཚང་མ་འི་ཕོ་རིག་
ག་སྐྲས་ཏེ། དེ་ནེ་ཕོ་དེ་ཚང་མ་ཕིང་བཅུག་འདུག་པ་ལེ། དེ་དུས་པའི་
ཀ་ནེ་ང་དང་ང་རྒྱས་མེད་ཀྱག་ད་ང་དང་ཡང་ཞིག་ཕེང་མཐོང་བཏང་
སྟེ་ཡིན་ནོག་པ་ལེ།

དེ་སའི་ཀ་བསྐྱེབས་ཏེ་ནེ་འི་ཁོ་མ་བདེ་མོ་མཐོང་བྱེན་ཀ་ག་ལེ། བག་
དོན་ཞིག་ཚོག་ཞིག་ཡོང་བྱེ།

དེ་ནེ་མ་ནེ་ང་ང་དང་ད་མ་ནེ་ཀ་ནེ་ཀ་རུ་དགོན་པ་མཐལ་ལ་ཆ་དགོས་
ཞེན་ཡ་ལེ། དེ་ནེ་འབག་གསག་བྱེས་མ་ནེ་གསག་བྱེས། ང་མ་ནེ་རིན་
པོ་ཆེས་ཅི་ཟེར་ཀུན་ཚང་མ་ད་རིན་པོ་ཆེ་རེ་རེ་ན་ལྱང་རེ་རེ་གཟུང་
བྱེས། ང་མ་ནེ་སེ་ལྱང་ཞིག་སལ་ན་ཡ་མ་ནེ་བརྟོ་ག་རྡའི་ལྱང་སལ་
ནའང་ཡ་འབག་གེ་ལྱང་སལ་ནའང་། ད་རིན་པོ་ཆེ་རེ་རེ་ན་རེ་རེ་
མཐལ་ལེན་ཞིག་དེ་ནེ་ཆ་བྱས་ཚང་མཐའང་སལ་ན་དེ་ནེ་ང་དང་ང་རྟེང་
ན་བྱེན་རླབས་འཐུག་སོན་འཐུག་སོན་ཞིག་དང་ང་དང་ང་ཚོས་བསག་
གེན་སག་གེན་ཞིག་དང་བྱེན་རླབས་འཐུག་སོན་འཐུག་སོན་ཞིག་དང་།

Translation:

White and black pebbles are brought in, (the candidates) are not allowed to sit near them (so they cannot see them), and water is poured into a pot. An *on po* or a lama recites prayers (called *spyan den*) over it, and then (the stones) are dropped (concealed) (in the water), and if it is a *lha*, the *lha* without any hesitation takes out (the correct stone). Prayers are said to the Dorje Sempa of the east, Rinchen Jungnas of the south, to Donyotdup of the north, to Snangwa Thayas of the west and to Nampar Snangzad in the centre; they all receive prayers. Then the *lha* will pick the (correct) stone (out of the water). And so the *lha*'s authenticity is established.

Then the monks *bring* forward an *lha-ibex* made of *tsam pa* pastry. If the ibex circles to the right (it is good); if it is not a *lha* it circles to the left. (If it is *de*), it circles in the water to the left in its silver bowl. And if all that runs according to plan, the gods can distinguish between *lha* and *de*. That is then the verdict (*ka*) of the Vajrapani of the east, the Ratnasambhava of the south, the Amogasiddhes of the north, the Nangwa Thayas of the west and the Vasocana of the centre.

Everyone is then handed mustard grains which they throw and in this way the *de* is thrown away and thus separated, and then the men are supposed to take incense, and the women *kha tags*... (unintelligible)...

The next task is to find something hidden away. The prayer bead strings of everyone present are hidden somewhere. The candidate must find them all again. We (candidates) remember nothing during this session. But I have seen how such a distinction between *lha* and *de* is established.

When the proceedings reach this point, everything looks lovely – it looks like a wedding festival.

Then we (shaman candidates) go to many monasteries and perform prostrations many times and recite mantras. And now we must receive from all Rinpoches the teaching of Buddha, the mantra lessons, the lessons of Vajra Guru, lessons of prostration. We go from Rinpoche to Rinpoche, we go on praying and receive their blessings (*chin lab*).

The route to shamanism from the *tsha ba tshu ba* state ("madness") to controlled *lha*-possession is portrayed in these narratives as clearly as in all the other accounts that young and old shamans have given me:

1. *Tsha ba tshu ba* (*nyos po song*) is in every case the first essential requirement prior to embarking on the road to shamanism.

2. There follows the examination by a Rinpoche and the obligatory *ka* (his diagnosis and his written order or contract to a shamanic master; the authentication of a genuine *lha*) as well as the requirement to fulfil Buddhist practices of worship.

3. The commencement of instruction from a shamanic master. Learning and teaching proceed in trance. The first thing taught is the method of going into controlled *lha* state as well as all compulsory preparatory arrangements prior to a shamanic séance – and above all the preparation of the *nyer shod*, the Buddhist offerings.

4. A dramatic event for all shaman candidates is then the "test" or "intermediate test", the distinction and separation of *lha* and *de* in a large group setting, in which family, neighbours, shamanic masters and Buddhist monks participate.

5. After this big examination, the shamanic instruction continues just as intensively, including devout Buddhist prac-

tices (pilgrimages, praying, prostrations, mantra recitals, meditation, reading scriptures, etc).

6. The young shaman will begin his own practice as soon as he has mastered his *Iha* state, the preparation for séances and the key shamanic methods of healing therapy, *did phin ches* and *khab phin ches* (*dib* = liquid poison, *khab* = solid objects/needles, *phin ches* = sucking out.)

This is the "normal" way, but, as is evident from the fates of some of the shaman candidates – see, e.g. Deldans sustained "madness" – things do not always go to plan.

Some candidates do not want to respond to the *Iha* calling, a shaman's vocation is, after all, very difficult. Then shamans and lamas are asked to terminate their *Iha* possession. It is generally maintained – at least by all shamans and also by the Rinpoches – that one cannot stop a *Iha*. *Tsha ba tshu ba* will return. And the candidate will eventually acknowledge and accept his calling.

Also, not all candidates will pass the big test at the first attempt, about which, however, no-one would speak openly. Of course, the authenticity of the *Iha* state is not fundamentally brought into question when the candidate fails: indeed the Rinpoche has already given his *ka*, that a *Iha* is certainly present. It is, therefore, a case of the *de* simply being too strong. More teaching and learning is required – until a new final test or a second intermediate test is set.

6. THE SHAMANIC SÉANCE

What are the shamans expected to perform? People come to him with every kind of problem imaginable: physical pains, worries, sleeplessness, help to seek out a missing object, requests for prophesising, interpersonal conflicts. They come for themselves, and they also come with their sick animals.

A shaman heals, as I have described, exclusively when in an altered state of consciousness, he heals only in trance. When in trance he is *lus gyar*, a borrowed body. He has lent his body to a god which is possessing him. He *is* the god. He sings, prays, speaks, prophesises and heals as this god.

The onset of the *lha* state is heralded by dramatic bodily reactions such as shaking, sneezing, hyperventilation, etc., and full trance can be recognised when it is no longer the "shaman" speaking as a person, but as a god. A god speaks with a completely different voice, often unintelligible, often also in another language (a mixture of Tibetan and Ladakhi). In this *lha* state healing can then take place. The shaman in trance is now the god who has come to possess him. Many shamans can be possessed by several gods, one after another.

The most common form of healing, that the shamans of central Ladakh perform, is the sucking of something bad out of the patient's body. To do this he places a suction tube (*pu ri*) on the exposed part of the patient's body (see Illustration 25), where the "bad" is lying, sucks through the skin and spits out the black repugnant substance into a bowl. Sometimes, a shaman sucks directly by mouth (see Illustration 26).

From the body of the animals – this is always done directly by mouth – (I have seen for myself how a shaman presses his mouth deep into the hide of the yak) the shaman brings out whole needles and nails.

Or he heals with the "fire sword" (see Illustration 27): a knife is heated over a flame. The shaman firstly draws the glowing blade across his tongue, then he puts it close to the afflicted area on the patient and blows – as though the heat of the sword should heal internal or external wounds.

The shaman also blesses patients and instructs them in connection with Buddhist teaching. All this happens quite hectically and the shaman's physical treatment of the patient is often very rough. You are sure to find bruisings where a shaman has sucked some dark force out of the patient.

Illustration 25: Using the pu ri to suck from the patient's vertex; the patient grimaces in pain

The dramatic element of a shamanic séance is the induction of the trance. One certainly cannot avoid being impressed by this drama even after taking part in a good number of shamanic healings. Also, all patients are, as the faces reveal, (see below, Illustration 32) very deeply ensconced. The room is full of incense. The shaman is surrounded by his sacral requisites and he is wearing his vocational clothing – the crown, the shawl and the cloth over his mouth.

In a monotone, sonorous voice the shaman recites mantras endlessly. Mantras are sequences of holy syllables. The shaman continuously beats the small *da ru* drum (colloquially *da ru*, but in Sanskrit *da ma ru*) in a hypnotic, crazy rhythm, with bells (*tilu*), likewise constantly ringing. Every now and then perhaps a cry, a wild gasp for breath, a dramatic groan – and then the bombardment of the senses with *da ma ru, tilu* and mantras resumes immediately. There is no question about it: the atmosphere heats up. The participants are spellbound. It is quite evident from their faces: they observe and listen most intensely, many clasp their hands together poised for prayer. If, on looking around in the crowded room, one sees a disinterested face – then it can only be that of a foreigner, who has come here accidentally and understands nothing and above all will not allow himself to become involved under any circumstances, or simply does not want to believe that a shaman, without trickery, can suck black substances from a person's body...

It remains to mention briefly how a shamanic sitting concludes. The shaman retires from treating patients, chants mantras, his body swaying, then suddenly falls forward (when giving treatment he is always sitting or kneeling on the floor or on a pedestal), he throws off his shamanic costume, one hears a long-drawn whistling (the sound of the *lha* withdrawing), his body trembles and convulses, he then lies motionless for a moment, sits himself up finally and looks around the room absent-mindedly, and perhaps says, as though surprised, "Oh...!" as though he had been unaware of the patients until now... He has now returned to a state of normal consciousness.

Illustration 26: Sucking by mouth from the patient's eye

I have portrayed a séance of this kind in order to clarify how "madness", which was the departure point on the road to shamanism, converts itself to trance later on when the shaman is in practice: inducing the trance in a carefully and consciously controlled, ritual-based process, and emerging from it is controlled with equal care – this is how the so-called "madness" has been transformed. "Illness" is transformed to a focused means of healing.

7. REPUTATION AND POPULAR PERCEPTION OF THE SHAMANS AND THE KEY ROLE OF THE BUDDHIST RINPOCHES

The public perception of the shaman in Ladakh (still excluding Changthang, because no studies are available) can only be described as ambivalent. Anyone who considers himself to be a "modern" Ladakhi would never admit to ever seeking the help of a shaman, or even to having a little respect for one. At the same time, in practice, however, the shaman is held in high esteem from people in all walks of life.

Once again, I may cite my Ladakhi assistants to illustrate an example – who covers the whole spectrum from unwavering deference to bewilderment, as well as an extraordinary ambivalence:
Sonam Wangchuk has finished his university education and works on his doctorate. He is a very well educated, highly intelligent, polite, reliable and a slightly reserved young man. He helps me transcribe dialogues from tape recordings of shamanic séances, and of conversations involving information and instruction sessions. He does not bat an eyelid when he joins me in a shamanic séance. He never utters a word of criticism. But he admits that he would prefer not to be seen when he accompanies me to visit a shaman.

Illustration 27: Woman shaman using fire treatment: the knife blade is heated over the fire and drawn across the tongue (above) in order to then blow over the area causing pain (below)

145

Thinley Gyurmet is a monk and most certainly a highly educated and gifted young man. He has overcome every hurdle to write his doctorate thesis on the philosophy of Buddhism at the Benaras Hindu University. No one takes such pains as he does on the word for word transcription of difficult texts. However, he views the shamanic Buddhist prayers, as well as the invocations, mantras and conjurations as a "remarkably slovenly" and "uneducated" form of Buddhism. What the shaman does is all magic and humbug. Yes, all monks and lamas would think as he. (Which is not true since I have encountered monks at shamanic séances not infrequently, having "evil" sucked out of them or seeking advice; see also Chapter 6).

Sonam Norboo is one of the most highly esteemed Ladakhi personalities. He is at home on the international scene, he works in the field of documentary films, primarily with the Japanese. In these projects, he is the manager and the main organiser. It is his job to overcome all kinds of hurdles, to open doors, to evade, win over or charm the bureaucrats and to make possible what the film team needs. This is also his truly impressive role in my research. With shamans, shamanic apprentices and shamanic helpers one must first of all build up a contact; with a Rinpoche one must apply for an appointment for a long time; to travel to Changthang one requires a permit which has to be processed through many bureaucratic channels. Sonam Norboo arranges all this, and, with his exceeding charm and winning smile, is successful on nearly every occasion. Sonam Norboo does not believe in shamans. Or so he says. In his behaviour towards them, however, he shows deep respect. And, with eyes beaming, he never tires of telling his stories about the most incredible acts of healing he has witnessed or heard about: he believes it all!

Of all my collaborators, I have worked the longest with Tsultim Kubet: as early as September 1994 on my first field trip to Ladakh we teamed up together. Tsultim was a monk from the age of six to sixteen, and as a monk and subsequently at university he received extensive Buddhist education. He is, therefore, very well versed in all things relating to Buddhism. In his eyes, Buddhism and shamanism are in no way contradictory. He has a deep belief in shamans. On attending shamanic séances, he always also has his own problem to present, seeking advice from a shaman with hands together poised for prayer. There is also a shaman in his family: his daughter was called to shamanism through the usual *lha* illness. Only recently in 2000 did he experience a crisis of faith in shamans. In the Kashmir armed conflict of 1999, his 19-year-old son was in the war and was missing for months on end. "Is he alive?" Tsultim wanted to know, "Is he alive, is he alive?". The shamans he had asked replied over and over again "Yes. He is alive!" But then he was discovered dead. Tsultim never recovered from the death of his son right up till his own death in February 2001. "The shamans are liars", he declared to me in December 2000 as we were working on some shamanic prayers. "Really? Do you think they're all liars?" I asked cautiously and softly. "Yes", he replied ferociously. And I: "Do you think that Sonam Murup (whom we frequently visited) lied?" "No", answered Tsultim, "not he. " And *lha pa* Thundup from Sumdo in Changthang, whom we saw in June?" "No, not him either."

The Rinpoches, the highest dignitaries in Tibetan Buddhism, are the most respected and influential personalities in Ladakhi society. Therefore, their role and their opinions regarding shamans carry particular weight. In a research project together with a collaborator, we attempted to find out more about the key role of the Ladakhi Rinpoches in religion and politics (RÄTHER & RÖSING 2001). I cite a number of statements made relating to shamans from the conversations with Rinpoches and then once more point out their key role in the legitimisation of a shaman.

Bakula Rinpoche was by far the most respected Rinpoche in Ladakh (he died in 2003). Thiksey Rinpoche is also held in high esteem. Both were or are also very actively involved in politics. It is extremely difficult to get hold of them and to make an appointment and time enough for a proper conversation.

Nevertheless, with Bakula Rinpoche (see Illustration 28) I was very lucky. He was just relaxing his residence in Sankar, directly behind Sankar monastery. Sankar is a village just outside the gateway to Leh. I personally think it is the most beautiful village I know in the whole of Ladakh. Every morning when I am staying in Leh, I go to Sankar and pay a short visit to the monastery. And so it happened quite by chance one morning that I heard that Bakula Rinpoche was there – and furthermore that he had time for me. I was able to have a long conversation with him (HI-36).

Bakula Rinpoche believed that shamans perform a thoroughly worthwhile function. This is, however, confined to physical and not spiritual concerns. Certainly, he had been concerned about the selection of new shamans and made decisions as to whether there was a *lha* within the candidate or not. (Sonam Murup also cites Bakula Rinpoche as having performed this function for him.) But Bakula Rinpoche had been out of Ladakh for so long (he was the Indian ambassador in Mongolia), and therefore, he no longer took part in the selections. He would, by no means, turn anyone away and would certainly take care of them, but they simply do not come to him any more, he said.

Thiksey Rinpoche, too, is in no way disinclined towards the shamans, though he refers to the specifically narrow realm over which they have "jurisdiction".[3] Naturally, their standing is well below that of a Rinpoche; after all, a Buddhist cannot seek refuge with them. They occupy themselves solely with sucking. (The sucking up of harm and evil.) *"They are of benefit for temporary aims only in this life, like taking out needles and sucking. They cannot do anything for the next life. They go for temporary (gnas skabs) aims."*

---

3 Cited from a conversation by H. Räther with Thiksey Rinpoche on 29.9.2000.

Illustration 28: Bakula Rinpoche

Thiksey Rinpoche confirms that there are far more shamanic callings today than in the past. And why is that? Thiksey Rinpoche is of the same opinion as many other Ladakhis (on this subject see KRESSING & RÖSING 2001b), who among other things discuss Tibet's fate as a reason for the proliferation of shamans. Thiksey Rinpoche says: "*Mostly they (the lhas) have come from Tibet because they could not rely on the Chinese*".

Togdan Rinpoche[4] speaks in very similar terms: "*One reason (for the increase of oracles in Ladakh) is Tibet, there was the spread of communism, that is why many lha come to us. The communists don't believe in lha.*"

What Thiksey and Togdan Rinpoche mean to say is as follows: in communist-ruled Tibet, where Buddhist and/or shamanic religious practice by the Tibetans carried a high penalty by the Chinese rulers, the *lha* found they had no more bodies to possess and through which they could speak and heal as a *lha*. As a result, there are many free-floating *lha*. The bodies they borrow – *lus gyar* – are now to be found in Ladakh. And Chogon Rinpoche adds[5]: a sign that these *lha* come from Tibet is that the shamans in trance speak Tibetan ... (which some in fact do, see e.g. HH-10, HH-11).

Chogon Rinpoche appears to be very open minded. Firstly, he points out, as does Thiksey Rinpoche, the very limited scope of responsibility and competence of all shamans. For sucking out *gnod pa*, impurity and illness, e.g. perhaps resulting from black magic (which one cannot cure with medicine), – that is what they are good at. "*For this if you consult an oracle, it is most useful.*" Even he himself has consulted a shaman – once or twice, he says. One occasion was when his Rinpoche teacher was very ill. And then, according to him, the shamanic *lha* are guardian deities of Buddhism and, therefore, it is beneficial to contact them:

---

4 Cited from a conversation by H. Räther with Togdan Rinpoche on 12.8.1999.
5 Cited from a conversation by H. Räther with Chogon Rinpoche on 12.12.1999 at Bodh Gaya.

I went once or twice. The reason was these oracles are sacred (*rtsa chen po*). For example, I think that for myself for travelling I don't need the help of the *lhas*. With respect to practising *dharma* if we consult *lhas*, that is good. It is of benefit for practising the *dharma*. The reason for obeying the *lhas* is because we call them *dharma* protector (*chos skyong*). Those oracles are *dharma* protectors. *Chos skyong* means protector of Buddha's doctrine, like a body-guard. For practising *dharma* they are beneficial.

Schas Rinpoche[6] is less positive in acknowledging a positive, if limited role of shamans. He believes there are only one or two "genuine" shamans; most of them are quacks or frauds. And for Schas Rinpoche, one of the key criteria for authenticity is quite clearly the ability of a shaman to suck a needle out of the body of a patient.

This is what Schas Rinpoche believes:

There are maybe one or two which are genuine, but mostly I don't believe in that. Maybe one or two of them are good but in the rest I mostly don't believe ... Most of them cannot control their mind... Then many of them are liars, even if something doesn't exist or is not happening, still they will say it is happening... They are more today because many of them are lying and people have faith in them... In reality, it is difficult to get benefit (from the oracles), but sometimes because of (their) faith, when (the oracle) says something, the person feels like healed. Sometimes it happens straight away. In reality, there might be some one or two real good oracles. They are beneficial. If there are some like that, then it is safe (to go there). These days there are some kind of oracles who take out needles. I think that is very surprising. Whether they are really doing this or whether some of them are false – if they are really doing this, then I think that is surprising. If they are really doing this, then I think they are real oracles, one or two of them.

6 Cited from a conversation that H. Räther had with Schas Rinpoche on 14.8.1999.

It was with Stakna Rinpoche that I was able to discuss the shamans most thoroughly (see Illustration 29) (HI-21). Of all the
Ladakhi Rinpoches, he is also the most important for the shamans.
He is the only Rinpoche in Ladakh who is actually staying and living in Ladakh and thus also readily available. And included in his
duties is the task of taking care of people who are brought to him
because they are "mad" and who want to know whether the
"madness" might be a symptom of an *lha/de* struggle, with a calling to become a shaman.

From all corners of Ladakh these "cases" come to him – and
Stakna Rinpoche estimates (although with some uncertainty) that
within the last 2-3 years he had around 60 shaman candidates
coming to see him, some 40 of whom he assessed as "genuine".
The genuine, like the "normal mad", will then be sent by him to
the shamans in office; the former for training and for separating
lha and *de*; the latter as patients, whose "madness" will be healed
by the shamans.

How does Stakna Rinpoche find out whether someone is possessed by a *lha* or has "normal madness"? To do this he refers to
special *sutra* books. From these books he extracts the diagnosis. If
there appears to be a *lha* he provides certification in writing, and
from then on an experienced shaman takes over the training.
However, Stakna Rinpoche does not let go of the candidate entirely. Time and again, they must still come to him for, as a shaman, they must follow many Buddhist practices and have their
mind purified. If they do not take this kind of spiritual training serious they would only fall behind to the *de*, and become "simple
madmen".

Stakna Rinpoche confirms too that there has been an impressive
proliferation of shamanic callings. And his diagnosis in the first
place is a criticism of society: today there is great progress, life is
becoming increasingly complicated, there is more wealth and af-
fluence. This makes people more unsettled within themselves,
stoked up by greed and envy. In the past, people were more "innocent", uncomplicated and helpful. Today, however, people are

Illustration 29: Stakna Rinpoche

no longer ready to help, today everyone is looking out for himself; today there is so much competition. "The devil is coming more and more". And as a result, people are ill far more frequently. And for precisely this reason one needs shamans – to remove the poison from people.

Second to this, so believes Stakna Rinpoche, public opinion and publicity have played a substantial role in the proliferation of shamanism. One day, he told me, a famous Yogi came to Ladakh and had publicly declared that all shamans were charlatans and that charlatans were not wanted. Consequently, the number of young shamans immediately decreased ... (and the shamans took to the streets to demonstrate; see e.g. HI-24).

No, he himself would certainly not go to a shaman, at least not to a village shaman – that was quite unnecessary. However, he would certainly consult the monastic shaman, the oracle of the monastery at Mato, and ask him whether this or that project was good. There would be no sucking involved (monastic oracles never suck, they only prophesise); it would be to seek KNOWLEDGE. Stakna Rinpoche added that he had no objection to a monk or lama going to a village shaman as long as all other options for medical treatment had been explored and not helped.

There is no question that for Stakna Rinpoche shamanism is a very real and genuine phenomenon. For him, trance indicates the presence of a *lha*, the taking over of a human body by a god. In trance, the *lha* speaks through the shaman. When a *lha* speaks, the person to whom the body belongs does not remember it. Deep trance and amnesia unavoidably go hand in hand, Stakna Rinpoche maintains.

If one brings together these remarks, statements and opinions to appraise the shamans, one cannot help but notice much ambivalence. On the one hand, the cosmopolitan and more educated Ladakhis and many of those who work in tourism, the Indian army and in the *pashmina* trade, often feel that shamanism is obsolete and irrational; they proclaim (loud and clear) to be non-believers (KRESSING & RÖSING 2001b). But it is also a fact that precisely these "non-believers" turn to the shamans in times of need.

154

One thing is certain: the Buddhist clergy does not believe there is any contradiction between shamanic practice and Buddhist faith, but quite clearly assigns to shamanism its rightful place, even if many of them see the shamans' scope of responsibility as being very limited and believe the number of "genuine" shamans to be relatively small. What is also quite plain to see is that the one Buddhist dignitary of Ladakh, who today plays the most important role as a key figure in shamanic calling – Stakna Rinpoche – does see shamanism very favourably.

However, what neither he nor any other Rinpoche nor any of the Ladakhis professing to be most committed Buddhists has ever verbalised, is a completely different matter: that the shamans are an essential element for the STRENGTHENING of Buddhism. This will become clear when we visit the shamans in remote Changthang in the ensuing chapters.

CHAPTER 4

The enigma of trance and amnesia

1. SHAMANIC TRANCE: INTERNAL AND EXTERNAL VIEWS

In September 1994, I took part in a Ladakhi shaman's healing séance for the first time – with tape recorder, camera and notebook as is fitting for an ethnological researcher. This first experience with shamans from the Tibetan culture left a deep impression on me. I was impressed above all by the dramatic nature of the trance. What an incredible performance, I thought, and on thinking this, the double meaning of the word "performance" naturally entered my mind.

A shaman's trance, as we have defined it – is an altered state of consciousness into which the shaman enters by constant drumming, raffling and singing, and then heals with an altered state consciousness and with altered behaviour and voice. However, describing trance as a state of altered consciousness is "western" talk. It is the language, meaning and understanding of science. From the shaman's perspective, it is the STRANGER'S viewpoint. It is a concept which, in offering us a familiar cultural perspective, enables us to understand unfamiliar consciousness and behaviour.

For the shamans within the Tibetan culture, trance, as presented, is not only something completely different, but, much more, it is something all-encompassing. From their OWN point of view, trance is not an altered state of consciousness. Far more, it is first of all a complete loss of consciousness. The only thing remaining is the body, an outer shell. And secondly trance is the process of a god taking over this empty body. The god penetrates this empty body.

So the shaman lends his body to the god, and in so doing becomes this god: he heals as this god, he speaks with the inspiration and sagacity and the knowledge of this god, he acts with the power of the god and speaks with its voice.

This is perfectly expressed by the Ladakhi terms relating to "altered consciousness", and "trance":

TRANCE IN THE SHAMAN'S LANGUAGE

ལྷ་སྣང་ང
lha nang nga
(to be) inside the lha

ལྷ་སྐྱོད་དེ
lha skyod de
arrival of the lha

ལྷ་སྐྱོད་ཚར་འདུག
lha skyod tshar duk
the visibly completed arrival of the lha

ལྷ་གཞུག་ཆེས
lha zhuk ches
lha staying, lha state

When the shaman re-emerges from this lha-state, when the lha god withdraws from his body, he possesses his normal consciousness once more. But there remains – at least this is what all shamans without exception assured us – a thick and impenetrable, indeed a hermetically-sealed screen of amnesia around all lha-related events. The shaman does not remember the actions, the words – and I cannot even say "his" actions or "his" words, for they were not his but those of the lha. Neither does he remember the patients, nor the context regarding healing, nor any disturbances, interruptions or other events. With the withdrawal of the lha (and the return of everyday consciousness), all memory of lha events is wiped out.

In the following pages, I would like the shamans to have their own say about these events, i.e. to document views from the "inside":

what THEY understand by "trance", how they sink into trance, how they feel when in trance, what happens after the trance, and how they explain the amnesia. But I shall continue to use the word "trance" as an abbreviated concept – meaning throughout what they call the "*lha*-state".

2. THE INTERNAL VIEW I: LHA-STATE AND AMNESIA

For a shaman, it is not easy to describe how one moves into trance or to portray one's consciousness when in trance. A woman shaman attempted to describe it as follows (HI-10):

དགས་དཔོ་ཞིག་གོ་ནང་ནེ་ང་ན་ཡིན་ནོག་ཡ། དང་ན་ཚོག་པོ་ང་ན་མ་
ནེ་སྒོག་པོ་སྒོག་པོ་ཡོད་དེ་ཡིན་ནོག་པ་ཡ། ད་མདང་དེ་ལྡུ་སྒོད་དེ་ཧུས་
པའི་ག་སྒོག་པོ་སྒོག་པོ་འབྱེར་བྱེས་པོ། ག་ཚོན་ཆེད་ང་ན་པ་ཏུ་མེད་
ཀྱུག་པ་ཅེ་པ་ཏུ། དེ་ནེ་ཡང་ན་པོ་གཞུག་སེ་ཡོང་ང་ཚོག་པོ་གཞུགས་པ་
སང་ཁོང་ག་ནེ་ཅེ་ཟེར་རད་ང་དང་ང་ཚེ་པ་ཏུ། དེ་ནེ་རང་དང་གཞན་ཞེས་
ས་མ་ནོག། ལྡུ་སྒོད་ཟ་ནེ་ཅེ་ཟེར་རད་དཀོན་མཚོག་འི་པོ་མོལ་བཞིན་
ཡོད་ཐིན།

དགས་ང་ལག་པ་བྱབ་འཁྲུན་ཅེག་ན་ང་དང་ང་ཅེ་པ་ཏུ་པ་ཏུ་ཡོད་མེད་
པ་ཡིན་ནོག་ཡ། ཁ་བ་འལ་ལ་བ་འལ་དེ་ནེ་ཅེ་བཙོས་ཅེ་མ་བཙོས་མི་སྲུ་
ཡོངས་སུ་མ་ཡོངས་ཆང་པ་ཏུ་མེད་ཀྱུག། ཁོ་ཁོ་རང་ང་ཅེ་ཐིང་ཁོན་ཅེ་
མ་ཐིང་ང་རང་དང་ང་རང་ང་ཅེ་ཟེར་དེ་ནེ་པ་ཏུ་ཡོང་ང་མེ་རག་ལེ།

ཅི་སྐྱབས་ཁོང་གན་ན་དེ་ཅི་བཏང་ས་ཡང་ཞིག་ག་ཅི་སྐྱབས་གན་པོ་ང་ལ་
ད་མེད་ཀུག། དེ་པོ་ཁོ་རང་ལྡུ་ནང་ཅི་ཟེར་ནའང་།

སྒུན་འཇེན་བན་འཇེན་མི་བཙུག་ག་བཙུག་བཙོས་དེ་མ་ནེ་སྐྱོད་ད་མ་ནོག། མ་
ནེ་ལྱང་ང་ཕྱིང་དེ་ཡང་སེམས་པ་པོ་གནན་མི་སེམས་པ་ཚོག་ཞིག་ལུས་
ས་ནོག།

དེ་ཆེན་མོ་གུན་ཡོངས་སེ་ཞན་འདུག་ཟ་ན་ད་ཡིབ་ཡིབ་བཙོན་ལ་མ་ནེ་
ང་རང་དང་ང་རང་གདོང་ཆེན་མོ་མིག་རིག་རིག་བཙོ་གན་ཞིག་ཡང་
སེམས་པ་པོ་གནན་མའི་སེམས་པ་ཚོག་ཞིག་ལུས་ས་རག།

དེ་ནེ་ཡང་ལྱུ་ཆབ་ལྱུ་ཀྱུལ་ལ་ཅིག་དང་ནེ་ང་དང་དེ་གཟུགས་པོ་འལ་གན་
ཞིག་ཚོག་ཞིག་གཉིད་གསད་གན་ཞིག་ཚོག་ཞིག་ནི།

Translation:

At the moment we are sitting here together, aren't we? – And whilst we are sitting like this we all have the same "souls" (*srok po*). The soul is inside us, isn't it? But yesterday, when I was in the *lha*-state (*lha skyod de*) my soul was away from me. I've no idea where it went. And then (something else, the *lha*) comes into me, something pushes its way in, we don't know what (the *lha*) says, we just don't know. When we are in *lha* state we cannot distinguish between people we know and those we don't know. What do we say in the *lha* state? (We say nothing at all) it is the god that speaks (through us).

When I wash my hands (preparing for the séance) – I don't remember anything more. Nothing at all. That's how it is. When I have rinsed out my mouth, I no longer know what I am doing and what I am not doing, who is coming, and who not; I just don't know. What the *lha* sucks out or doesn't suck out, what is said – I cannot say.

Even what I teach, the information I impart, I do not remember afterwards. Whatever the *lha* says when it is in me I don't remember.
(It is not easy to go into *lha* state). One must say numerous prayers of invocation; without these it won't work. Without these there is no stable (*lha*-state) and your consciousness (*sem pa*) remains the same as other, normal people's.

When I am sitting and the (*lha*) comes over me with force and strength, I begin to tremble and my field of vision becomes enormous and my eyes roll upwards – that's what it feels like. And my consciousness is like that of another (creature) in my body.

And when I emerge from the *lha* state, my body feels completely exhausted; it feels as though I am coming out of a deep sleep.

Another woman shaman tries to compare the *lha* state with a dream: (HI-18):

ང་དེ་ལུས་པོ་ཡང་ཞིག་ག་བཏང་དང་སེ་ཡིན་ནོག་པ། དཀོ་བཏང་དང་
པ་ཡང་ཞིག་གི་སེམས་པོ་གཞུགས་ཏེ་ང་དེ་སེམས་པོ་ནེ་ག་ཚོ་ཞིག་ག་
འདུག་གད་ཡིན་འདུག་གད་ཀྱུག་ལ་ལེ། ད་འོ་ན་རྟེན་ཞིག་གི་གཉིང་
ལམ་ཞིག་ཚོག་ཞིག་མཐོང་བྱེས། མཐོང་ན་ཡིད་དུ་ཡོད་དེ་ཡིན་ནོག་པ།
ད་ན་ལྷ་སྐྱེད་དེ་དུས་རིག་ག་དེ་པོའང་ཡིད་དུ་མེད་པ་ཡིན་ནོག། པད་
སེམས་ཉེད་པོའང་ག་རུ་འཁོར་རད་འཁོར་ས་མ་ནེ་མེད་ཀྱུག་པ་ཁོ་ལ་ད་
མེད་མ་ནེ་མ་ཚ་ཡིན་ནོག་སྲང་། སེམས་ཉེད་པོ་ད་རང་དེ་སེམས་པ་

162

ཡིན་ནོག་པ་ཡ། ལྷ་སྐྱོད་པའི་དུས་ལ་རང་ངེ་སེམས་པ་འང་པ་ཏུ་མེད་པ་
ཡིན་ནོག་པ་ད། རང་ངེ་སེམས་པ་རང་ངེ་བསྐུབྱ་མ་ཐུབ་བ་ཡིན་ནོག།

Translation:

Our body is given over to someone else. Another consciousness (*sem pa*) possesses us and our own consciousness goes elsewhere. We see, for example, a stone in a dream, and when you have a dream you remember it. But if you are in the *lha*-state (*lha skyod de*), you have no memory. No-one knows where your own spirit (*sem nyid*) might be floating. The spirit (*sem nyd*) is what we also call consciousness (*sem pa*). In a *lha*-state of mind we do not know our normal consciousness (*sem pa*). We have no control over our consciousness.

Another woman shaman (H-14) also compares the *lha* state of consciousness to dreaming – but to emphasise the difference. She mentions likewise "signals" which for her invoke the *lha* state: the preparatory activities that every Ladakhi shaman performs prior to the séance (washing hands, preparing offerings, etc) as well as the scent of incense:

It begins normally, she says, when she washes her hands before the séance. Then "it" starts to happen. She then goes into the room and begins to prepare the offerings (*nyer chot*), the seven small bowls, with tea and water, with barley corns and with *tsam pa* flour. And then "it" comes, and there is the incense (*shuk pa*), and after that she cannot remember anything. Now she is no longer conscious in conventional terms (*sem nyid*) and she has no memory. She does not know where she is, nor what she is, or how she is. When you are asleep, she explains, you are also not conscious; consciousness goes away. Dreams come to you. You do not know whether they are real or not real. When you go into the *lha* state (*lha zhuks*), you are also not conscious. Your body is there but your consciousness is gone. The *lha* is there. What the *lha* sees is real. The *lha* does not see dreams. The *lha* "sees" the patients' problems. The *lha* acts on one's behalf. You yourself do not know anything. You remember nothing (*yid du lus sa ma nok*).

Similarly, the shaman Dechen, whose background and career development we already know (HI-16): As soon as she starts washing her hands at the start, it's as if things aren't quite normal; or sometimes a little later, when preparing the offerings. In the *lha* state, she no longer sees anyone, she does not know what is going on around her, who is coming or going, who is there or what is being said. She is without consciousness (*sem nyid*). Her body becomes "incredibly heavy", her body expands increasingly. She lends her body to something else. The *lha* is like air, she explains, and can permeate everything. Her body is at the *lha's* disposal, and the *lha* invades it like air.

As it is with other shamans when washing their hands or preparing the offering bowls, so it does to Sonam Murup (HI-11) on lighting the butter lamp: with this preparatory act he is launched into trance, into the *lha* state. As this happens, something yields within him, something seems to disappear, he says. (Sonam sometimes calls it "heart" [*snying*] and sometimes "consciousness" [*sem pa*]). And then – according to him – there remains only the *lha* (one of his most important *lha* is called Nezar Gyalpo). And from that moment on, it is not he, Sonam Murup, with his normal heart and his normal consciousness: *that* is lost. It is the *lha* that is speaking.

A question along the lines of "Do you remember you gave the patient a bundle during the healing séance?" or: "Do you remember sucking the black magic (*dschadu*) from her body?" does not make sense any more. Sonam Murup can only ever say: "I didn't give anyone a bundle. I didn't suck anything out (of anyone). It was the *lha*. Anything said or done is the work of the *lha*":

མཆོད་མེ་ཕུལ་ལ་ཅིག་པད་ལྷ་སྐྱོད་གཀ། དེ་ནེ་ང་དང་དེ་སྙིང་དེ་སྱོར་ར་
ནོག་མི་སེམས་པོ།......དེ་ནེ་སེམས་པོ་སྱོར་ར་ནོག་མ་ནེ་དེ་རྒྱག་པ་ཁོ་
ཆོས་སྐྱོང་ཡིན་ནོག། དེ་ནེ་སྙིང་ཡོད་པ་ཡང་ལྷ་ཆབ་གཡོལ་ལ་ཅིག་ཡང་
ཁིང་རང་དེ་སྙིང་ཆབ་དེ་ནང་ང་ཡོང་ང་ནོག། དེ་ནེ་ཁོ་རང་སྲུང་མ་དེ་ཁོ་
རང་གཞུགས་སྲུད་གཀ་པ་སྱོང་དེ་ནང་ང་ཆང་ཁོག། ངའི་སྲུང་མ་རྒྱལ་པོ་
པེ་གར་ནེ་ནེར་རྒྱལ་པོ། དེ་ལྷ་སེ་གཏང་ག་ནག་ངའི་མ་གཏང་ག་ནག་ཏ་
དུ་ཕིང་གཀ། ང་ག་ནེ་ཉེན་ནེན་ལྷ་སེ་བཅོན་ནོག་ཅི་ཆང་མ།

Translation:

When I light the butter lamps, the *lha* comes to me. My heart (*sni-yng*), my consciousness (*sem*) disappears. We completely lose our consciousness. And then we are possessed by a *lha*. When the heart yields in this manner, only the *lha* is present; only the *sung ma* (*lha*) is occupying your body. My *lha* are called Gyalpo Pegar and Nezer Gyalpo. *I* had given a bundle to the patient? No. It was the *lha*. I don't give the patient anything. *Dschadu* was extracted? But I'm not able to do that. Whatever it is, it's the *lha* that's doing it.

Sonam Murup also mentions the profound amnesia that, as all sha-mans maintain, does follow trance. He, too, uses for comparison a person's state of consciousness when dreaming, to help explain the similarity. The consciousness of sleep that produces a dream which is remembered (see both citations above), does not help us to under-stand the *lha* state – however, a state of sleep consciousness which produces a dream that is *not* remembered does help to understand the *lha* state:

མཚན་ལ་སེམས་ཉིད་པོ་སྟོར་ར་རོག། ང་དང་ངེ་མཚན་ལ་གཉིད་ལམ་
མཐོང་ང་ཚོག་ལ་ འི་མཚན་ལ་གཉིད་ཡོང་ང་མེ་རག་ག། དེ་གཉིད་དེ་ང་
དང་ངེ་གཉིད་དེ་པད་གསད་མེད་སྟོར་སོང་སྟེ་ཡིན་ནག་པ་ང་དང་ངེ་ཡང་
གཉིད་སད་ད་ཚིག་གཉིད་སད་ད་ཚིག་སེམས་ཉིད་དེ་ཡང་ལོག་སྟེ་ཡོང་ང་
རོག།

Translation:

During the night one loses (normal) consciousness. If we have a dream at night while we are asleep, i.e., we sleep at night and if it's a very deep sleep from which we awaken, then (the dream) is completely lost to us. And after sleeping, when we awaken, our consciousness returns (without our remembering the dream).

And so it is when in trance. When one awakens from trance, one can say – expanding on the analogy of the above passage – and when the trance was deep, then one has no recollection of it (yid du ma nok). This "there is no memory" is like a REFRAIN in all shamans' reports:

དེ་སེམས་གཉིད་སད་དེ་མེད་ག་རོག་ཡིད་ད་ཡོང་ང་མ་རོག། དེ་ཡིད་ད་
ཡོང་བྱེ་མེན། ཡོང་བྱེ་ན་དེ་ནེ་འ་ཚོན། ཡིད་ད་ཡོང་བྱེ་མེ་རག། དེ་བོ་
ཡིད་ད་ཡོང་ང་མ་རོག།

Translation:

If one's consciousness is cut off there is no memory.
There is then no memory of any kind. If I were able to remember anything, how would I have been able to heal?
Memory does not come to you.
There is then no memory.

3. THE INTERNAL VIEW II:
SPAR KHA, THE SPIRITUAL POWER

One day I asked Sonam Murup (HI-8) about the role of incense in the shamanic séance. For him, the incense (*shuk pa*) is also a fundamental element for invoking the *lha* state. As soon as he inhales the incense, the *lha* manifests itself. Without incense, he says, one cannot call on the *lha*. At this point I enquire: "But all of us who participate at a séance breathe in the incense too. So why don't we fall into trance?"

This leads Sonam Murup to a very important point. There is more to the *lha* state than simply washing one's hands, preparing offerings, lighting butter lamps, inhaling incense – or anything else one might mention that is supposed to invoke this state of mind.[1]

What also belongs to this process is *spar kha*, the spiritual power. "Ah – of course. The shaman must have strong *spar kha*, mustn't he?" I anticipated. "No", says Sonam Murup, " his *spar kha* must be low – and that is in fact the prerequisite for a *lha* state."

གཞུག་བྱེ་དེ་སྤར་ཁ་མེད་མཁན་ལ་གཞུགས་ས་ཚོག།

Lha state is only possible with low *spar kha*.

This is, in fact, one point that really every shaman, every non-shaman and every Rinpoche in Ladakh maintains: shamans have a chronically low *spar kha*. This is already evident in the form of the "madness" at the outset, Sonam Murup explains; he has indeed described

---

1 It is remarkable that the particular elements which the scientists take pains to define as the stimuli of going into trance – hyperventilation, trance through the monotonous drumming and changing etc. – are never suggested by the shamans themselves.

how crazily he used to behave (see his report in Chapter 3). Only when the *spar kha* is low can another being, a *lha*, occupy a person.

Many people, especially the Rinpoches, have very strong *spar kha*. *Spar kha* can also fluctuate – depending on troubles and worries, illness and black magic, prayer, religious practice and ritual activity (primarily the displaying of *lung sta*, prayer flags).

One can best understand *spar kha* if one draws an analogy to a psycho-immunological state. To a physically strong person, whose psycho-immunological constitution is good, misfortune and illness can have less impact.

These psychosomatic concepts have been known to us for a long time. In an analogous sense, *spar kha* could be understood symbolically as a psycho-immunological concept:

If a person has problems, so teaches Sonam Murup, if one is chewing over worries, broods and despairs, then the *spar kha* drops. One is more likely to become ill. One is also more prone to be put under a jinx or be possessed by evil spirits; if someone works black magic on a person with a low *spar kha*, the black magic will be more effective; this weakened person will be easier to "poison".

Also *ti mo* and *ti po* can more easily possess a person whose *spar kha* is low. *Ti mo* is the evil spirit of a jealous woman, and *ti po* the spirit of a jealous man. These spirits are sent out by people who have a very strong *spar kha*. They infiltrate the person and induce motivations and tendencies foreign to that person, and give them expression in the subject's own voice – e.g. "Now jump off the roof, do it – jump now!" And the victim of the jealousy attack says in his or her own voice: "I'm jumping off the roof now!" And according to the belief, the victim does indeed do this if no-one intervenes. – Here is an example that my collaborator Sonam Norboo never tires of telling: it is something that he himself experienced, and the woman involved very nearly *did* jump off the roof.... To a person with a strong *spar kha*, *ti mo* and *ti po* could not possibly affect them.

It is everyday common knowledge in Ladakh that shamans suffer from a chronically low *spar kha*. But, I asked Sonam Murup, doesn't that cause a very paradoxical and dangerous situation for the shaman, if he has a case of *ti mo / ti po* to heal? After all, *ti mo* and *ti po* illnesses are very common and people come to the shaman to be cured of it. How then does the shaman, with his weak *spar kha*, wrestle with the strong *spar kha* of the *ti mo* spirit? This question to Sonam Murup only went to show that I had still not fully understood his explanations regarding trance. But he was patient and repeated his explanation: "It's not ME wrestling with *ti mo*, it is the *lha*!"

But even for the *lha*, Sonam Murup assured me, this struggle was not an easy one. *Ti mo / ti po* are very strong. The victim had to be whipped, one had to tug on his middle finger and at his hair to make *ti mo* reveal the name of the "sender". Only once one knew the name could one begin to heal. The name had to be written in blood on a piece of paper; the paper had to be kneaded into a small clay or pastry anthropomorphic figure, and then this figure had to be burnt. And when it is burnt this paper transforms into flesh... so Sonam Murup teaches. A *ti mo* healing is rather violent, as I was able to see for myself (HH-13); it was painful to watch Sonam Murup's patient being thrashed and whipped and pushed here and there until finally in the depths of her torment she gave a name ... In that moment he released her from her ordeal.

So the shaman's *spar kha* is very low. Moreover, in yet another respect *spar kha* has very much to do with Tibetan-Ladakhi shamanism. *Spar kha* is the actual true focus of the healing: it will always fundamentally be a question of enhancing the patient's spiritual strength (to raise the psycho-immunological threshold so to speak) – and to weaken the spiritual power of the enemy or the enemy's strength (RÖSING 2002a).

Blessings of the patient with incense and a diamond sceptre, prayers and mantras, prescriptive religious practices and the installation of *lung sta* (prayer flags) on the roof of the house or on a mountain – this all is used by the shaman (and moreover by the Rinpoche), as a means of strengthening the patient's *spar kha*.

To have a strong *spar kha* is in general unequivocally desirable. But the chronically low *spar kha* of the shaman is not simply a "feature" or characteristic: it is the very essence of being a shaman. This is also one of the reasons for the ambivalent status that shamans have. Anyone who wants to demean them will draw attention to their weak *spar kha* first of all.

The other side of the coin regarding this ambivalent status is, however, the accepted Ladakhi knowledge that every shaman without exception must be certified by a Rinpoche and that the shaman has to observe the Rinpoche's prescriptions in keeping with intensive Buddhist religious practice. Shamans are always particularly pious people, i.e. diligent practising Buddhists. Sonam Murup, the best-known shaman in central Ladakh, specifies, therefore, next to the low *spar kha*, a further requirement for being a shaman: one must be a person with a pure heart; he is speaking of that kind of purity of heart that one gains through prayer, prostrations and pilgrimages. When one has pursued all Buddhist practices, one becomes a good person. That is also when the *lha* comes. If one has been a bad person – why should a *lha* wish to enter your body? (*Mi sok po cho at te zhuk cho na – ka ne yong ngen ko*? HI-23, p.42). Only when people are pure (*gtsang ma*) are they able to go into deep trance (*ur po skyod ches*).

4. THE EXTERNAL VIEW I: TRANCE AS THEATRE?

Many shamans have impressed me by their personality – most especially Sonam Murup, whose generosity, openness and humour was to me unsurpassable. Also, their séances have often greatly affected me. But that did not prevent me from observing very precisely – and remaining sceptical.

And, not infrequently, during a séance in which a shaman, in his deep *lha*-possession which he (allegedly) knew nothing about – I had the impression that this shaman, male or female, was very probably perfectly aware of what was going on, and knew precisely who were present and what one had to perform for them.

Ayu Lhamo may be mentioned as an example. Sonam Murup considers this woman shaman to be his most successful student. Today, she is over 60 years old. Indeed her practice is thriving most spectacularly. Not least because she increasingly and very willingly makes her services available to the tourist industry. The Ladakhi tourist guides organise bus trips to visit her!

When I visited her and documented her healing séances and had long conversations with her, she had not yet set forth on this tourist racket, but one could see it coming: Ayu Lhamo seemed to be unusually inclined to show off. I do not question her significance, nor her accomplished healing ability, but in comparison with the other shamans I cannot help realising that she very much eulogised her success: to this end it helped her, so it seemed to me, to keep conveniently remembering the things she had previously claimed to have forgotten.

It was also quite plain that she was trying to impress my Ladakhi collaborator, Sonam Norboo. Sonam Norboo, as I mentioned, is a very highly respected man. She thus had every reason to want to impress him. The patients had already left and she continued to perform, continued to speak in the altered voice of the *lha*, but delivered – which one can discern quite easily from the tape recording – a coherent lecture on the significance of all those *lha* that enter her body. At that point, her gaze always wandered to Sonam Norboo, as though she wanted to make sure that he was listening. And if he happened to nod her speech continued with renewed vitality. Theatre, I thought.

Even Sonam Murup, whom I respected with the utmost sincerity, aroused some scepticism in me on a number of occasions. For me, it was inexplicable how he could suck a rusty nail from the body of a yak. Beforehand everyone could inspect his mouth, his sleeves, and his empty hands. Following all these checks he presses himself into the animal's fur with arms spread; places his mouth on its body and sucks without interruption until, completely exhausted and dizzy, he sinks backwards into the arms of his assistant and weakly spits the nail into his hand. Impressive. How does this work?

What I also found most impressive was his phenomenal strength when in trance. He was, after all, very old – over 90. Prior to a séance he was sometimes very tired, and spoke and moved very slowly. And in trance he would then engage in a wrestling match with *ti mo*, unique in stamina and strength.

But – and herein lies my doubt – what was that sword all about? Once again, I had lots of questions which were all thwarted because of the amnesia. He could not tell me how he healed one illness or another, only the *lha* knew that. However, he was prepared to go into trance and to ask them all my questions as a *lha*. This séance (HH-10) took place at the house of his grandson, Ngawang Chimba. No sooner than a shaman goes into trance with drums, bells and chants, than patients from nearby fields all gather, including people from the neighbouring houses. Even my co-workers – especially Tsultim who particularly revered the shamans – always took the opportunity to hear prophecies through the shamans.

After attending to all these patients, Sonam Murup, in a trance voice, called for his sword. It all became very dramatic. It was almost unbearable seeing how dangerously he lashed out with this weapon, endangering himself and us. Certainly, Ngawang Chimba did take some care – but Sonam Murup's movements were as quick as lightning as he let his sword whistle past so close to our faces. And we were all horrified. Sonam, however, ceased his antics and laughed – but also with some malice. Later, in one of my long conversations with Ngawang Chimba (HI-27), I asked what the sword was all about. Chimba answered: foreigners are so disbelieving. And therefore the *lha* wanted to impress them. In other words: the *lha* had made some decisions entirely based on worldly considerations...

It was also clearly possible for Sonam Murup to call up a particular *lha* at my request! This *lha* of Sonam Murup is called Shang kong ka (VOLF 1994, p.192), is feminine, has a bad knee which causes constant pain (Sonam Murup squirmed in pain and groaned) and is brazenly indecent and crude. Shang kong ka told Sonam Norboo how he amuses himself in bed, reproaches Tsultim for an affair and related to me in lurid detail my alleged smutty fantasies. All of us, including Ngawang Chimba and the *lha* itself creased up with laughter. I felt it was a priceless comedy, quite the most wonderful piece of theatre.

In addition to these experiences, there are also less dramatic observations. Allegedly, the *lha* speaks with an altered voice. Certainly, that is what it usually does. But sometimes the shaman (perhaps through inattentiveness), lapses into his normal voice. Many *lha*, as it is said[2] come from Tibet, driven out by the Chinese, which is why Ladakhi shamans often speak Tibetan while in trance: in their normal state of consciousness they would not understand a word of it (according to their own explanation). But what's with this Modern Tibetan Study Book lying there in the shaman's living room, which was quickly hidden away when my gaze fell upon it?

In other words: I had my doubts about the authenticity of trance. Is the trance not just for show, simply a clever act? I believe that my scepticism and these questions do not detract from the shamans' worth, and it has in no way lessened my esteem for their ability. For whether it is "real" trance or "real" theatre, it does not necessarily have any bearing on the curative effect of their performance.

---

2 See the many testimonies to this effect in KRESSING & RÖSING (2001b).

The curative effect I have experienced myself in many ways (after a shamanic sucking session the pain had definitely subsided), and the vast majority of patients when questioned afterwards confirm that. One can also observe it. If a woman, weeping bitterly and in despair, leaves the shaman's "practice" in a calm and relaxed frame of mind following a séance, and explains that she now knows what is to be done, then one can safely conclude that it has been a successful healing.

It is also not difficult to analyse context and constellation of a shamanic healing séance in terms of "western" scientific concepts of Symbolic Healing (RÖSING 1988/1995) and to identify various cross-culturally valid healing factors in their performance (RÖSING 1997).

5. THE EXTERNAL VIEW II:
AMNESIA AS A DEFENCE MECHANISM?

If I already had mild doubts about the trance state, then my scepticism regarding the universally "claimed" amnesia of the shamans was even greater. Certainly, the claim of amnesia is an impressively consistent explanation and is maintained by all shamans, shamanic assistants and shamanic associates without exception. But this can also be for reasons outside matters of trance. I went in search of these reasons with considerable patience.

On the background of available comparative research on shamans, I also felt justified in systematically cross-examining the phenomenon of amnesia:

There are, after all, shamans in other parts of the world (apart from those one finds in western countries and who are with relative certainty commercial plastic shamans). We can look at shamanism around the world and search for that element of amnesia that appears to be such a fundamental constituent of Tibetan shamanism.

And one realises: amnesia is by no means universal. Quite the contrary. Secondary analyses of shamanic research, such as that by PETERS & PRICE-WILLIAMS (1980), show that out of a total of 42 cultures that practise shamanism, only 20 per cent include the element of amnesia. And more recent findings by KRESSING (1997) put this figure at only 14 per cent.

But this only serves to make the questions regarding the whys and wherefores of shamanic amnesia in Tibetan culture all the more pressing. My hypothesis was: there is no amnesia and the claims of amnesia are a defence mechanism. In this respect, the justification of such a possible defence tactic is not the question at all; it is of far greater value to study and understand the need for amnesia and the need for justification.

Why should I not discuss this question with the shamans themselves? I did do this in circumstances where I had a sufficiently trusting relationship, in order to also discuss these rather thorny questions.

I seemed to have just such a trusting rapport with the shaman Dechen. I, therefore, had very searching conversations with her on the question of fluctuations in the depths of trance, on partial memory and on amnesia as a defence mechanism (HI-25).

She told me there were three different *lha* who had access to her – they each had a different function in the healing process. One *lha* would make prophesies (when patients wished to know what the future held), the second was the sucking *lha*, and the third was the *lha* of fire (healing treatment by blowing over a glowing hot knife). And, so she said, when these *lha* changed, she would for a moment be "unpossessed", and a trace of (normal) consciousness would surface briefly. Sketchy, vague and fleeting, as though in a dream, she would then see a few "real" faces float before her eyes – but within a few moments the next *lha* would enter her and she would not remember anything further.

"And" I wanted to know "are my sort of questions burdensome? Have not other researchers already paid you a visit so as to ask you similar and additional tiresome questions?" "Of course", she said plainly.

"And so" – I now asked her directly "is the claim of amnesia not then a DEFENCE against such uncomfortable questions?" "No, of course, not", Dechen replied, really very surprised and continued in a straightforward manner: "What would I be defending? We don't remember anything. Why would we want to lie?" And when I asked her if I could speak to her shamanic assistant, her brother, immediately after the completion of our own discussions, she unreservedly agreed at once. The conversation with the shaman's brother followed (HI-26) – we were alone, without the shaman. Whatever I asked he always replied "No, she does not remember. No, she never says anything about a séance, as she simply remembers nothing about them..."

I had a similar conversation along these lines (HI-22) with Tsering, also a student of Sonam Murup with whom I had become acquainted at a number of healing séances. Sonam Norboo was present during these conversations and as always we recorded them on a tape recorder – naturally with the permission of the shaman.

I asked this shy but very alert young lady if there were such thing as trance fluctuations. Initially she said at once: "I don't know" but then elaborated: "Before the *lha* is fully present you do remember something (*go ma yid du yong nga rak le*). But then, when the *lha* is there you don't remember anything anymore (*te ne yid du yong nga mi rak*)."

Shamanic teachings proceed under double trance – both the instructor and the student are in a state of trance. Did she not perhaps remember something at the start of the instruction by Sonam Murup? Yes, at the beginning certainly (*O, go ma yid du yong nga rak le*). And how Sonam taught her to go into trance, did she remember that? She did not. However, she clearly remembers that he frequently thrashed her harshly, e.g. if the sacrificial offering were not prepared correctly or if she were only partially in trance. And in full trance? "Then", she answered, "you don't remember anything".

Now I challenge her a little. I informed her that in other parts of the world there are also shamans. They go into trance too. And in fact they have a good recollection of what happens! So why is that not the case here? She says quite simply: "I don't know; we, in any case, don't remember anything, there is nothing in our memory." (*Yid du yong nga mi rak le, chang yid du lus a mi rak le.*)

Finally, I question her directly about amnesia as a defence strategy. Nevertheless, a great number of foreigners come to this young shaman because a close relative of hers is a tourist guide. And he is keen to include her on the tourists' program. "Don't they all ask her lots of questions? Doesn't it get tedious? Aren't some of the questions sceptical, from non-believers? Is that perhaps why you say that you cannot remember anything?

Once again, I received a very innocent answer: "Why shouldn't we say that we don't remember anything? What would I gain from lying? What would be the point of that? Why should we want to lie?", she answered (quite plainly). (*Koa rdzun tang ste nga a chi top pen le?*)

But then followed a dialogue (HI-8) that had made me particularly perceptive in relation to the function of amnesia. It was a conversation with my most important shamanic master – Sonam Murup.

It was on the day that he said he would take me now "officially" as his "student" and, as a sign of this adoption, presented me with a *pu ri*, a shamanic suction pipe: he announced that he was prepared to allow me to attend all his healing sessions. He even made a number of concrete and constructive suggestions as to how we would do it – with him living in Thiksey and me in Leh – bearing in mind the fact that the people call him to their house – which was of course largely unpredictable. Sonam Murup does not conduct group healings and generally does not heal at his home – as for example many shamans from Leh – but rather within a family context, in the home of the patient. However, Sonam Murup had some good ideas on how I could be contacted swiftly, so that I would be able to reach Thiksey on time and thus take part in his séances... Sonam Murup had no qualms at all, and was completely open, friendly and full of enthusiasm.

However, there was one other person present during the conversation: Dolgar, Ngawang Chimba's wife. Ngawang Chimba is, as I previously mentioned, Sonam Murup's grandson and he very often acts as Sonam's shamanic assistant (see HI-23 and HI-27) and therefore knows a great deal about his healing practice. When Chimba helps, the healings take place in his house. And this means that his wife, Dolgar, is also there. Dechen, the daughter of Ngawang Chimba and Dolgar, also attends to the *meme*, Sonam – the grandfather – in his own house since the death of his wife. Thus Dolgar is not infrequently at Sonam's house and if a healing session is taking place, then she also participates.

At the end of September 1998, my collaborators Sonam Norboo and Tsultim Kubet and I spent a few days on the 300 pages of text of this same conversation transcribed by Thinley Gyurmet, and we attempted to translate it.

We could often be heard in fits of laughter – over the "psychodynamics" of this conversation, the ways and means adopted by Dolgar as she persistently interjected in an attempt to control and steer the conversation. Furthermore, she interrupted Sonam Murup audaciously and quite unembarrassed whenever he set out to say something she did not want him to say. My collaborators, as well as I, had the impression that Sonam Murup was completely open, unaffected and indeed very innocent, and was prepared to explain everything – but was repeatedly put in check by Dolgar. We just had to laugh when her tactics became to plump and gross ...

And what was her intention? Her intention was unequivocal: she wanted to tell us that *memele*, the grandfather, remembered absolutely nothing about a healing session, that shamanic amnesia remains impenetrable.

That morning Sonam Murup had conducted a healing séance. What did the people want? What problems did they come to him with? Sonam Murup was just drawing breath to give his answer, when Dolgar interjected: "He doesn't remember, not a thing. The people come in and sit down. And they only ask their questions when he is in trance. And when he's in trance, it's not him there; it's not him speaking. It's the *lha*. And after his trance he remembers nothing, nothing at all. He never remembers anything! If we don't tell him what is said then he would never know."

And so I asked Sonam Murup: "Surely you have been told after the séance what was said?" Once again Dolgar jumps in: "We've never told him anything". And echoing her words Sonam Murup said: "I've never been told anything." Dolgar: "*Memele* remembers nothing. *Memele* is uneducated" (cannot write). (As if that had anything to do with his memory.)

And Sonam Murup outwits her and says to me: "What I do remember is the séance that we had together last year when a woman patient..." (and Sonam Norboo and Tsultim and I burst into spontaneous laughter at this point in the transcript). However, Dolgar interrupted: "We were all there on that occasion. And on that occasion we *did* tell him about it – that's why he remembers it – otherwise he doesn't remember a thing! If we don't tell him anything, then of course he doesn't know about it, he cannot remember anything."

Tired, Sonam Murup comments: "Well, okay. I can't remember most (!) things...."

Why was it so important to Dolgar to defend the story of hermetic amnesia? Sonam Norboo and Tsultim thought that one reason might be: from the conversation, shaman Sonam Murup's readiness to be completely open with me is indisputable. However, if he were frank and gave details about other patients who might then find out about this, would that not cause problems? Dolgar was probably concerned about this. She certainly would not want problems with other people...

Like Sonam Norboo and Tsultim, I also think that Dolgar, for reasons of protection – though for another kind of protection – tried to defend the "theory" of hermetic amnesia, as well as the assertion that she and her family do not reveal to Sonam Murup anything about a healing séance which they have witnessed. Ngawang Chimba as shamanic assistant to Sonam Murup and with whom one could have good and open dialogues (HI-23, HI-27), has equally reinforced this assumption which has also been my own experience with Sonam Murup:

Chimba says (HI-23): Memele can be uncharacteristically aggressive, dirty, unreasonable and coarse when under trance. He then makes sexual innuendoes and tells dirty jokes. I can confirm that – see the encounter with Shang kong ka mentioned above.

It is quite clear – as far as one defends the amnesia "theory" – that one cannot call Sonam Murup to account. It is the work of the *lha*. It is the *lha* that is speaking. And it is the *lha* that is behind the inappropriate behaviour when it occurs – and not Sonam Murup. If *he*, Sonam Murup, had any recollection of events, then it would not have been the *lha* but he himself behaving inappropriately, for he would not be in trance. It is not only shamanic belief but also generally received wisdom that authentic trance (*lha*-possession) is accompanied by total amnesia of the *lus gyar* – of the person who has lent his body to the *lha*. Even the Rinpoches hold this view. This, for example, is what Stakna Rinpoche says (HI-23):

ལྷ་བ་ཁོ་རང་བཙན་པོ་ཁྲིག་མ་ཡོང་ན་ཡིད་དུ་ཡོང་ང་རོག། ཡིད་དུ་ལུས་ས་རོག། ལྷ་ཁོ་རང་དུ་ར་ཁོ་རང་ཨ་མི་ལི་ལྷ་ཡོང་ང་ཅིག་བིལ་གྱལ་ཡིད་དུ་མེད་མཁན་ཆ་རོག།

Translation:

If the shaman is not fully immersed in his *lha* state, he will remember. If he is deep in the *lha* state then he will certainly remember nothing.

The concept of amnesia, as far as one can gather from the events described and the information available, has a most important function in the social organisation of shamanism: it protects the profession.

In the conversations with Ngawang Chimba there does also come into play another possible protective function of amnesia: protection from those constantly delving and enquiring foreign researchers, by whom in fact Sonam Murup, more than any other shaman in Ladakh, had been plagued.

This siege on shamans from all angles by western researchers is formidable. Among those researchers have been: BRAUEN (1980), DAY (1989, 1990), FRANK (1983), KALWEIT (1987), KAPLANIAN (1981, 1984, 1985), KAPLANIAN, RAAB & RABOUAN (1992), KUHN (1988), SCHENK (1994) and VOLF (1994) who have all studied the shaman Ayu Lhamo as well as her eminently more impressive shamanic master, Sonam Murup from Thiksey, about whom there are even three films, in which one can also see Ayu Lhamo (SCHLENKER 1975/1983).[3]

Sonam Murup is only one example for the invasion of Ladakhi shamans from all sides by western researchers.

Other shamans are also sought, observed and questioned time and again, such as Lhamo of Skara, recently deceased, who was pursued by Brauen, Day and Kaplanian; and Lhapa of Phyang, sought by Day and Kuhn; Lhapa Largyal by Day, Kaplanian and Schenk; the Lhapa

---

3 It says much for his great personality that he nevertheless met me and welcomed me – the last of these people prior to his death – so willingly, openly and warm-heartedly.

of She by Day, Kalweit and Kuhn; the Lhapa of Agling by Brauen, Day and Kalweit..., to name but a few examples.

Against this background the question emerges whether the Ladakhi shamans' "alledged" amnesia is perhaps an artefact of western research. Particularly conspicuous is the fact that this puzzling amnesia gives rise to a rather bothersome paradox.

6. THE PARADOX OF AMNESIA AND THE PATH TO CHANGTHANG

The paradox of amnesia has several components. It is most evident when one takes a transcultural perspective and compares how, in various cultures – our own included – the role of the doctor or healer is defined in terms of specific jurisdictions and limits. It is an obvious assumption that the doctor knows more than the majority of the laymen, that he is an expert in healing, that he is in a position to teach his expertise at any time, that he takes responsibility for the treatment he gives, that he devotes himself to his patients, that the quality of his treatment is consistent, and, last but not least, that he will allow a researcher to examine his activities and will make himself understood.

In the case of the Ladakhi shamans, however, all of these assumptions must be thrown overboard. I shall mention only six aspects regarding the paradox of amnesia:

(1) The Ladakhi shaman is an expert in healing
  without the knowledge of healing

The first paradox is that, in the case of the Ladakhi shamans, we have a professional healer before us without any "personal" specialised knowledge of illness and without any specialised knowledge of healing – in other words, a doctor who personally does not know any more about illness and healing than the patient! The *lha*, of course, does.

Naturally, the shaman in Ladakh shares the knowledge of illness which is pertinent to that particular culture – he understands the concepts of illness and knows which illness originates from where, which every Ladakhi knows – i.e. common knowledge. Therefore a shaman can explain to me at once what *dschadu* (harmful magic) is, what *ti mo / ti po* possession is, and what a *lu* illness is, etc.

Knowledge of illness must be distinguished from knowledge of healing and healing *performance*. Normally, healers are experts in the knowledge of healing and in healing performance. In Ladakh, however, the shamans – Sonam Murup, for example – do NOT have such a specialised knowledge of healing; i.e. it is not accessible to them. Like everybody, they know that *dschadu* illness must be sucked out. And in the case of a *dschadu* illness what can one do apart from that? They do not know. And HOW does one suck it out (is it a question of healing technique?) They do not know. They are amnesic. Somebody else knows it: the *lha*.

(2) The Ladakhi healer cannot teach

If a shaman's knowledge is not available to him, the shaman then also cannot teach it, at least not him personally – only a fleeting, temporary "strange being" can teach it: the *lha,* which happens to be "inside" the shaman.

(3) The Ladakhi healer offers therapy without responsibility

The career of a healer in virtually all cultures is usually embedded in the ethics of medical treatment. The healer is responsible for the treatment he administers. The Ladakhi shaman, however, is NOT responsible for his activities as a healer. This is indeed an extraordinary situation.

(4) Doctor-patient contact is unavoidably limited to one minute per patient

Beyond doubt, trance is a highly strenuous achievement, and it is a delicate process. Shamans therefore prefer to heal in the morning when they are at full strength. However, they cannot remain in trance for as long as they wish – all shamans would tell you that. Consequently, one must be quick with the patients. Thus the one-minute-per-patient contact is an inevitable consequence. Indeed, the healer-patient contact, in the case of shamanic séances, is incredibly hectic, sometimes really very superficial and hurried. No patient ever has a chance to describe the history of their illness in any depth – that is out of the question in the time given. The haste is programmed into the performance: trance is fragile.

(5) The healer's key attribute in therapy is unstable

Also a certain discrepancy between reality and what one claims to be reality is part of the scheme. All Ladakhis – including the Rinpoches – share the conviction that authentic trance goes hand in hand with amnesia. As a result, amnesia becomes the hallmark of a GOOD shaman. And if in reality the state of trance fluctuates slightly whilst the séance is in progress – then one must DENY it, otherwise one is not a good healer.

(6) A healer's knowledge cannot be probed

Transculturally a Ladakhi shaman can only communicate his knowledge in very small extracts; shamanism in Ladakh is virtually impenetrable. I have tackled this paradox more thoroughly in another publication (RÖSING 1997). Needless to say, shamanic amnesia is a formidable obstacle when conducting research.

Amnesia is an obstacle to research not only because one cannot ask the shaman any questions after his healing session (or because – pointing to the all-knowing *lha* – one receives no answer), but because it is also so difficult negotiating the conditions under which one can proceed with research. It goes without saying that I never use the tape recorder without the permission of the healer. Similarly, I do not take any photographs without explicit agreement. However, it is not much help to me if I do manage to agree terms prior to a séance. The shaman may say 'yes', but the *lha* can still threaten to flog me (see HH-5) because I have my tape recorder with me.

This last point – the grandiose obstacle to research – was for me the most dramatic aspect of the paradox; after all, I set out to investigate concepts of illness, healing knowledge and healing therapy of the shamans. And I tried to think of different ways in which I could possibly get around the problem. I developed a strategy of recycling the waste of amnesia: I analyse the little "bits of rubbish" which are those small "lapses" in amnesia that occur during the gentle fluctuations in the depth of trance, and I cautiously "recycle the waste" as I term this approach (RÖSING 1997).

But one of the most direct ways to approach this hypothesis of amnesia as a defence strategy against foreign researchers, i.e. the shamanic amnesia as an artefact of western research, would be to seek out a shaman who had had little or no contact with outsiders. And that is what brought me to the inhospitable region of the Changpa nomads in Changthang adjacent to the Chinese border. That distant Changthang, I knew, had scarcely been touched by western researchers.

CHAPTER 5

A key event, an embodied experience and the displacement of the question

1. IN SEARCH OF THE SHAMANS IN THE VAST LANDSCAPE OF CHANGTHANG

In Changthang, I was incredibly lucky every time.

When in June 2000 for the first time I undertook this expensive expedition[1] to Changthang, my explicit and single goal was to meet a shaman who had had as little contact as possible with foreign researchers (or observers or visitors).

One of the most important shamans in Changthang was called Lhapa Thundup – that I already knew. Like all inhabitants of Changthang he is a nomad, and he moves from place to place with his herd.

And so we set off to find our nomadic shaman, Lhapa Thundup, in the vast, wide landscape of Changthang.

After crossing the Indus Bridge at Mahé, where travellers are very closely inspected by the Indian military, it is about one-and-a-half to two hours to the small settlement of Sumdo. It was here that I had intended to ask for Lhapa Thundup for the first time. Did anyone know him? Did anyone perhaps know where his herd was grazing? Where might he be these days?

The answer I received was: "He has just arrived in Sumdo. Yes, we called him. A girl is ill." Five minutes later I was standing in front of Lhapa Thundup (see Illustration 30). I established a good rapport with him very quickly. His healing séance for the girl would be that evening. Could I possibly join him? "But of course", he said quite simply.

What I did not know at the time is that there are two other shamans in Changthang who take care of people in the region. The second, Lhapa Ngawang, is an uncle of Lhapa Thundup. I did not get to know him on my research expedition in 2000 – he spends most of his time a long distance off in the remote region of Terasong, which can only be reached after several days' hiking or

---

1 The preparations involved are in fact substantial. One has to take along all food, water, fuel, and accommodation (tents).

Illustration 30: Shaman Thundup

riding. Nevertheless on that expedition, I did become acquainted with Ngawang's son, Lhapa Sonam Lathar, a lively-minded young man, who followed in his father's footsteps, and thus also heals as a shaman himself. This young man had frequently encountered strangers even though none had ever attended one of his séances or questioned him. His father, however, he believed, had never encountered any strangers in his whole life to date.

Indeed meeting his father – the long and painstaking route over the windswept plains of Changthang on foot or horseback (so I thought) – would have to wait until my 2001 expedition.

The second expedition had two aims. Firstly, for very specific reasons (see below) I was intent on seeking out Sonam Tashi, Lhapa Thundup's shamanic assistant – also a nomad, and equally elusive in the vast expanse of Changthang. And secondly, I was determined to go to almost any length to meet that second shaman, Lhapa Ngawang.

With these two goals in mind, I returned to Sumdo in June 2001 and began with the question: Where is Sonam Tashi, where is Lhapa Thundup's shamanic assistant? And once again a nice stroke of luck: the shamanic assistant was watching over his herds not far from Sumdo. Work began on that same day.

After a few days we proceeded towards Lake Tsomoriri, near to which, in Thugu, Lhapa Sonam Lathar, the shaman's son, had his tent as I understood. I had hoped that he would tell me where I would find his father in the remote Terasong; I had hoped to be able to hire a horse and a guide from him to get to Terasong.

But none of that was necessary. I reached Thugu. I visited Lhapa Sonam Lathar in his tent and was welcomed most warmly. There was a great number of people in the tent. We greeted each other. His wife immediately prepared butter tea. We chatted, I passed round the photos from the previous year – which really contributed to the atmosphere (see Illustration 31) – and finally asked him about his father. His father, Lhapa Ngawang, was sitting next to him in the tent! And in the evening a healing séance was scheduled to take place.

I soon realised that fortune was smiling on me for my Changthang research.

In this account of my Changthang research I shall firstly return to the year 2000 and to Lhapa Thundup, the first Changthang shaman whom I met.

2. THE FIRST HEALING SÉANCE WITH LHAPA THUNDUP

This first healing séance of Lhapa Thundup (HH-14) which I attended took place at the kitchen in a hut. The whole family participated as well as a few additional people from the village. At times, there were up to twelve people in the small dark room.

Incense fills the room creating a dense haze. The Buddhist altar has been built up, the shaman sings his prayers and puts on his costume.

After about twenty minutes, the shaman starts to tremble with increasing vigour, his singing fades, he has a tormented expression on his face, his eyes keep rolling upwards, the shaman looks around him, jerking and twitching, as though some great danger were approaching. Then a quiet whistling sound can be heard, heralding the entry of the *lha* into the shaman's body. The song changes pitch, Lhapa Thundup puts on his shamanic crown and begins drumming and ringing the bell.

Lhapa Thundup's opening prayer which is chanted is only partially intelligible. However, the basic structure is quite recognisable. Essentially, it consists of four critical kinds of content which are paralleled and reflected in the song's intonation, even if the content is not actually comprehensible word for word.

The first part consists of the mantras, the best-known being *om-ah-hung*. Many others are indecipherable.

Secondly, there is a long series of invocations of dignitaries in Tibetan Buddhism (Rinpoches) – first of all the Dalai Lama – to

Illustration 31: Convivial atmosphere in the tent – my photos from last year being passed around

whom Lhapa Thundup pays his respects and who are called upon to give protection.

But protection from what? Here all inclemencies and mis-chieves (*nod pa* and *dib* are the key terms) are listed – this is the third style of content, a record of all the problems and dangers people confront on a daily basis. And it soon becomes clear how dangerous the world is for people. Above all, there are countless evil spirits that roam around everywhere and can attack people. They are non-human spirits like the *tsan* and the *de*, but also many evil spirits expelled from humans such as *ti mo, ti po, gon po, gon mo* and *son de*. Besides these harmful spirits, clearly there are in the world a great number of defilements which can occur as a result of forbidden contact, forbidden touching, by bad food, in-correct medication and dangerous encounters (strangers, refu-gees). The whole nosological universe, and the whole world of illness which a shaman has to cure comes into the frame:

Causes of illness and sources of dangers in the Ladakhi world. From the opening chant of a séance by the shaman Lhapa Thundup (HH-14)		
ཤིན་འདྲེ	shin de	Evil wandering spirit of a dead person
སོན་འདྲེ	son de	Evil wandering spirit of a living person
ཏི་མོ་ཏི་པོ	di mo / di po ti mo / ti po	Evil spirit of a jealous woman (-mo) or of a jealous man (-po)
འགོང་མོ་འགོང་པོ	gon mo / gon po	Witch, warlock
ཕོ་འདྲེ་མོ་འདྲེ	pho de / mo de	Male and female daemons
རོ་གྲིབ	ro dib	Defilement through bodily contact
འབངས་གྲིབ	bangs dib	Defilement through contact with a woman who has just given birth
ཕོ་གྲིབ་མོ་གྲིབ	pho dib mo dib	Defilement through man or woman
ཤ་གྲིབ	sha dib	Defilement through consump-tion of unclean meat

194

སྨན་གྲིབ	sman dib	Defilement through incorrect medication
ཡུལ་གྲིབ	yul dib	Defilement through something impure in the village
གཟའ་གྲིབ	za dib	Defilement through planetary spirits
ཡུལ་བཙན	yul tsan	(evil) village spirits
གནོད་པ་ཐམས་ཅད	nod pa thams chat	All collective evil

All these factors are dangers that surround man – and it is from all these hazards and defilements that the shaman, in his opening song, pleas to the Dalai Lama and to all other Rinpoches for protection.

Against all these evils – and this is the fourth kind of content of the prayer – the shaman sets the Buddhist prayer formula of the threefold refuge heralding the emphatic plea for all six classes of living beings to be released from the *samsara*, the cycle of rebirth, to achieve complete Buddhahood:

1. ཨོཾ་ཨ་ཧཱུྃ།…

2. རྒྱལ་བ་ཡོད་བཞིན་ནོར་བུ།…རིན་པོ་ཆེ་…

3. ས་སྐྱ་གོང་མ་རིན་པོ་ཆེ།

4. སྟག་ལུང་བཀྲ་སྐྲུལ་རིན་པོ་ཆེ་མཆེན་ནོ།

5. ཀ་རྨ་པ་མཆེན་ནོ། ཨོཾ་ཨ་ཧཱུྃ་ཧྲཱི་…

6. བླ་མ་ལ་སྐྱབས་སུ་མཆིའོ།…

7. བོགས་སུ་གྱུར་པའི་བླ་མ་ལ་སྐྱབས་སུ་མཆིའོ།…

8. དང་པོ་ནད་ཀྱི་སྐུ་འཁྲིད་པ།

9. གཉིས་པ་ནད་ཀྱི་ཚངས་ཁྲིན་པ་…

10. ཐམས་ཅད་པོ་འདྲེ་དང་མོ་འདྲེའི་གནོད་པ་

11. ཐམས་ཅད་དུ་མོའི་གནོད་པ་ཞེན་འདེ་གནོད་པ་...

12. ཡུལ་བཅུན་ཆེན་མོའི་གནོད་པ་ཐམས་ཅད།

13. ཨོཾ་ཨ་ཧཱུྃ་ཧྲཱི་...

14. སྨན་གྱིབ་དང་ཁ་གྱིབ།

15. རོ་གྱིབ་འབངས་གྱིབ།

16. ཡུལ་གྱིབ་གཟའན་གྱིབ།

17. ཐམས་ཅད་དག་གོ།

18. དག་པའི་སངས་རྒྱས་གནས་གཙང་གི་གནས་སུ་འཕྲངས་ཀྱི་...

19. ཨོཾ་ཨ་ཧཱུྃ་བཛྲ་གུ་རུ་པད་མ་སིདྡྷི་ཧཱུྃ།

20. བླ་མ་ལ་སྐྱབས་སུ་མཆིའོ།

21. སངས་རྒྱས་ལ་སྐྱབས་སུ་མཆིའོ།

22. ཆོས་ལ་སྐྱབས་སུ་མཆིའོ།

23. དཔལ་མགོན་གྱི་དམ་པ།

24. ཆོས་སྐྱོང་སྲུང་མ་ཡེ་ཤེས་ཀྱི།

25. སྐུན་དང་ལྷུན་པ་རྣམས་ལ་སྐྱབས་སུ་མཆིའོ་...

26. ན་ལེ་ཁྲོ་བའི་...ཨོཾ་ཨ་ཧཱུྃ།

27. སྐྱབས་གནས་དམ་པ་རྣམས་ལ་སྐྱབས་སུ་མཆིའོ།

28. འགྲོ་དྲུག་འཁོར་བར་འཁྱམས་པ།

29. གཞན་དོན་རྟོགས་པའི་སངས་རྒྱས་ཐོབ་གྱུར་ཅིག

30. ཀུན་ཀྱང་བྱང་ཆུབ་མཆོག་ཏུ་སེམས་སྐྱེད་དོ་...

31. སྐྱབ་མགོན་འབྲུག་ཆེན་སྤྲུལ་པའི་རྩྭ་...

32. ཡུང་ཐོབ་པའི་བླ་མ་ལ་སྐྱབས་སུ་མཆིའོ།

196

33. སྐྱབས་ཀྱི་ལྷུང་ཐོབ་པའི་བླ་མ་ལ་སྐྱབས་སུ་མཆིའོ།

34. ས་སྐྱ་གོང་མ་རིན་པོ་ཆེ...

Translation:

1. *Om ah hung...*
2. His Holiness, Dalai Lama ... Rinpoche,
3. His Eminence, Sakya Rinpoche,
4. Staglung Tsetul Rinpoche, I cherish you,
5. I cherish you, Karmapa. *Om ah hung hri ...*
6. I seek refuge in my teacher ...
7. Refuge in my teacher who is my assistant.
8. First of all we must recognise evil,
9. before we can heal through purification,
10. all the evil of male and female daemons,
11. all the evil of *ti mo*, all the damage caused by *shin de*,
12. all the evil from the great *tsan* of the village.
13. *Om ah hung hri ...*
14. Defilement by medicine and meat,
15. Defilement by corpses and people,
16. by settlements and by our planet,
17. all that must be purified,
18. born in Buddha's pure land.
19. *Om ah hung Vra Padma Siddhi Hung,*
20. I take refuge in my teacher (mentor),
21. refuge in Buddha,
22. refuge in learning the dharma,
23. refuge in the shining holy deities,
24. that are the dharma protectors,
25. and awaken with eyes of wisdom.
26. *Om ah hung ...*
27. I take refuge in the holy places of protection,
28. may all six classes of *smasara* living beings,
29. achieve full insight into (the nature of) Buddhism ...
30. and come to full enlightenment ...

31. Dukchen Rinpoche, reincarnated ...
32. I take refuge in my teacher and master,
33. and in my teacher of mantra learning,
34. the outstanding Sakya Rinpoche ...

After these mainly Buddhist invocations, there follows in the shamanic opening songs more, and partly pre-Buddhist invocations – primarily invocations of *lha* deities. The *lha* are usually named after the place where they reside, the *lha tho*, which is also worshipped and decorated. With the naming of these *lha tho*, the shaman wanders virtually the whole length and breadth of Changthang, naming many places, mainly mountain passes and crossroads. And also the *lha* are asked to give protection, primarily from *nod pa* – evil and misfortune – and from all the numerous *dib* – defilements, and other lurking dangers for man.

With the invocation for protection from the five Buddhas which feature on his shamanic crown, the invocation of all Buddhist guardian deities (previously non-Buddhist gods that were converted to Buddhism according to the myth of Padmasambhava, and who rose to guardian spirits of Buddhism) as well as the white and green Tara, the *kandoma dakini* "angel", and again the Rinpoche, the *lha tho*, the Tara goddesses, with all them Lhapa Thundup's songs move through the broad spheres of both Buddhist and shamanic religion.

This wandering to and fro between Buddhist and shamanic invocations without defining any boundary, with no differences nor divide – that is one of the primary features of the multi-faceted – though often so dark – prayers of Lhapa Thundup. And this absence of religious division follows right through to his identity as a shaman:

Thundup under trance has a very specific *lha*. The *lha* god that possesses Lhapa Thundup in trance is called Paldan Lhamo. At this point, my collaborator Tsultim (who, as previously mentioned, was a monk up to the age of 16) remarked – not without some fury – as follows:

"Paldan Lhamo is a being who became enlightened, Paldan Lhama is a (female) Buddha. A female Buddha cannot be the *lha* of a shaman. It's not possible. But Paldan Lhamo has many students, – or, one could say, many physical appearances – and one of those forms may in fact be that of Lhapa Thundup's *lha*. But this is really not quite legal." So spoke Tsultim.[2]

For Lhapa Thundup, however, the questions regarding (Buddhist) legality are quite irrelevant. He *is* Paldan Lhamo, Paldan Lhamo and nobody else. He does not need this talk about students or appearances. In the eyes of Lhapa Thundup, Paldan Lhamo enjoys the same elevated status as Buddha Avalokiteshvara and Buddha Amitayus: all are worshipped. The shaman sings:

1. ཁྱེད་རང་ག་ནེ་ག་ནེ་ཡིན་ནའང་
2. འཕགས་པ་སྤྱན་རས་གཟིགས། མགོན་པོ་ཚེ་དཔག་མེད།
3. དེ་དང་གཅིག་སྐྱབས་མགོན་ཡིད་བཞིན་ནོར་བུ་དང་གཉིས།
4. དཔལ་སྤྲུན་ལྷ་མོ་དང་གསུམ།
5. དེ་དག་ལ་གསོལ་བ་གཏབ་ན་ཁྱེད་ཁར་
6. སེམས་ཁྲེ་དེ་རྩུབ་རང་ན་ཡོ་མ་རེ་ཡ་ཁོ་རེ།

Translation:

1. Wherever you are,
2. Buddha Avalokiteshvara and Buddha Amitayus are the first,
3. (of those worth invoking) and then the Dalai Lama,
4. and thirdly Paldan Lhamo,
5. if you pray to them,
6. you will have no more worries – heed my word!

2 On this subject see also VOLF 1994, p. 190, p. 195, Footnote 40.

Whereupon the shamanic assistant, Sonam Tashi – as always when the shaman sings a message of wisdom – proclaims emphatically:

1. ཕྱིན་རླབས་ཆེ་མོ།
2. མི་ནི་མ་རིག་གི་མུན་པ།
3. ལྷའི་འོད་གསལ་ཀྱི་འདྲ་བོ་···
4. མི་ནི་མ་རིག་གི་མུན་པ་
5. ལྷའི་མ་རིག་གི་མུན་པའི་ཏེ་མའི་འོད།

Translation:

1. The greatest blessing all over,
2. we humans live in the darkness of ignorance,
3. but *lha* is like light ...
4. to be a human being means darkness,
5. *lha* is a ray of sunshine in the darkness of ignorance.

After a further 20 minutes, the girl sitting in the "audience" is called. She kneels before the shaman, and he, singing and continuing to play his hand drum, feels the girl's pulse. It is quite plain to see: the whole body of the little patient is physically "drawn in" by the drumming: through the shaman's hand feeling the pulse, his bodily trembling is transferred to the girl.

From the pulse shaman Thundup feels what is wrong with the girl. And he speaks not only of piety and gods in his prayers – he also gives many concrete instructions on what the patient, who has been infected by the *lu*, should do, and how to conduct herself, in the next seven days. She may only drink thin tea and must not put sugar in it – and she must also observe a *ka stan po* – "mouth control", i.e. she must exercise restraint in eating. And under no circumstances should she go outside bare-headed and without shoes. The wearing of head gear and shoes is a mark of respect and this is how she must pay her dues to the *lu*. She must certainly also avoid going out in the midday heat and keep away from water – the reasoning behind both of these requirements is that around noon and near water insects are most prevalent – and with it the greatest danger that man will kill them ... and, on top of all these precautions to help strengthen her he also gives her a *shu nga*, an amulet, prepared from some strands from his shamanic crown – consecrated in the name of the five Buddhas depicted in his crown.

Apart from the little girl, other participants at the healing séance bring their problems and questions. A young man asks about the current well-being of his herds and what he can do to ensure its continuity. My collaborator Tsultim Kubet asks if he should accept my invitation to come to Germany to work for a few weeks on the transcripts, or whether there may be some hidden danger. Lhapa Thundup's answer: there are no dangers but he must prepare himself through intensive Buddhist practices: make *pujas*, light butter lamps, visit monasteries. As a deeply committed Buddhist who believes in shamanism, Tsultim had already done this – and so he came to visit me in Germany (November/December 2000).

After a whole number of participants at the séance had brought their worries and questions to the shaman in a similar way, Lhapa Thundup sang once more – a long message of warning to everyone (HH-14 as dictated by Sonam Tashi, HI-42):

> You should make *pujas*!
> Look at my five Buddha crown
> And my sacrificial shawls on the altar.
> You should listen to me
> And think only good in your hearts.
> You should have clarity (of mind) from deep within your hearts.
> If you have this clarity of spirit,
> Then do not discard it ...
>
> You should not fight with the enemy,
> do not keep company with people who do wrong,

Otherwise you will become accustomed to it.
In this world of *samsara*
there are so few honest and believing people ...

If you all follow my good words of advice,
then *lha* and *lu* will be happy,
and the *lan de, shin de* and *son de* are defeated
by the *lha*, the *lu* and the eight Buddhas.
We are surrounded by evil spirits and gods.
If we are not wary of one another,
if we play games for luck and profit,
then the spirits of the dead (*shin de*)
and other evil spirits
will look at you with eyes wide open.
People who are careless and play games,
are lost in ignorance.
Do you understand?

Respectfully, with hands folded as in prayer and with spellbound gaze, everyone listened (see Illustration 32).

And all of us had to heed all this advice. But Lhapa Thundup does yet more for the small patient. He performs on her those healing acts which up to that time I had never seen a central Ladakhi shaman do: he places the shamanic drum on the patient's body (neck, chest, abdomen), puts his mouth around the edge of the drum and starts breathing out from the depths of his abdomen – a deep and long sound of breath fills the whole room. The shaman takes in more air and repeats the action, and again... these are acts of purification and cleansing (see Illustration 33).

3. THE CAREER OF SHAMAN THUNDUP

After this first healing séance by Lhapa Thundup, we invited him to breakfast for the following morning. We told him we had a lot of questions. He was very willing to take part in some conversations. He came to our tent the next morning. The cook had prepared a really excellent breakfast with several courses and Lhapa Thundup ate heartily. Today he was wearing his peaked cap with 'MAGIC' printed on it.

After a wonderfully long conversation, I was then keen to know how much contact he had had with foreigners – my prime interest being in relation to my hypothesis regarding foreign RESEARCHERS who sat in on his séances, took photographs and wrote notes and then subsequently possibly asked questions for hours on end...

Lhapa Thundup had allowed an outsider to participate in his séances on two occasions. One was a Japanese, whom he did not allow, however, to take photographs; that was a long time ago and he did not hear anything more from him. The Japanese had not had any questions and there had been no conversation following the séance.

The second contact was with a Frenchman (FÖLLMI & FÖLLMI 1999). This Frenchman filmed the seance. He did not have any questions. No, he had never sat down with strangers before and answered questions as we were doing. For the first time ever he was telling his life story to a stranger, he says. I thanked him for his confidence and he smiled engagingly.

Here now is an account of his life story in his own words. For his own particular healing power Lhapa Thundup refers primarily to his consumption of 360 mantra notes:

> How did I become a *lha pa*? Firstly, I must mention that my father was a *lha pa*. And for me the *lha* manifested itself (*lha thon yong*) when I was 13 years old.

> Then 14, 15, 16, 17 up to 18 years of age I was possessed (*bam te*). That was a very difficult time. For example, on a number of occasions I vomited blood. And it was a Tibetan *lha pa* at that time who put an end to this. When I was 25 years old, I was at the monastery of Hemis when the Cham plays were taking place. Togdan Rinpoche was there and I went to visit him in his room.

Illustration 32: Devotional attention to shamanic ritual actions: clients at a shamanic séance conducted by Lhapa Thundup

It's as though I lost consciousness and could not stand, and I trembled and this is what happened to me – and I did not feel at all well; I was shaking terribly. And then I went down the steps and that's all I remember.

That happened to me on the day of the Hemis festival. There, in the room I saw the photograph of Stagtsang Rinpoche. He himself was not there, just his photo. And then, as I said, I went down the steps. But whether I reached the monastery courtyard or not, I don't know; I can't remember (*yid du med kan la song*); everything suddenly got lost (*te ne pa ta med kan la song*), I lost all memory, yes, that's how it happened to me.

I really did not understand what was going on with me; I don't really know. And then somehow I got down to the *du khang*, where the eight gurus are; I don't know how exactly, it was terribly hot; it was as though the room was full of butter lamps, I felt ashamed of my peculiar behaviour. And then the Guru Rinpoche's masked dances began and I left, and was ashamed of everything that had happened...

And then Karmapa Rinpoche came to the village of Gya in Ladakh. It was incredibly crowded. And he said to me immediately: My dear young man: I believe you are a *lha pa*, a *lha pa*. And I prostrated before him and said I felt so crazy (*nyo*). And his holiness, the Karmapa, said to me: you must do good for all living beings, you appear to be a good *lha* (*lha yag po*). That's what he said to me.

After that I went to Takthok monastery where Tsetul Rinpoche is, and paid him a visit. And I asked him: I keep going crazy (*nyo tak*), what is it all about?

He sat on his throne and there was a small table in between and I sat at the other side of it. And he offered me tea. He used a mirror and prepared offerings and said prayers ... And then this mirror was the mirror, the mirror ... and while he prayed he lifted it up and displayed it and I began to tremble violently and lost consciousness (*sem*) and as he lay the mirror down again everything was over...

When I have a turn of madness (*nyo song ste*), I remember nothing (*te ne yid du med pa*). And I said: "I am Paldan Lhamo" someone told me. Someone said that, in front of the Rinpoche, I said "I am Paldan Lhamo". And he said that if a beggar or a person from the lower caste comes, I (should) do good to him and to everyone; the *lha* is for everyone, do good for everyone...

I received mantra-instruction (*nyaks ge lung*) from Staglung Rinpoche. He did not teach me how to handle *ti mo / ti po,* not that; nor how you find items that had been lost; that is not their business, but apart from that he did teach me all the relevant things (*lung tsang ma*).

Above all, he gave me a small cardboard container as big as a matchbox. All my teaching was contained in it, he said. There were 360 minute notes on Tibetan paper, the letters were in red and he told me I should eat one note each day. But don't drink *chang*, he said, and don't eat meat, and then you will be a very strong *lha*. And so I ate them all up. On each piece of paper there was a mantra written in red ink.

4. THE PASSAGE INTO TRANCE

It is not easy for Lhapa Thundup to go into trance. Lhapa Thundup wonders endlessly how there could possibly be shamans, who – on washing their hands prior to a séance (which they all do) can fall into trance straight away – what sort of shamans are *they*? Or there are apparently shamans, so he hears, who only have to talk about trance and they fall into one immediately. And what sort of shamans are *they*? How can one go into a real trance without *ser*

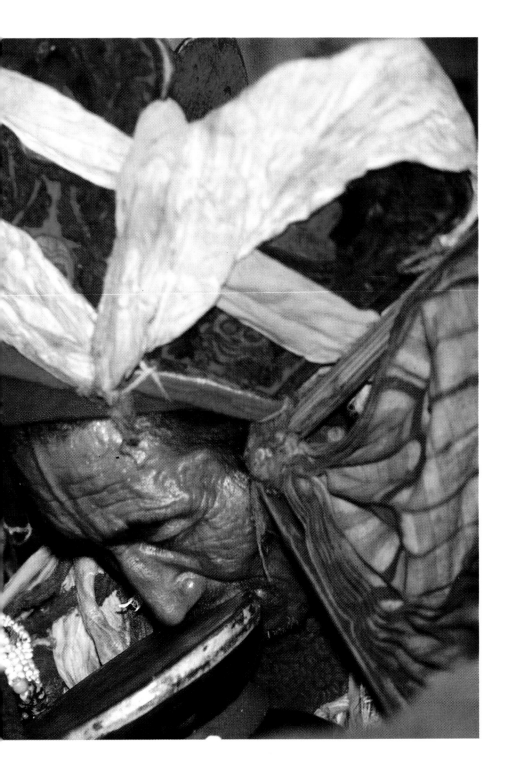

kyem, without *puja* ...? This would mean that *anyone* could become a shaman!

For him, there are at least three conditions that have to be fulfilled: he must prepare the Buddhist altar and the offerings (*nyer tschod*), he must recite or chant Buddhist prayers (*ser kyem*) and he must recite invocations (*chan den*) – only then does he become "unconscious", "as though crazy". Then he continues his story:

He sees changing colour formations and wild animals and hideously large insects – those are *shin de* and *son de* spirits. He himself rises higher and higher, he says, and the people around him disappear further and further into the background; they become minutely small, he floats high up somehow and the mirror which he uses for prophesising becomes enormous. Chitti-pati figures (skeleton players from the monastic Cham plays, mainly performed by children) spring up and attack him, jumping and tumbling on his body; it is frightening but sometimes amusing too. He sees the colour red and the mountains come in very close to him.

Lha appear in great numbers, all in different forms, also appearing as animals – a wild donkey, a great bird. It is because he has received *lung* (instruction from a Rinpoche) that all this happens to him; he had also been forewarned that he would see many things and he should take care, but not be afraid.

Beams of light emanate from all four corners, the *nyer tschod* appears in the form of wolves, snow leopards, tigers. The grains turn into yaks. Everything looks larger than life. All these things are *lha*. He must give the offerings to the *lha*. Then these figures will disappear, he says.

And black and white colours descend from the heavens and enter the mirror. In the mirror Guru Rinpoche (Padmasambhava) and images of the eight Buddhas appear.

Lha emerge in multitudes – 360 in total – because he had eaten 360 mantra notes. There are 360 illnesses and he has 360 *lha* at his disposal to resolve the problems. There is one *lha* for pains, another *lha* for questions relating to the whereabouts of stolen goods, one for blowing (*snag*) ...

His most important *lha*, however, is Paldan Lhamo. She normally appears on a walnut-coloured mule. It is the scornful Paldan Lhamo that turns up. But the gentle Paldan Lhamo is also coming. She rides a white horse, is as beautiful as a bride and wears a magnificent *pe rak,* he says.

The *lha* do not, however, simply appear spontaneously; he must call them. When patients ask questions, he looks into the mirror. A *lha* appears in it. He puts the question to the *lha* and the *lha* answers. Depending on the nature of the patient's problem various *lha* are called upon.

The *lha* that come to him are not like the *lha* that are found in Leh. His *lha* come out of the blazing fire from four corners. One must handle them with great circumspection.

In the morning, all *lha* stay more or less congregated together – just as people sit together in the tent – then it is relatively easy to call on them. Therefore, he prefers working in the morning. After that they disperse, as do people. It then becomes a painstakingly difficult task for the *lus gyar* to invite each one individually. By the evening the *lha* are again clustered together and so once more it is easier to call them.

When one calls a *lha*, *sem nyid* (consciousness) retreats from the body, he explains. As it retreats, darkness prevails. When the *lha* moves into the body it becomes light once more. And when the *lha* departs, *sem nyid* returns. And after that one cannot remember anything.

But where does he get all these details from – I wanted to know – the colours, the wild animals, the outsized insects, the colour of Paldan Lhamo's mule? That is, he says, the path to the *lha* state, the long and laborious path. Once a *lha* has entered his body, he has no recollection of events.

5. SECOND SÉANCE: THE KEY EVENT

Lhapa Thundup wore not only a huge, impressive watch on his wrist, but also one around his neck. And he was very precise with times. At exactly 9 o'clock – as he had already announced to us – he terminated our conversation. He had a healing séance to go to right away, he explained, and he needed to call together the *lha* before they dispersed for the day.

Another healing séance? That came as a surprise – and (for the researcher) a real blessing. May we take part, make a tape recording and take photos? He had not objections to this. This second healing séance of Lhapa Thundup became for me an indelible key experience. For this reason I wish to describe it now in more detail.

SHAMAN THUNDUP'S HEALING RITUAL FOR SONAM DISKIT AND TASHI
GONPO ON 26.6.2000
THE SHAMAN'S ASSISTANT: SONAM TASHI

Place, time, participants, reason for healing

The healing séance takes place in the kitchen of Tashi Gonpo's hut in the small settlement of Sumdo in Changthang, Ladakh. It begins at 9 a.m. and finishes at around 11 a.m.

The main patient is a woman, Sonam Diskit; she is about 40 years old. She has consulted the shaman because she is short of breath and has chest pains.

She lives with her father Tashi Gonpo, who is also participating in this séance. Sonam Diskit is a widow with three children. The oldest son is already at high school in Nyoma, a small town at the edge of the Changthang high plains, a 6-hour walk and bus journey from Sumdo. He wants the shaman to prophesise: will he pass his school exam? The girl is about 12 and the youngest, a boy, 4 years old. The children are at times also present during the séance.

Besides the patient's family the following people also participate: the shamanic assistant, Sonam Tashi, my Ladakhi collaborators, Sonam Norboo Spurkhapa and Tsultim Kubet, and I.

The appearance of Lhapa Thundup

Lhapa Thundup sits down in his normal daily clothes in the kitchen (see Illustration 34), on the carpeted floor, in the corner of the room in front of the Buddhist house altar. He wears beautiful shining turquoise stone rings on both hands, he also wears a turquoise stone (gem) on his ear (secured by a thread through his ear lobe) and one around his neck. Around his neck he wears a *dzi* stone[3] as well as a watch. A second large, prominent watch adorns his wrist. He has his hair pulled back and tied in a pigtail. Draped over his pullover and trousers he has a wide velvet coat.

Preparatory activities

Lhadap Thundup begins his preparations slowly and leisurely. He squats or kneels in his place. Firstly, he must prepare the Buddhist altar with the usual seven offering bowls. The offering bowls for tea symbolise a holy lake; one of the *tsampa* offering bowls is the holy mountain of Kailash, the other the heart of the shaman, he murmurs, as he proceeds cautiously. During these preparations people continue to chat – about everyday matters; the goats, the sheep, school, the weather.

The shaman begins with monotonous prayers, singing of Buddhist mantras reeled off, and accompanies his praying with many tea libations. The others continue uninterrupted with their everyday chat. However, with the lighting of the butter lamps on the altar a certain atmosphere of formality pervades and the conversations subside.

---

3 Regarding the meaning of the *dzi*-stones see EBBINGHOUSE & WINSTEN 1982a, 1982b; LIU 1980; NEBESKY-WOJKOWITZ 1952.

Dressing for the séance

Lhapa Thundup removes his threadbare velvet coat from his shoulders. The monotonous recitation of Buddhist prayers and mantras continues. At the same time, the shaman gets dressed – still squatting or kneeling: firstly, he ties a red cloth around his head, like a cap, then tucks a wrap around his shoulders and finally he threads another piece of cloth around his head and ties a piece of bright cloth in front of his mouth. In the meantime, his assistant (Sonam Tashi) has prepared the incense bowl and a thick haze of incense fills the room.

Drums, bells, singing

The shaman takes his small precious *da ma ru* (hand drum) out of his bag of ritual props and begins to drum. At the same time, the droning singsong becomes clear singing. Thirty minutes have passed since the start of the healing session.

A few minutes later under constant drumming and singing the shaman's whole body begins to tremble; he looks wildly around him, continues to drum; the vibrating and shaking of his body gets stronger, and now with trembling hand he reaches for his magnificent shamanic crown adorned with wings and bands, and fiddles with it erratically as his sings and drums on.

After a few minutes, the drumming and singing stops. He lays the drum down and puts on his crown with both hands. With the sheer chaos of countless dangling, shaggy braids it is quite evidently not easy to fasten the crown at the back of the head; it takes him a considerable time to fix. Then the *da ma ru* drumming resumes, with Buddhist singing. Forty-five minutes have now passed since the start of the séance.

Illustration 34: Lhapa Thundup giving explanations

The drama of the trance

His singing gets faster. In addition to the *da ma ru* (in the right hand), he reaches for the bell, and rings and drums and prays more and more wildly (see Illustration 35). He is shaking rigorously all over from head to toe. The tension in the room rises and is reflected in the faces of the participants. No one dares to say a word.

All of a sudden, Lhapa Thundup, in a wild precipitous and passionate gesture, lays down drum and bell, jumps to his feet, takes a leap in front of us, he bends right over us (we are all sitting on the floor), cutting a formidable figure – with giant wings and countless numbers of brightly coloured long braids dangling and jostling from his crown – and sings before us.

There is so much vehemence in his movements and in his facial expression, and, with his glare, equally wild, everyone visibly winces and stares paralysed with fear, their breath caught: everyone is clearly afraid of the shaman's physical aggression.

He looks wild. He comes right up to each person, one by one; everyone can feel his breath, everyone can see his face dripping with sweat while trembling and vibrating in every fibre. At the same time, he continues to sing to us uninterrupted and with great intensity, and sometimes with alarming breathlessness. His face twitches, his lips tremble, it is breathtaking (see Illustrations 36 and 37).

Diagnosis and recommended treatment

After some minutes, he returns to his carpet in front of the altar, reaches for the *da ma ru*, calls the patient to him, feels her pulse as he continues to drum and sing; and then speaks to her for a long time – no drum, no singing. He tells her where her pains are coming from, and what she must do and what she should not do, which Buddhist rituals she must adhere to, how long she must allow for healing and whom she should consult (an *am chi*, a Tibetan doctor), if she is not cured after one week. Whatever happens she must not drink cold or hot water; everything must be done in moderation.

If she does not abide by these instructions, the shaman says, her condition may deteriorate substantially. But, after all, he continues, we are all human beings and illness is normal. We fight illness through *sem pa* – through our consciousness, this consciousness must be pure and clear. Whoever understands this message, he says, will not get into difficulties. If she, the patient, works on her consciousness and retains moderation in all things, then he can help her. Otherwise misfortune threatens...

Ritual healing with the da ma ru breathing

Then Lhapa Thundup puts the *da ma ru* to her neck, to her head, to her temples, on her chest, on her back; each time he places his mouth round the edge of the drum and blows on the drumskin, causing the drumskin to make an impressive, long, deep, arresting, gentle breathing tone that resounds around the room. As a *lha*, a god, he breathes the healing forces into her, as Sonam Tashi later explains to us (HI-41): then the patient, kneeling before him, must bow right down to the ground and is blessed by the shaman with the *vajra*, the diamond sceptre.

Other patients; prophecies and admonitions

Sonam Gombo is also treated in this way: feeling of the pulse, *da ma ru* breathing and *vajra* blessing. From time to time, Lhapa Thundup interrupts the *da ma ru* blowing, in order to beat the drum violently, before he continues the blowing once again.

The son asks if he will pass his exam. Lhapa Thundup takes out a small round "mirror" (a plain brass plate) and stares into it for a long, long time before he gives his answer. In the mirror the *lha*, the god, spoke.

Illustration 35: Lhapa Thundup with da ma ru-drum and bell reciting mantras

Emerging from the trance

The shaman begins drumming energetically and ringing the bell once more, and following the calmness of his prophesising his body begins to tremble and shake once again – wildly gesticulating with the drum and bell: it all appears very dangerous – as though the shaman might injure himself or attack one of us.

The shaman assistant slips behind the kneeling Lhapa Thundup and holds him tightly with both hands, in an attempt, apparently, to prevent him from falling backwards.

Suddenly, the drumming and ringing ceases, the shaman rips the crown off his head, then the red headcloths and finally the mouth cloth which has long since slipped out of place. He collapses with a massive groan and lies like that for some time. Sonam Tashi puts corns into his hand (shamans scatter them around to consecrate the room) – but his attempts at scattering the corns is so weak that they scarcely roll more than a few centimetres from him. He is exhausted (see Illustration 38).

After a while Lhapa Thundup sits up and looks around him as though he does not know where he is and who he is, and what is, or has been, happening here. He wipes the sweat from his forehead, smiles, slightly perplexed, and then says weakly and in a friendly tone: Juley – hello!

In the light of my scepticism regarding trance and amnesia, the healing by Lhapa Thundup has become a key experience for me. I now "understood" – and indeed not in a left-hemispheric, rational, logical or scientific way, but in a right-hemispheric, intuitive, emotional, even virtually a trance-induced way – that the shamanic trance *can* be completely authentic.

Quite according to the traditional pattern, the shaman went into trance through song, drumming and sounding a bell; while under

Illustration 36: Lhapa Thundup in deep trance: chant about the state of the world

221

trance the patient Sonam Diskit and her father Tashi Gombo specify the problem – the daughter's chest pains – and the shaman diagnosed the origin of the illness. But then the shaman leaped to his feet with such fury (shamans usually heal while crouching) – that EVERYONE present (not only I, the stranger) were startled, and indeed drew back, horrified. Heart racing frantically, I quickly drew all my research equipment to my side on the floor – tape recorder, camera, notepad and pencil – to rescue them from his threatening behaviour, and shuffled back – like everyone else – as far away as was possible, with the wall behind us.

With his impressive appearance, shaman Thundup stood before us, bent over us and sang down to us for many minutes with indescribable intensity. Time and again, his face came very close to mine; I felt his rapid breathing, I saw the beads of sweat and the trembling in every fibre in his face – his lips, eyelids – he sung with an expression of such power and strain that I was afraid he would collapse at any moment. However, he sang on and on; it was absolutely captivating. After a few minutes, our fear subsided and we were suddenly drawn into this song: I was almost drawn in with him. My breathing followed his short breaths, I suddenly realised; gradually it was as if I began to hear the song also emanating from within myself, like a sounding board within my own consciousness. And I had truly understood – right in my soul, in my heart, in the right-hand side of my brain (which all seems rather unscientific and taboo in a strictly scientific context!) – what trance is, and that a state of trance does indeed exist – real, authentic and deep shamanic trance, and I understood that one can get infected by the trance and that the contagion gives rise to a state of consciousness which makes one receptive to things in a completely different way – and certainly receptive to the potency of suggestion of shamanic healing ...

With this key experience, I cannot necessarily explain what trance is, nor can I necessarily give a logical account. However, I can say that on this occasion I have certainly witnessed its complete authenticity.

222

Illustration 37: Lhapa Thundup in deep trance: chant, prayer and admonition

6. THE NEW QUESTION: WHAT DID HE SAY?

I was completely dazed following this healing séance. I immediately asked my collaborator Tsultim: "What was the shaman singing when he leaped up?" "I didn't understand", Tsultim replied, "I was frightened." I asked Sonam Norboo. He had not understood either, and he, too, had been scared. However, after we had composed ourselves to some extent, I sat the whole day with Tsultim over the tape recorder. But still there were only fragments that we understood!

Illustration 38: Lhapa Thundup – collapsing at the end of the séance

Now, finally, I had really experienced for the first time what trance is. I had understood that trance can be overwhelmingly powerful. Now I could quite easily imagine that, having been in such an entirely different state of mind, one would indeed NOT be able to remember, in the "normal" functioning mind of everyday consciousness, what had happened. The searching question of amnesia as a defence strategy had not become irrelevant, but, (in the light of my experience) now took a lower priority.

But I did not wish to rest on my "unscientific" *embodied understanding*: on a scientific level I wanted to at least understand SOMETHING of what happens in trance. I certainly wanted to understand what the shaman had sung to us with such vehement power and intensity. WHAT DID HE SAY? What did he wish to communicate to us? What message did he have, what warning, what advice, what story, what threats, what promises? I was completely fixated in my desire to find the answers, no matter what lengths I had to go to. And that should indeed be possible since, after all, I had the song on my tape recorder.

This additional new and burning question: "What did he say?" consumed a substantial amount of research time, effort and (other) resources for a full year. The results can be found in the following and final chapter.

CHAPTER 6

The great shamanic chant, resolution of the questions

1. FATHER AND SON;
TWO OTHER CHANGTHANG SHAMANS

As previously mentioned, in June 2001, I undertook another field trip to Changthang. And what luck I had this time too in finding the "still missing" shaman, Lhapa Ngawang (father of Lhapa Sonam Lathar) and then above all to find Sonam Tashi, Lhapa Thundup's shamanic assistant – this I mentioned earlier. Fortune had indeed smiled on me.

Firstly, I would like to allow the two Changthang shamans, whom I have not yet introduced, to give their accounts. They speak of their personal development, their healing practices, their *lha* and their amnesia. With the elderly shaman, the father Lhapa Ngawang, I also had the opportunity to witness and document a healing session.

Given this background, it will be possible to clarify similarities and differences between the nomadic Changthang shamans, on the one hand, compared with the shamans of central Ladakh – on whom I had previously concentrated – on the other (see Appendix A). These differences are also linked to the economic, ecological setting in which these two groups of shamans operate.

2. THE YOUNG SHAMAN, SONAM LATHAR

The young shaman, Sonam Lathar – 39 years old – is tall, slim and wears "modern" clothes (see Illustration 39). He usually wears a Coca-Cola peaked cap. He is Lhapa Ngawang's son and Lhapa Thundup is an uncle. He had never been questioned by strangers and no stranger had as yet attended his healing sessions.

Twenty years ago, Sonam Lathar tells me, the *lha* came to him:

228

Illustration 39: Shaman Sonam Lathar with his son

ང་རང་ཚ་བ་ཚ་བེ་ཚིག་སོང་། དེ་རྫུག་གི་མ་ནེ་སྨྱོ་ཉི་ཚིག་སོང་།

Translation:

I sort of went mad. I seemed to go crazy.

Upon this happening he consulted a Rinpoche who confirmed that his was no "normal madness" but possession by a *lha*: however, *lha* (the god) and *de* (the evil spirit) were still in combat within his chest. He, the Rinpoche, separated *lha* and *de*, and started teaching him. From that time only the *lha* came to him, and even then only when called upon. After that his father taught him.

Both are in practice – father and son. How are their duties divided? The father, Lhapa Ngawang, remains mainly in the remote Terasong region and so he heals mostly there, while Sonam Lathar heals primarily in the villages and other locations in the regions of Korzok, Kyaga, Chhumur and Churtse. When both of them are in the same area and patients ask for a shaman, whichever of the two is available will go.

What are the reasons for the patients coming? They come if they are feeling physically unwell; if they wish to be relieved of the burden of some ailment or worry (*ngan chod chig*, the wrong doings of others), if they have lost something and wish to know where it is; if they have questions – what they should do or how the future looks, and if they need fire therapy (*me ngag be ngag*[1]) or some kind of medicine.

No, neither he nor his father treat animals; they do not suck needles out of a yak's fur (*khab phing*), they are completely unfamiliar with the practice of sucking (*dshib bib*). For sick animals, they make *pujas* and give them medicine. But each person does

---

1 In the language of Sonam Lathar and his father there are some remarkable linguistic peculiarities: the repetition of a word with a change of consonant, primarily b: *me ngag/be ngag; dschib/bib; chho ga/bo ga; kab ko/bab ko* etc

heal in a slightly different way, he says. Lhapa Thundup draws out the malaise with the *da ma ru* drum (*da ma ru bo tang nyam po then na nog*) but neither he nor his father does that. They have other methods of healing.

He and his father are familiar with the following treatments: performing of religious rituals and prayers (*chho ga bo ga, kab ko bab ko*), administering medication, blood treatment (*khrag bag tang ches*) and treatment with fire (*me be tang ches*, or *me ngag*).[2]

Father and son are possessed by the same *lha*. A long time ago, the father went on pilgrimages to Tibet to the holy mountain of Kailash. It was there that the *lha* first came to him. It was Kailash Rinpoche himself, that came to him. He is also known as Kangs Rinpoche, or Kang *ri lha tsan*. On asking whether Kangs Rinpoche and Kangs *ri lha tsan* are the same, Sonam Lathar answers: "Kangs *ri* stands for Kangs Rinpoche and the place where the *lha* Kangs Rinpoche came to the father was *tsan*. And no other *lha* has come to him or his father.

And how does he go into trance (*lha zhugs*)? He says prayers and as he does so the *lha* comes in and takes over. And once the *lha* is there, he remembers no more. He cannot remember any-thing:

ལྷ་གཞུགས་ཡ་ལེ་ང་རང་འིན་ན་ཁོ་རང་ནེ་ཕྱ་ར་ལྱ་ཏེ་བརྗེ་ཚོང་མེ་ལྱ་ ར་གསོལ་ཀ་ཚིག་མེ་གཏང་ང་ནོག་གསེར་སྐྱེམས་གཏང་ང་ནོག་ནེ་ ནེ་ཁོ་རང་དང་མཉམ་དུ་ལྱ་གཞུག་ཕྱེན། གཞུགས་ཆ་རང་ཅང་ གཞུགས་ཆ་རང་མ་ནེ་ཅང་པ་ཏ་ཆ་མེ་རག། དེ་ཡོང་ང་མེ་རག་དེ་ ཡོང་ང་མེ་རག་ལེ།

---

2 With an iron object (*sa bug*) "bad" blood (*khrag tsog po*) is drawn out − mainly from the head, hands, feet and from any specific area where the problem lies. The heat treatment involves the heating of the blade of a kni-fe, which the shaman places over the area in pain and blows.

Translation:

The *lha* comes when I say prayers and prepare offerings; that's when he comes. Once he is there I know nothing about what's going on. He comes – and I remember nothing any more.

Lhapa Sonam Lathar sees social changes everywhere he goes. In some places, there is now electricity, people are familiar with radio, and many have ovens fuelled by gas cylinders. But the shamans are held in just the same respect, he says, as they have been in the past; quite simply, people need them. So can he do something for my sore knee? "I don't know", Sonam Lathar said, "only the *lha* knows".

3. THE SHAMAN LHAPA NGAWANG: HERMETIC AMNESIA

There was a tangibly warm and relaxed atmosphere in the tent of his son, Sonam Lathar, where for the first time I met the father, shaman Ngawang, who stays mainly in the region of Terasong. We were most welcome to participate in a healing séance that was to take place here on that day; he would be pleased to speak to us too.

For the healing session, thirteen people had gathered in the spacious tent, amongst whom there was a monk, who devotedly watched the shaman the whole time with hands clasped together as in prayer (see Illustration 40). The shaman's son, Lhapa Sonam Lathar, was his assistant today.

The healing séance began at 9.45 a.m. with the usual preparatory activities and was over by 11 o'clock.

The shaman prepares – in silence – the *nyer tschod*, and places the requisites ready. The incense bowl is prepared and the butter lamps at the altar are lit. With great care, Lhapa Ngawang unwraps

Illustration 40: Buddhist monk in a shamanic séance (with Lhapa Ngawang). In the background a traditional container for making butter tea and modern Chinese utensils of plastic and tin

233

the mirror – it is a round, shining sheet of metal (similar to Lhapa Thundup's mirror); it is placed upright in the bowl full of barley corns. Barley corns are an integral feature in every shamanic séance; under trance, a shaman throws the corns around: a gesture symbolising the blessing of those present.

Finally, towards 10 o'clock, the shaman begins to chant in a quiet, droning tone while he dresses in preparation for the séance: he ties a large white cloth over his mouth and a red one around his head. He hangs a cape over his shoulders and finally he places the crown on his head, which, adorned with an abundance of dangling, shaggy braids, is as impressive as that of Lhapa Thundup's.

The chant becomes louder, the shaman begins to beat the drum and sound the bell (see Illustration 41), he shakes a little, he groans a little.

Illustration 41: Lhapa Ngawang in trance. the da ma ru-drum in the right hand, the bell (not visible) with brightly coloured braids in the left. Background: daylight streaking through the tent hand-woven from yak hair

This appears to be a sign that he has reached a state of trance, for now the son, Sonam Lathar, steps before him with the utmost respect, kneels down and – acting as his assistant here – brings the first patient's enquiry to him. It is mine: how is – a thousand miles away – my husband, Ré?

The shaman puts corns onto the *da ma ru*, shakes them around a little and looks for the answer in the position of the corns. After that, in silence, he will draw out with great care and attention from his many pockets, six different "medications", plastic bags with brown, green and red powder, taking a bit of each and putting it on a piece of paper, folding it and tying it up and finally handing it over to me with instructions. The instructions were spoken in his normal voice, not chanted. The contents of the one bag Ré should rub into his skin; the contents of the other should be administered with tea and drunk, the corns he should scatter over the feet of a woman that wants to harm him. During all this time there was no drumming, no bells, no change from his normal voice.

Then comes the next question – from the monk; it is a question about land. Again the corns are placed on the *da ma ru*, their position read and advice given.

Lhapa Ngawang appears to be much more interested in the concerns of two nomadic women, bowing down low and kneeling before him, whom he blesses firstly with his sceptre and then with the incense bowl and then with the braids from his crown, whilst continuing his chanting and drumming (See Illustration 42).

The women get up, the shaman's chanting continues but gradually becomes quieter; he takes off his crown, shakes himself a little and finally looks at us and greets us: Juley! He has come back.

The following day we have a long conversation (HI-43). Indeed, Lhapa Ngawan did have a foreign development aid worker attend a healing (session), though he did not take photographs, nor did he ask questions, and he did not want anything. And on one occasion he helped a tourist who had had an accident. He had not encountered any other strangers.

Illustration 42: Lhapa Ngawang, carrying the incense bowl, blesses women bending down before him on the floor

He was only 13 years old when the lha came to him (his father was not a shaman). At that time, he was in Tibet on a pilgrim trail to Kailash. Near Kailash, there is a monastery with many doors. There is one door, and one door only, through which you can only pass – without any hesitation or uncertainty – if you are possessed by a lha. The 13-year-old boy chose that very door. And ever since this incident he has been healing as a shaman (!).

Today he is 71 and has over 170 families in Terasong to take care of: that is a lot of work. In return, however, the residents help him to collect brushwood and dung and to look after his livestock.

No, he did not receive instruction; the *lha* had all the (necessary) knowledge. Twenty-five years ago, he also began to distribute medicine (Tibetan medicine, that otherwise only the traditional Tibetan doctors, the *am chis*, do).

Which medicines treat what? He does not know. Only the *lha* knows that. How many *lha* does he have? 360 – he cannot name them all. He only knows this while he is in a trance (Sonam Lathar said he only has one).

Which *lha* was present in yesterday's healing session? He does not know. After a séance he cannot remember anything.

"OK", I say, "I'll tell you one thing that happened: you gave me something for my husband Ré. What was it?" He does not know.

"So, my husband – I continue – does have a problem, as I told you in the séance (he is in a wheelchair)." No, the shaman did not know.

"OK then, and you gave me some medicinal preparations. What kind?" Only the *lha* knew that.

"And you gave me corns which Ré is supposed to scatter at the feet of a woman that wants to harm you" "Aha?!" the shaman replies, rather astonished. Apologetically he adds: only the mirror knows about all that, the mirror into which I look (he was not looking into his mirror), that is the *lha*. The *lha* knows the answer.

So here the amnesia appears to be hermetic. And so I told Lhapa Ngawang of my shamanic teacher Sonam Murup from Thiksey (whom he knew by name) and how he insisted that trances *can* vary in depth and that following a phase of lighter trance one can remember a little afterwards. How is it for Ngawang? Certainly, he is also familiar with fluctuating depths of trance. But he cannot remember what that is like....

4. ASSESSMENT OF THE QUESTION OF AMNESIA

Following my talks with Lhapa Ngawang, who effectively had not had any experience of foreign researchers asking questions, and claimed hermetic amnesia, the question of amnesia as a defence strategy had been answered to a large extent as far as I was concerned. Hadn't I sought out the least accessible shaman in Ladakh only then to hear that his amnesia was airtight?

Claiming amnesia is a common narrative amongst all shamans throughout the whole of Ladakh. It is part of their professional reality and the way they portray themselves professionally. To me, following the key experience in Lhapa Thundup's healing séance, this element – whether genuine or staged – was no longer the critical question. Most certainly, there is such thing as authentic deep trance and indeed there also exists trance as good theatre. And likewise profound amnesia certainly exists as well as mere claims of amnesia.

Amnesia as a "claim" is fully justified in the overall context of the Ladakhi shamanic complex. Two premises regarding Ladakhi shamanism that are completely unquestionable are: only in deep trance is a shaman (considered to be) in the *lha* state. Deep trance and hermetic amnesia go hand in hand. Sonam Murup thrashes his shamanic pupils when he – or correspondingly the *lha* who is teaching – has the impression that their trance is not complete! Partial trance is punishable. This reflects the fundamental values of the Ladakhi shaman.

At the same time, trance is an uncommonly difficult condition to establish. The shamans' accounts regarding their trance, as well as the clearly apparent exhaustion following trance, shows that the whole process of going into trance (and indeed remaining in it) must involve great physical exertion. It is only justified if this trance – my means of claiming amnesia – is protected!

Without deep trance (which can only be proved by the presence of complete amnesia), the shaman would lose his credibility, his professional role, the patient's faith in him, and his powers of healing. Therefore, he MUST claim amnesia so that the true "depth" of his trance remains unknown and is thus protected. And furthermore, he must claim amnesia because otherwise he would be called to account for any possible violent or indecent behaviour during his trance (see Chapter 5).

Amnesia is certainly not only a defence strategy to shield the shaman from intrusive strangers: that I had certainly understood following all my experiences. The claim of amnesia may, I think, be a defence strategy on certain occasions – or perhaps a more accurate description would be a protection strategy – but it is a protection of the shaman in view of his own professional status.

In any case, the question of amnesia that had brought me to Changthang had in some respects been answered. The answer, however, is more differentiated and more specific than the original question. The alternative, whether there is "really" amnesia or not, does not make sense. Sometimes, amnesia may exist, deep and complete. Sometimes, it is only claimed. And, as was revealed, the question regarding the purpose, the meaning, the necessity of claiming amnesia in the shamanic complex as a whole, is in fact far more intriguing than the question of its authenticity.

However, the question which arose on my first expedition to Changthang is not yet answered: what was the message – conveyed with such impressive intensity from the depths of what was clearly an authentic trance and communicated in the form of a great shamanic chant – that contained so much force and energy?

5. SONAM TASHI, THE SHAMANIC ASSISTANT

Apart from the search for the shaman Ngawang, there was a further (and indeed my most important) reason for another expedition to Changthang in 2001: to decipher the long shamanic chant which I had documented in 2000. I had already been busy working on it for several months previously:

Shaman Lhapa Thundup's chant was on tape. All tape recordings from my fieldwork are transcribed, i.e. are written down, in the original language and writing – Ladakhi in Tibetan script – line for line. For this purpose I have experienced native collaborators from Delhi and Leh who are well versed in the Ladakhi language and Tibetan writing.

Now shamanic chants and prayers under trance are especially challenging to transcribe: the shamans speak incredibly fast, often in "secret" (and partly even private) language; their speech is often incoherent or rambling and may be cryptic, containing riddles. However, with a great deal of patience we, in the transcription team, have always managed to fathom out many passages (See Appendix C).

Lhapa Thundup's trance chant, however, is different. Five different transcription co-workers applied themselves to the work – and none managed to make sense of any of it. "Don't understand a word!", every single one of them said.

And so, for me, after this there were two – but only theoretically two – remaining ways in which I could attempt to transfer this trance chant into text and decipher it. I would have to ask either the shaman himself or his long-standing helper who assists at his healing sessions.

The key experience had brought home to me the fact that there is indeed such thing as a genuine deep trance and with it there can also be genuine hermetic amnesia. After this experience, the thought of asking Lhapa Thundup himself about the contents of his shamanic chant, or even playing back the tape of his chant "line for line" in order for him to explain it all to me, was not something I had given any serious thought to. My key experience when I witnessed the trance phenomenon for the first time "from the inside", enabled me to understand – as I expounded in Chapter 4 – the internal perspective of the shaman himself: that the *lha* had sung the chant and not he, Lhapa Thundup. The *lha* understands the content of the chant – not he, Lhapa Thundup.

It would have been quite alien to me, merely for the benefit of my research in this case, to want to evade, undermine or surmount these premises of shamanic thought by replaying tape recordings and asking questions.

Therefore, the only option available to me was to seek out the shaman's assistant. He is Sonam Tashi, about 55 years old and is also a nomad. Above all for this reason – to find the nomad Sonam Tashi – I once again undertook the major task of organising another field trip into Changthang, with my local collaborators, with jeep, tent, food, fuel, drinking water. As mentioned earlier, one cannot simply go and set up camp with the nomads and expect them to support you; one has to take everything along – the nomads already have too little as it is!

With the jeep we drove up the Indus to Sumdo. And, as mentioned, we found him straight away. He was happy to help us with the transcription of the chant. Certainly, we would have to adhere strictly to allocated times, fitting around the daily work routine of shepherding and milking – but that still left us several hours a day to work together. We sat on the floor in the tent, Sonam Tashi, the shamanic assistant, three of my collaborators and I. We put on the tape which I had recorded the previous year at the shamanic séance, and listened. We asked Sonam Tashi: "What is he saying? Do tell us what he's saying, please!"

Sonam Tashi had no trouble understanding. He knows the shaman, and naturally he also understands the Changthang dialect which had already presented us with problems. The difficulty lay on another level. It proved to be almost impossible to explain to our nomad Sonam Tashi, who was illiterate, that we wanted him to dictate to us word by word from the tape and that we also wished to understand it word for word.

We played a passage from the shamanic chant. And Sonam Tashi told us long stories and anecdotes and had many associations. We played the tape for another minute. Again, long and rambling stories. We could not make Sonam Tashi understand why we should want it explained word for word: – why should we need that? Hadn't he explained everything? The following day we tried again – and again. At first, I heard as many different versions of the "translation" by Sonam Tashi as the number of times we played back the tape recorder. It was very rewarding, however, how we then met on middle ground: Sonam Tashi finally "dictated" to us – although certainly simplified – a version of that trance chant.

It is the most wonderful text that I have transcribed in 18 years, be it in relation to my Andean research or my Himalayan fieldwork. It is a chant that, in a fascinating way, bridges the gap between the bloody, violent images of the original shamanic religion (i.e. the pre-Buddhist religion) and the myth of the Padmasambava and of Buddhism with its spiritual values of freedom from violence. However, before I present the shamanic chant I must clarify my methods of approximation – a piece of work full of compromises!

6. METHODS OF APPROXIMATION

In my attempts to understand Lhapa Thundup's shamanic chant, I approached the text from four different angles. I shall briefly outline these four approaches so that one can also judge how literally the ensuing documented chant has been translated and assess the authenticity of its content.

It is one of my tried and tested research techniques to listen word for word to my tape recordings of healing rituals or conversations with medicine men or shamans immediately after the event. This is not just to audit the recording, but above all to elaborate on my hand-written notes with additional material that the oral records call back into memory, and to help me organise the contents to complete a preliminary draft of the translation.

I had written up Lhapa Thundup's healing séance in just this way on that same day, together with my collaborator Tsultim Kubet – and it was also Tsultim who dictated to me the first few fragments of this chant. He, Tsultim, who had been present at the séance, usually managed to understand parts of the content once he had listened to the recording a few times. This was my FIRST approach to the content and it made a summary of the chant possible (Version 1). I have to thank Sonam Tashi, the shamanic assistant, for the three further approximations.

After several days' work with Sonam Tashi as protagonist, as well as my collaborators, the following three approaches were adopted, and from them came three further versions:

Sonam Tashi listened to the tape with the shamanic chant for the first time and, as well as an abundance of anecdotes and associations – he offered a cursory global version of the content (Version 2). After lengthy and exhaustive explanations, after many trials and numerous exercises, fresh commentaries and then further trials, Sonam Tashi finally attempted – with the help of Sonam Norboo – to "dictate" the shamanic chant "word for word" to Sonam Wangchuk (Version 3).

However, this third version is by no means a literal translation: firstly, Sonam Tashi did not merely dictate: he also omitted much material and added a great number of explanations. Secondly, Sonam Norboo constantly and unrestrainedly interwove what he thought were helpful comments into the "dictation". Thirdly, Sonam Wangchuk certainly did not always keep abreast of the writing – and so our "technician" (P. Fa Tkaczyk), who monitored the counter numbers on the playback and recording equipment, found that the shamanic chant was always longer that the shamanic assistant's "dictation", and that Sonam Wangchuk's control-reading of what he had written was always shorter than Sonam Tashi's dictation...

Finally, there was one more approach. Released from the pressure of the "dictation", Sonam Tashi heard the shamanic chant once more – in small sections, pausing at intervals which were decided by him and Sonam Wangchuk together, and relayed what the shaman says in his own words. And both of my Ladahki collaborators translated this into English straight away, and this was also taped (Version 4).

Of these four versions,

- the first global description of the content by Tsultim Kubet;
- the first global description by Sonam Tashi;
- attempt at dictating by Sonam Tashi; and
- reproduction of the content of the chant , in small sections, with simultaneous English translation,

there is clearly no definitive word for word translation of the chant. Nevertheless, in noting consistent elements present in all four versions in their extraordinary multiplicity, the essential message of the chant is quite clear. The following version is a carefully compiled representation of the CONSISTENT ELEMENTS that arise from all four approaches to the transcript translation of the chant. The chant, as it is conveyed below, is therefore not complete, although the extracts documented are certainly authentic.

7. THE GREAT SHAMANIC CHANT

At first, just by means of illustration, there is a short (by no means complete, as mentioned) extract from the third approach, by Sonam Wangchuk:

ང་དཔལ་ལྡན་ལྷ་མོ་ཡིན།
ང་དཔལ་ལྡན་ལྷ་མོ་ཡིན།
ཁོ་རེ་ང་བཛལ་པ་ཆགས་ཡོད་པའི་དུས་འགྲོ་བ་རིགས་དྲུག་ག
ཕན་ཐོགས་དང་མཁན་ཡིན།

ཁོ་རེ་ང་བདུད་ནག་པའི་ཡུལ་ལ་འབྱུངས་ཏེ་ཡ་ཨ་བ་གཅིག

བདུད་ལ་བསྐུལ་བས།

ཡུམ་ཨ་མ་བཙན་ལ་སྐུལ་ལེ་ཡིན།

ཁོ་རེ་ང་སྟེང་ལ་རབ་ནེ་ལ་དད་པའི་དུས་བྱུང་མི་རིགས་བཅུའི

ཁོང་པོ་འདི།

བྱང་ལ་ཨ་དག་ཁྲག་སྟེང་ཁྱིལ།

འབྱོང་པོ་འབྱོང་བཅུ་ཡི་ར་ལོ།

འབྱོང་མོ་འབྱོང་བཅུ་ཡི་ར་ལོ།

ནང་པའི་ཚོས་ཀྱི་གདན་ས་བོད་རྒྱལ་པོ་ཁྲི་སྲོང་ལྡེ་བཙན་དང་བླ་མ་

ཨོ་རྒྱན་པདྨ་ཁ་ཞབ་ཡག

ང་ཇམ་སྙིང་ཅེ་ལ་མ་དག

ང་དཔལ་ལྡན་ལྷ་མོ་བོད་ཡུལ་དུ་འབྱུངས་སེ་འདུག་ཅན་དོར་ལ

གུ་ཅེ

མ་ཅིག་དཔལ་ལྡན་ལྷ་མོ་པོ་བཙན་རིགས་མ་གསར་རྒྱལ་མོ

བོད་ཡུལ་དེར་རྒྱལ་ལུ་ཡུལ་ན་འགེས་ཡོང་།

བདུད་ལ་རྟེན་ནེ་མིང་བཅུ་ན་མཚན་ཏོག

བསོད་ནམས་འཇམ་སྙིང་ཕྱེ་ལ་མ་ནེ་དོན་མཛད།

ཏོར་བདག་མི་ཉེན་ཅིག

ང་མི་རོག་བཅུ་གསུམ་གྱི་ལྷ་གྱུར་ཡིན།

ཁོ་རེ་མཁར་ཆེ་གྱོག་པའི་པོ།

གྱོག་པ་ལྷ་དུད་ཆེ་རྒྱབ་ས་མེ་རྡུད་ཤུག་ཤ་པར་ས་འདུད་ཆེ་ཐབས་ལྷ

མོའི་

གོ་ཅེ་ཐབས་ལྷ་མ་ཡིན།

དེ་ཐུན་གཏང་ཅེ་ལ།

མ་ཉེ་ན་ཚམ་སྐྱིང་སྤྲོག་བདག་ཡིན།

མོ་མགོ་ཡུང་ཡོ་དག་ལ་མགོ་འདུན་འདྲ།

ཚོས་འདོད་པ་ཡི་ཐུབ།

Rather than translating this short illustration I will rather document those extracts from Lhapa Thundup's shamanic chant, which are consistent across the four versions.

The great shamanic chant

I am Paldan Lhamo, I am Paldan Lhamo.
Listen. Since the beginning of the world
I have done good for all six classes of living beings.
But I was born in the world of evil spirits.
For my father was born a daemon
and my mother a *tsan*.
And I was born a *lha*, a god,
called Paldan Lhamo.
My parents lived on eating corpses.
Every day they ate people, horses, donkeys and wild yaks.
From my parents' meals
the evil spirit Adag drank oceans of blood.

My father lived on the horns of one hundred male yaks,
my mother lived on the foreheads of one hundred female yaks.
Listen. When I was born in Tibet,
and when I was there,

Illustration 43: Lhapa Thundup singing the great chant

I gave advice in the form of a crow and as a *tsan*-daemon
to the powerful rulers of the Hor,[3]
I gave advice to Masar Gyalmo.
To be dependent on hundreds of daemons
and to call their names – that is not good.
Instead you happy people should recite the mantras of the world.
Don't listen to the voice of the Hor!
And in Tibet I met with King Tresong
and Padmasambhava.
Listen. Now I am here to bring you the teachings of Buddha.
It is the message of the king and of Padmasambhava,
that each and everyone in the world should follow the teachings
of Buddha.
And so I, Paldan Lhamo, have travelled to Sabu
and have spread the teachings.
And then I travelled to Naro Koson
and spread the teachings there.
I went to Paru and taught there too.

3 It is certainly an indication of the high status of that figure, if he is advising
the *Hor*. However, since he advises them while in the form of a crow and a
tsan, the power of the *Hor* can also be perceived as negative here. JINA
(1999, p.94) writes about the *Hor*: "The Chang Pa are said to have original-
ly migrated from "Hor" in Tibet around 800 A.D. The term *Hor* was first
applied to the Vighurs found in Kanchow, and the contemporary nomadic
Horpa of the West (*Nup Hor*) in Tibet may still bear their name. Later the
term was used for the Mongols of Genghiz Khan and it is from these that
the five *Hor* principalities of Khan (around Kandze and Beri) claim descent.
In the past, the Chang Pa and Ladakhis did not inter-marry. However, when
the Ladakhi king Singe-Namgyal married Kalzang Dolma, a girl from the
family of Rupshu Goba, the custom of intermarriage with Ladakhis began"
And MANDERSCHEIDT (1999a p.4) reports: "The search for Tibetan sources
on nomadism in Tibet was until then largely unsuccessful. The interest of
the literate clergy in historical matters was confined to religious writings.
Only the Tibetan national anthem, "Gesar Ling" that is spread all around in
Tibet in a great number of variations, portrays the mythological-historical
nomadic gender of the *Hor*. Even today Tibetans eagerly trace their ancestry
back to this glorious generation which shows the high status of nomadism
in the eyes of Tibetans."

And I went to Phayul
and met Tsering Chednga
and Gyalu Yulna
And we three spread the message of Buddha
in one hundred or two hundred places

And now there is only one lesson and that is the teaching of
Buddha.
If you people listen to us, you will be all right.
Otherwise we will cause you harm.
For thirteen generations I have been the *lha*.
Listen to my message.
You people should live in harmony.
But these days people are changing so much.
These days people are jealous and full of hatred,
they fight one another and argue.
More blood than ever before flows down the valleys.
There is war and violence and times are completely different now.
Even the climate has changed.
There are cyclones and violent storms.
There are all sorts of conflicts and violence.
The Ladahkis are in great crisis
with water supply.
Times are changing in our world!

But you are still engrossed in your small world.
You still have enough to eat.
Nevertheless you are not satisfied.
Very little has changed with you yet.
So you should be content.
You people are envious. You look and say:
He's got more than me.
You must not think like that.
Go about your work and be aware of your consciousness.
Everything depends on your consciousness.
If there is no clarity in your consciousness,
you will get into difficulty.

Always be pure in your consciousness.
If you do not control your consciousness,
then hell is within you.
There is no alternative to this approach.

Everything is dependent on your consciousness.
Your consciousness must be clear.
If you brood and brood and brood,
all you will achieve is internal tension
and you will cause problems for yourselves.

If you live with tension and languish in problems,
you will more easily become ill, do you understand that?
You need a clear consciousness.
Everything is dependent on your consciousness.

I am Paldan Lhamo,
I give you this advice.
And you should follow this advice.
If you don't believe me,
if you have no faith in the Buddhist teachings,
then that is your business.
Things only depend on yourselves,
do you understand that?
It depends on you where you stand and where you go.
Naturally not everybody has the same mind.
We are distinguishable by our consciousness and thought.
You think one thing, he another and that person something else.
However, everyone stands on their own two feet.
Each person is responsible for himself.
And I see to all of you. I treat you all the same.
I am not here for the rich, nor for the poor.
To me no-one is big and no-one is small.
I care for all people, all living creatures.
And I do it very well.
You must just listen to me.

You must be in harmony with each other.
You must try to build monasteries and palaces.
Tread carefully with the *lu*.
When in the village you manage to treat the *lu* well,
then they will also give you whatever you need.
Otherwise they will do you harm.

There are so many *lha*, so many gods.
There is Paldan Lhamo and many more.
They have been amongst us for thirteen generations.
If you show them respect
then they will protect you.
Otherwise they will harm you.
Listen. We can be in perfect agreement and inseparable on this path,
like knots in a horse's tail.
And so we shall also chase away the evil spirits
in lightning speed, as swiftly as the batting of an eyelid.
That is my advice.
But if you do not follow my advice,
I shall use my spiritual power.

8. INTERPRETATION AND MEANING OF THE TRANCE CHANT

I do not think this chant requires lengthy interpretation. I just wish to draw attention to a few points.

The teachings of Buddhism appear here against a backdrop of dramatic contrast. He, the *lha*, the god, that possesses the body of Lhapa Thundup, was born into the world of people-eating, blood-thirsty, evil spirits. Even the *lha*, then, when he was born in Tibet (this was 13 generations ago) served the powerful Hor and the evil beings – at least until he met Padmasambhava.

Padmasambhava was living during the time of the Tibetan king Trisong Detsen (755-795) (who is also mentioned in the trance chant), and, as history can confirm, he is one of the founders of Tibetan Buddhism. He conquered and tamed daemons and evil spirits – such as the parents of this shaman's *lha*. On encountering Padmasambhava and King Trisong he too, the shaman's *lha*, set out to spread the word of Buddha. And with precisely this message he also came to the healing séance here, and stood before his patients.

What is Buddha's message? One of the core concepts is that some of the problems we experience are produced by ourselves – because problems come with our formidable, greedy 'Me', because we mentally propagate it and brood, because we mentally cling to it, because we are so immodest, always wanting to be cheerful and happy; because by clinging to illusionary material things we pollute our consciousness. If we would only let go – let go of the illusion of the formidable 'Me'; let go of our desire to possess (the desire to be wealthy, to have everlasting happiness, eternal security etc); if we purify our consciousness, if we know in all clarity the origin of misery – which in part is always conditioned by ourselves – then there will ultimately be less suffering.

And precisely, this is the message of the shamanic *lha* to the patients, the family circle and all those present: you are responsible for yourselves, you must purify your consciousness. And he delivers this message in all intensity: "If you do not control your consciousness then hell is within you. THERE IS NO ALTERNATIVE TO THIS APPROACH."

Particularly impressive in this trance chant is how the shamanic *lha* extends the scope of his vision more and more broadly: on the first level, he speaks to the patients and he makes it clear that they are making themselves more prone to sickness if their consciousness is not pure (i.e. brooding, brooding and brooding) – thus it is a very "modern" psychosomatic concept of the origin of sickness that the shaman's *lha* is putting forward. In addition, he points out to the patients that since they are partly responsible for their illness, they therefore also have the means to contribute to their healing.

But here the *lha* does not remain within the close circle of patients and their families in this tiny kitchen in the hut; his advice is more far-reaching – on a second level – reaching the whole village community. Attentiveness, harmony, purity of feeling (no envy, no jealousy) and a clear consciousness is the central message here. People should treat each other with care, respect and attention as well as the *lu* and the *lha*. The *lu* are the underground spirits of the earth, the *lha* the gods of shamanism. They should do their work and retain purity of consciousness, live in harmony, and honour Buddha ("build monasteries and palaces").

He also makes clear to them the principle of reciprocity, of balanced mutuality: if people heed the *lha*'s message, things will go well for them, and the *lha* will protect them. If people treat the *lu* with care, then the *lu* will give them, the people, whatever they need. If people heed the message of the shamanic *lha* – then the *lha*, too, will be there to protect them and heal them. However, in all these statements there is a "but": nothing comes free. Carelessness has consequences. If people do not heed the message – then the *lha* will harm them, the *lu* will take revenge with illness and refusal and the presently acting *lha* will also impose his POWER (which in Buddhism is always non-violent force – thus spiritual power).

On the third level, the shamanic *lha* addresses the broader Ladahki community, which under the pressure of modernisation and its associated ethos of maximising personal gain, is threatened by envy and conflict. In addition, he speaks on a fourth level – a global level – of violence and war ("more blood is flowing down the valleys than ever before") and the changing environment ("even the climate has changed").

In this way, the shamanic *lha* extends his diagnosis of illness and of conditions giving rise to illness, from the individual to the village community and then more widely to the whole community and finally in a global context. And everywhere the message is the same: if we do not purify and guide our consciousness, then hell is within US, within the VILLAGE, in the WORLD. "There is no alternative to this approach"[4]

9. THE ECONOMIC AND SOCIAL REALITY IN CHANGTHANG AND LADAKH AND THE SHAMAN'S VISION FOR HIS COUNTRY AND FOR THE WORLD

Ladakh, erstwhile kingdom in the Himalayas and today a part of India, in its far northern reaches, is culturally Tibetan. This is defined primarily by language and religion. The languages of cultural Tibet (as opposed to political Tibet) (JONES 1996) belong to the Tibeto-Burmese languages (GRIERSON 1909/1967a, volume III). Also Ladakhi, (FRANCKE 1898, 1903, 1929/1979; HAMID 1998; KOSHAL 1976, 1978, 1979, 1982, 1987; NORBERG-HODGE & PALDAN 1991) including its variety of dialects like the Changthang dialect (to date in no way systematically examined), belongs to this family of languages. The second main feature of cultural Tibet – including Ladakh – is religion: Tibetan Buddhism with its elements deriving from the pre-Buddhist shamanic Bön religion.

This small country of Ladakh, culturally Tibetan and politically Indian, is one of the regions of the world that, in the shortest time, has been subject to the greatest amount of foreign influence as a

4 In Ladakh or West Tibet, the Buddhist dignitaries of Tibetan Buddhism, the Rinpoches, have very ambivalent feelings towards the shamans and their practice (See Chapter 3, Extract 7) – lu and tsan and dud and shin de and son de and all these evil presences, which the shamans believe in, appear to them (and justifiably so) to come from the sources of other religions. But when one listens to this shamanic chant one cannot help but recognise just how powerfully the Buddhist message is communicated , possibly more powerfully that the Rinpoches themselves can convey– the latter, indeed, lacking the dramatic religious-historical background of the vengeful pre-Buddhist spiritual world.

result of Hindu India, the Indian military and the massive influx of tourists.

This objectively-described experience of alienation naturally has far-reaching consequences on the economical, social and cultural sectors. It also has a massive influence on people's experiences, attitudes and values. It is this aspect of the Ladakhi foreign experience, which we – a collaborator and I – have particularly explored in a research project in Ladakh (KRESSING & RÖSING 2001a).

If one can identify a common link running through the many statements on the numerous changes experienced in Ladakh (statements from many and varied sectors of the Ladakhi community – from the Rinpoche to the simple lama and onwards through to the shaman and layman), then it is this: the charge against the receding values of modesty, contentedness and community spirit and the increasing trend towards the ideals of individualistic profit maximisation with its accompanying fundamental disposition towards greed, desire for maximum personal gain, envy, constant comparison with others and discontentedness.

Just to cite some examples, here are a few extracts from conversations I had with inhabitants between 1994 and 1998 in preparation for the above mentioned project on the Ladakhi perceptions of the societal changes in their country.

A Ladahki farmer and owner of a guesthouse says:

> There were many waves of foreign infiltration in Ladakh. First, there was the war with China in the early 60s and there was a horribly large Indian military presence. Then came the war with Pakistan and still more soldiers came along, all Indians, all Hindus. And streets were constructed, Indian workers came into the country. Then came tourism.

> Everyone had previously lived from farming. We were content. It was enough. We worked hard. Now there is easy work in the tourist business. You can make a lot of money very quickly. Young people are abandoning their studies. They'd rather see

money. The standard of education is plummeting. The standard of living is rising. Greed is proliferating. Envy is on the increase. Wickedness is spreading (HI-29).

A Ladakhi businessman expresses this view:

Everyone today is so much more egotistical. From an external view there is progress. Schools have improved. Health care is much better. The streets have become better. But accompanying the external progress there needs to be an inner progress. This is missing. The inner worth, i.e. the spiritual values are receding. The inner worth – that is the consciousness, our values, our character. Today every family has a son in the business. They all come for money. And everyone is getting greedy; plain, dismal envy is on the increase (HI-30).

In connection with my question as to why are there so many more shamanic callings today than earlier, Stakna Rinpoche answers by rebuking the trends of modern times:

It's true, in earlier times fewer *lha* manifested themselves. And today there are so many. It is probably because there is progress; envy, jealousy and negative feelings come as part and parcel with this progress. Previously, people were serene, without hate; they were content, they were placid, and they helped each other out. But now people pitch themselves against each other. Each person wants the most for him or herself. Everyone craves status, respect, wealth, and they gloat at others' misfortunes and are bad-tempered with one another. And shamans are useful. They suck out this evil (HI-21).

These conversations, however, do not relate to Changthang. In many respects, Changthang cannot be compared with central Ladakh, not only because of its nomadic economy but also with regard to the Hindu Indian presence as well as mass tourism which is definitely less in Changthang.

256

The social situation in Changthang and its problems are certainly different. But what is comparable is a change in values, which nearly everyone notices and which even shamans are already warning about in their chants.

What are the main problems for Changthang? The Changpa themselves pinpoint the start of all the problems – the severance of the good old days from modern times (HI-38) – as being in 1959, the time of the Dalai Lama's flight from Tibet. With him fled thousands and thousands of Tibetans out of their homeland annexed by the Chinese. There also fled from the Tibetan part of Changthang a great number of Tibetan nomads. 1962 then saw the Changthang border conflict between China and India and the frontiers were sealed off. Since then Changthang has been a militarily sensitive region and there is a dense Indian military presence.

Where previously the Ladakhi nomads wandered freely in and out of Tibetan Changthang – an area much greater than their own region – so these vast grazing lands were suddenly cut off. The "limitations" of their own grazing lands became all the more apparent with the arrival of nomadic refugees from Tibet, who now brought their herds to Ladakhi pastures. The danger of overgrazing is extremely acute. As early as 1990, S.P. Jina warned that without the rigorous implementation of countermeasures, Changthang's pastureland would become barren wasteland within a generation, supporting no life at all (JINA 1990).[5]

There were enormous social tensions between the Changpa and the Tibetan nomads because the latter do not respect the system of collective management of the pastureland and the allocation of pastures through the Changpa *go ba* (chief). In the Rupshu region, according to AHMED (1996), the Changpa nomads went to court and won: the Tibetans had to abide by the Changpa rules on the apportioning of grazing land.

---

5 This is a problem that also effects other nomadic societies. See the warnings by SCHOLZ (1991) and KHAZANOV (1998).

But what if they did not do so? Everywhere even today they are accused of two transgressions. One, the Tibetan nomads contribute heavily to overgrazing by taking their herds out for a longer time each day than the Changpa, much to the latter's annoyance. Secondly, the Tibetans are wealthier and will therefore more readily overstep the clearly demarcated pasture boundaries: although they do incur penalties as a result they have enough sheep and money to pay.

In general, the reality is that Tibetans are much keener businessmen than the Ladakhis. There is also no Ladakhi who would not acknowledge this, admit it or accuse them of it. It makes no difference which way one looks: whether to the Ladakh Buddh Vihar in Delhi[6], which the Tibetans have almost completely taken over with their market; or to the Tibetan settlement of Choglamsar near Leh, or to the Tibetan nomads of Ladakhi Changthang – one will always be able to observe the Tibetan business acumen.

In Changthang, today, this takes the form of, among other things, Tibetan trading – with China, precisely. From China come cheap consumer products, introduced by Tibetan nomads or other traders. In by-passing the traditional trade routes of the commercially precious *pashmina* wool between nomads, with Kashmir being the most important processors of it, an increasing number of Tibetan middlemen are emerging and the *pashmina* is in part going to China. JINA (1999) is by no means reticent in speaking out against the Tibetan exploitation of Changpa.

But still the reduced grazing land, the influx of Tibetan nomads and the accompanying great danger of overgrazing as well as the social tensions with the Tibetan nomads are not the only problems of Changthang.

---

6 The Ladakh Buddh Vihar in Delhi is a Ladakhi "enclave" in the middle of Delhi. The land was granted to them by Nehru. There is also a Ladakhi monastery and a hostel for pilgrims. With the annexation of Tibet by the Chinese and the consequential streams of refugees, the Tibetan poured into the Ladakh Buddh Vihar area. Today, it is almost entirely taken over by Tibetan business life: the Tibetans run a thriving market, restaurants, guesthouses. There are only three of four ground owning Ladakhis left.

The squeeze on pastureland has not resulted from these factors alone, but from the population growth of the Changpa nomads themselves. Most authors (AHMED 1996; JINA 1995, 1999; also see GOLDSTEIN 1981, BEALL & GOLDSTEIN 1981) account for the population growth as being a result of the decline in frequency of polyandrous marriages. In fact, today, there are more monogamous marriages than previously, polyandry is unambiguously on the wane. This is not ultimately a result of foreign influences through the Indian administration and military, which, even if to a lesser extent, reach as far as Changthang: polyandry is officially prohibited and is considered backward (see the studies of FAHLEN 2000 on the decline of polyandry in central Ladakh as a reflection of social change).

If there are more people in Changthang, then of course the population density of the livestock increases too. There is no scope for growth in either agriculture or bartering – and so, today as previously, the primary source of income is livestock.

Furthermore, the Changpa nomads stay much more "at home" the whole year over than they used to be. Previously, the region was central for trans-Himalayan trade. Changpa nomads undertook months-long trade journeys. They were always accompanied on these treks by a substantial proportion of their livestock – after all sheep are also their beasts of burden. Today not only are these extended periods of absence on the decline because the trans-Himalayan trade has been completely squashed, but also because the Changpa nomads – when they go on trade journeys (e.g. to Leh to sell meat and wool) – no longer need livestock as a means of transport. Why not?

This is partly to do with the Indo-Chinese war of 1962. Since then the region, as mentioned, is part of a high-security military zone and is under constant surveillance by the military. Streets have been built. Today one can drive from Leh right to Korzok, deep in Changthang on asphalt or gravel tracks. Heavy goods vehicles and jeeps use these roads. Today the Changpa no longer transport any goods on the backs of their sheep – they go by truck.

The population growth and the shortage of pastureland do also lead to migration. If, according to counts by AHMED (1996), in the region of Rupshu there are only 399 people, then the migration in 1992-93 of only three tents (which is nevertheless 38 people – see AHMED 1996, Footnote p.339) is really quite considerable. One could argue that the migration is perhaps a healthy counterbalance to the population expansion with the ensuing growth in herd sizes which is, after all, the major problem. But it is only the poorest people who migrate, those who cannot survive on the meagre herds that belong to them.

As a result of the road network, the opportunities for schooling for Changpa children have indeed improved greatly. Nomadic schooling (where a teacher moves around with a tent community) has proved to be a failure. But today, since there are now reasonable truck connections, a nomadic family can always send at least one son or another to school in Nyoma or Leh. Furthermore, once these children as youths had entered their new environment, they often do not want to return to their nomadic parental tent. This situation also gives rise to a whole host of tensions relating to values. These children have experienced the consumerism of Ladakh's small towns and they bring their demands and expectations back to Changthang with them.

Another major contentious issue is tourism. Luckily, in Changthang, it is still in check, thanks to the rigorous restrictions imposed by the Indian frontier administration. But its traces have been quite recognisable in Changthang for a long time. Changthang was open to Indian tourists in 1993 and to foreigners in 1994. As mentioned, only small groups may enter Changthang for a limited time and on prescribed routes. One of the most visited regions is of course Lake Tsomoriri – a truly enchanting, beautiful landscape. Because of the extreme cold, tourism is essentially restricted to July and August. However, that is also the breeding season for the rich variety of bird life on the lake. As early as 1994, BHATTACHARJI complained about the crests of scum on the waves of the lake, the increased algae, the litter on its banks, and the hitherto unwitnessed swarms of flies (see also BHATACHARJI 1993).[7]

Quite apart from the effect of tourism on the environment, there have been quite a number of other consequences. Suddenly, there is paid employment for a Changpa inhabitant: he can open a tea shop on the roadside and sell tea, or he can offer his services as a guide for trekking tourists. And this has a great impact on the monetary value of work in Changthang. Today no Changthang shepherd would take another person's herd to graze even for a day at the rate of pay he would have received for a whole month ten years ago. Today the inhabitants want to have far more money in their hands. With their fine tents, elegant clothing and sophisticated, specialised equipment, tourists also bring with them new demands for consumer goods. And so the spiral of material desires, the value of maximising individual profits and consumerist thinking circles onwards.

And this is precisely what far-sighted Changpa nomads can see so clearly. Perhaps, along with the Buddhist clergy, it is just these shamans, who – as a result of their contact with a whole range of human problems which they attend to with their ability to heal – have this far-sightedness. From this perspective we can once more refer to Lhapa Thundup's great shamanic chant. He chants with great urgency and force:

> You people should live in harmony.
> But these days people are changing so much.
> These days people are jealous and full of hatred,
> they fight one another and argue.
> More blood than ever before flows down the valleys....
> Times are changing in our world....
> You still have enough to eat.

---

7 And so one can read with very little enthusiasm an announcement of the North Bavarian News on 25.8.01, that a certain Pit Schubert would like to include Lake Tsomoriri in future in the travel catalogue of the Munich Summit Club.

But you are still not satisfied....
So you should be content.
You people are envious. You look and say:
He's got more than me.
You must not think like that.

Highly condensed but nevertheless very clearly, the shaman in this way has made a social diagnosis and he warns people to unreservedly surrender to these value changes (more materialism, envy, comparisons with one's neighbours, competitiveness) that have been brought about by these social developments. It will only lead to misery. And he also tells them how to counteract this:

Go about your work and be aware of your consciousness.
Everything depends on your consciousness....
Always be pure in your consciousness.
If you do not control your consciousness,
then hell is within you.

Work on your consciousness (it should be pure, pure in the Buddhist sense: without avarice and envy and hate and delusion) means, concentrate on one's own (inner) values. And I think it is precisely this message which we all should heed from the nomadic shamans. We cannot change all the conditions of so-called modern life; we cannot all become politically active and put in check all the abhorrent violence of our time, we cannot conjure up the mentality of modesty, concern and community spirit from the past – but in spite of this not one of us must remain passive in view of the evil in our present day: every change starts when one changes oneself, for one's way of living, one's own consciousness.

Shaman Thundup: "There is no alternative to this approach."

GLOSSARY AND COMMON ABBREVIATIONS

am chi	Tibetan doctor who heals with herbs, powders and pills; does not perform rituals
bag ma	marriage of a woman into the man's household
chag dzod	monastic administrator
chang ra	"northern goat" (that provides *pashmina*)
chi ru	wild antelope; provides → *shahtoosh*-Wool
da ma ru	a Ladakhi shaman's hand drum, an essential requisite of every séance
de	daemon, evil powers, adversary of the *lha* on diagnosing shamanic illness at the outset of a shamanic calling
dhar ma	the teachings of Buddha
dib lung	*dib* = defilement, *lung* = teaching. Teaching a shamanic candidate to suck out liquid impurities from a patient's body
dib phin ches	sucking out the *dib*
dud	evil spirit, daemon
du khang	the prayer hall of a monastery
go ba	a nomad from a nomadic community selected to be leader of their group for 3 years; one of his primary duties is to allocate grazing land
gon pa	monastery
gon po, gon mo	witch, (*po* = male, *mo* = female)
gur	the nomads' white (modern) tent
jadu	a Hindi word, but also generally used in Ladakh to mean 'black magic'
ka	an order and official certification: *ka* indicates the diagnosis and written certification of a "shamanic illness" by a Rinpoche which is handed to a practising schaman instructing him to separate *lha* and *de* within the candidate
khab lung	*khab* = needle, *lung* = teaching: teaching a shamanic candidate to suck needles (or other solid objects) out of a patient's body

khab phin ches	sucking out *khab*
kha tak	a white ceremonial scarf
lan de	evil spirit
la pok	teachings, also shamanic
lha lug kar po	sheep (*lug*) blessed by the white (*kar po*) gods' (*lha*) world
lha mo	*lha* = god, *mo* = suffix for female. *Lha mo* = goddess (woman shaman)
lha pa	*lha* = god, *pa* = suffix for male. *Lha pa*: shaman (male)
lha skyon	an alternative for "*lha*-illness", as distinct from *tsha ba tshu ba*
lha tho	the place where a → *lha* resides: a cairn (stack of small rocks) decorated with twigs, ritual artefacts and prayer flags
lu (klu)	spirits of the underworld
lu lug ngon po	sheep (*lug*) blessed by the blue (*ngon po*) underworld of the → *lu*.
lung sta	prayer flag; displaying of prayer flags strengthens the → *spar kha*
lus gyar	literally: body lending. The term used for Ladakhi shamans whose bodies are possessed by *lha* when in trance.
mag pa	marriage of a man into the woman's household.
mantra	sequence of holy syllables
me ngag (srag)	shamanic healing therapy using fire
nod pa	harm, defilement
nyer tschod	a Buddhist offering comprising 7 bowls; an essential part of every shamanic séance.
on po	a layman, but sometimes also a Buddhist monk, who specialises particularly in prophesising (but frequently also performs black and white magic too)
pe rak	Ladakhi women's head decoration richly adorned with precious stones; only worn on festive occasions

pha lha	the god of → *pha spun*
pha spun	the paternal relatives
phug lha	another word for → *pha lha*
polyandry	marriage of a woman to several men (if they are all brothers = fraternal polyandry)
polygamy	marriage of more than two partners
polygyandry	marriage of several men and women, having evolved from polyandry
polygyny	marriage of a man to several women
puja	a Buddhist devotion involving preparations for offerings, prayer and song
pu ri	a shaman using a sucking pipe to suck out → *dib*
re bo	Changpa-nomads' black tent
samsara	cycle of rebirth
sem pa	spirit, consciousness – that element of the mind which, according to many shamans, changes during *lha* possession (trance)
sem nyid	spirit, soul: word used by shamans to describe what it is that changes or disappears while in trance
ser kyem	drink offering
shahtoosh	the winter "down" the finest woollen underlayer of the Himalyan antelope → *chi ru*
shin de	the evil spirit of a deceased person
shuk pa	juniper, often used as an incense offering
son de	evil spirit of a living person
spar kha	spiritual strength
srog	the life force, without which one cannot live; *srog* is sometimes used by the shamans to mean that spiritual element which is changed or disappears during trance
sung ma	"guardian angel", *lha*, which possesses a shaman
tag ril	term relating to an oracle's activities, primarily in monasteries, e.g. during the selection procedure of the monastic oracle

thab lha	the oven deity in a tent
ti mo, ti po	evil spirit of a jealous woman (*ti mo*) or a jealous man (*ti po*)
tsam pa	flour from roasted barley
tsan	gods or spirits of the "earth world"; for Tibet see STEIN (1972) who describes them in "King, Powerful God of Space"; for Ladakh see main source: KAPLANIAN (1995).
tsan lug kro po	sheep (*lug*) blessed by the red (*kro po*) world of → *tsan*
tsha ba tshu ba	most frequently used expression for the "madness" indicating the starting point of a shamanic calling, when the diagnosis of a shamanic illness is still to be confirmed (→ *lha skyon*)
tshe thar	an animal consecrated to the gods to ensure the "survival"
yul	region, village
yul lha	god of a settlement / region
yul lha chen po	the most elevated (*chen po*) god (*lha*) of the region (*yul*)

HI, HH	indices used for the identification of written records, tape recordings, transcripts and visual material
HI	Himalayan research (H) / information (I) from conversations
HH	Himalayan research (H) / Healing (H) séances

266

APPENDIX A

Comparison of the Changthang shamans with the shamans of central Ladakh

My research on the shamans in Changthang now enables me to make some preliminary comparisons between them and the shamans of central Ladakh, the latter having been hitherto the only shamans studied by other researchers as well as myself (see Chapter 3).

The first result is that – as expected – the fundamental basis of shamanic healing for all Ladakhi shamans is the same. The most important similarities are:

1. the so-called "madness" indicating the starting point on the path towards the shamanic calling;

2. the affirmation of the calling by a Tibetan Buddhist dignitary;

3. the transformation of the "madness" into a controlled trance which can be induced at will;

4. the concept of a shaman's body being possessed by a *lha* god, representing the only subject that heals at a shamanic séance;

5. the claim of amnesia – that shamans remember nothing while in trance;

6. the basic components of a séance including the preparatory rituals, the preparation of the Buddhist altar, the Buddhist prayers and songs;

7. the most important requisites for shamanic performance: the shamanic crown and cape, the head and mouth cloths, the *da ma ru* drum, bell and *vajra* (diamond sceptre);

8. the most important duties for a shaman: healing man and animal, prophesising, and protecting people from misfortune and harm.

Following these similarities, the differences may appear minor – but they are noteworthy, as the three main differences are related to the ENVIRONMENT in which the Changthang shamans live.

These are the differences:

1. Changthang shamans have no bodily contact when healing animals. For the shamans in central Ladakh, however, it is an integral part of their healing practice (above all for the large and valuable animals such as the yak) to suck out needles and other solid objects from the animal's body – which the Changthang shamans never do. And this one can also understand. This treatment technique is, as all shamans confirm, extremely exhausting for the shaman. Assuming each family of nomads has between one and thirty yaks, which could all become ill, no shaman would be able to afford this procedure. Changthang shamans heal animals too. But this healing consists simply of blessing with incense and *puja* (HI-37, HI-38, HI-43).

2. Changthang shamans heal as "individuals": the individual shamans have tended to develop their own particular, idiosyncratic methods of healing that are a part of *their* shamanic healing practice, and nobody else's. Shaman Sonam Lathar's blood-sucking technique, Lhapa Thundup's blowing across his *da ma ru*, Lhapa Ngawang's use of herbs and powders from a store of Tibetan *am chi* medicine – all these are highly "individual" practices – as affirmed by the other shamans who do not practise these methods. Quite clearly, there are overlaps between father and son (Sonam Lathar and Ngawang) –

Sonam Lathar's blood-sucking technique comes from his father (he also wants to teach his son the art if *am chi*-medicine); – however, blowing across the *da ma ru* is completely unfamiliar to them, just as practising *am chi* medicine is for Lhapa Thundup.

In the case of the shamans of central Ladakh, I cannot ever recall a shaman using a healing technique which others would not have already used, or were learning.

It is quite clear that in the vast expanse of Changthang, there are so few opportunities for shamans to encounter other shamans directly or indirectly (i.e. through patients' accounts) and thus become familiar with other healing techniques. Thus, the development of individual methods is far more obvious.

3. A third difference concerns the outer appearance. Fundamentally, it is the same. But shamanic crowns adorned with a whole drape of long, wild and jostling woollen braids – one does not find such crowns with any shaman of central Ladakh. In this respect, the Changthang shamans are attired far more elaborately than the shamans of central Ladakh (and accordingly they are a much more impressive sight to behold!). The jostling woollen braids do, of course, originate from their immediate environment.

4. One may link these three differences to the Changthang environment, but there are also a whole number of other differences that are not apparently related. Sucking – whether on a man or animal – is a key healing technique for the shamans of central Ladakh; it is also the first method of healing they learn. None of the Changthang shamans heals by sucking – certainly not in the case of animals (see above), but similarly

neither for people. For their counterparts in central Ladakh as well as for themselves, *nod pa* and *dib* – harm lingering in the body – are the most common ailments, and must therefore be removed from the body. Indeed they SING it out, BLOW it out, or they EXTRACT the blood with an object. They do not use a suction pipe, nor do they suck by mouth.

5. A further difference, which would be worth examining more closely, relates to the technique of foretelling the future. Sonam Murup's technique of making barley corns dance around on the *da ma ru* drum during his reverberating song (see RÖSING 2002a) – is unknown in Changthang. Conversely, I have not seen the mirror - which both Lhapa Thundup and Lhapa Ngawang evidently use regularly – being adopted by shamans in central Ladakh; as VOLF (1994) reports, however, it is in fact used by a small minority there.

More important than such superficial, external differences, however, are of course the differences in content. In central Ladakh, I have never witnessed or heard such a long shamanic chant – so original in content, and also completely orientated towards the patients and participants and their world and time – as that of Lhapa Thundup. And in all my Ladakh research to date, I have never seen any chant like this documented. There is also a lot in the content of this chant (the shaman's mythological origin, his bridging the gap from the individual to the global etc) that I have not yet found in central Ladakh, either in a séance documented by myself or in reports published by other researchers. However, this is most probably also not a phenomenon peculiar to the whole of the Changthang region. I venture to suggest that one would not be able to find these contents with Sonam Lathar or Lhapa Ngawang. It seems to be the chant of ONE great individual shaman, who, deep in trance, grasps the significance of the evil in our times more acutely than anyone else.

APPENDIX B

Shamanism as a mental disorder?

It was not all that long ago that western researchers on shamanism qualified the shamans as "healing madmen", and shamanism as a form of mental disorder. And one can still find researchers with a similar opinion today. In her book on Ladakh, Janet Rizvi refers to anonymous "Western-trained anthropologists" who view trance as an "hysterical disturbance" and continues: "In this context, the *lha-ba* training at the same time develops and controls a pre-existing multiple personality syndrome" (RIZVI 1996, p.137).

Multiple Personality Disorder is a western psychiatric category; in the western context this syndrome is perceived as a mental disorder.

According to Rizvi, this "mental disorder" marks not only the outset but also the result of shamanic training – in other words, the training (on the basis of an illness already purported to exist) leads to the development of a mental disorder syndrome, termed multiple personality.

This account by Rizvi is at the very least highly misleading. To protect the research described in this current book from being similarly misunderstood, I would like to return once again to the "madness" as the starting point of shamanic calling, and the transformation of this "madness".

The shamans portray the starting point of their calling, this *tsha ba tshu ba* state, most impressively. They FEEL ill. They are viewed as being ill by those around them. Their family and friends take them from one healing practice to another. And the nature of the illness – even in their own eyes – is that of a mental disorder (*sem pa, sem nyid*).

Nevertheless, when using the shamans' words (*tsha ba tshu ba, nyos po*) in my preceding text, I have always put the word "madness" in inverted commas in order to make it quite clear that I am not using it in the psychiatric sense of the word. Whether or not the budding Ladakhi shaman's *tsha ba tshu ba* condition is diagnosed by a foreign psychiatrist as hysteria or schizophrenia or multiple personality disorder, is immaterial. What is critical is something else; and that is what Rizvi's explanation above – according to which the shaman remains in an abnormal mental state – so spectacularly fails to – pinpoint.

The critical point is that through the process of recognising and acknowledging the *lha* and through the shamanic training, the shaman's "pathology" is transformed, a process that is witnessed and identified also by others and by the shaman himself: he or she is transformed not only into a healthy person, but into a healthy person who cures other men and women of their illnesses. This to me is the very essence of the extraordinarily impressive cultural achievement of this shamanic complex.

Whether one views it from an external perspective or from his own, a Ladakhi shaman is in no way "ill". Much more, he has developed an extraordinary ability: under circumstances strictly controlled and dictated by himself, he is able to go into an altered state of consciousness (which is by no means a mental illness!) and – with equal control at a moment he determines – can come out of it again. All this is achieved without any form of assistance by drug taking to launch his consciousness into that other world, and, as its effects wear off, to bring him back into this world. His only means of assistance is his deep concentration as he chants monotonously along with his drumming and ringing. And his greatest asset, which he brings with him from his often crazily demanding and tormenting training – is the orientation of his consciousness on receiving certain signals conducive to bringing on his altered state of consciousness. A reservoir of certain "conditionings" as one would say in "western" language – that is his great asset.

272

These "conditionings" would not be possible during training if there were no points of contact. And the essential point of contact is his early experience of a non–spontaneous altered state of consciousness, that "madness" which is the starting point on the road to a shamanic calling.

Shamanic "madness" – that starting point of professional shamanic development – is, when viewed like this, quite immune to criticism. In all countries of the world, there are mentally ill people and there are probably also mentally ill people in Ladakh.

In other countries, such people are often removed from everyday life, placed in an institution and their condition veiled by medication. They become "manageable". And they become dull, unimaginative and lethargic. And they are a burden to others.

In Ladakh, however, they are transformed into people who go into society, participating actively, going about their everyday business and healing. In trance, their spirit unfolds, becoming animated and extremely active. They are not simply rendered "manageable". They manage themselves. They are a burden to nobody – much more, they unburden other people.

APPENDIX C

Language and method:
"Speaking anthropology" in the context of ecliptic language codes

1. DIFFERENT ANTHROPOLOGIES

1.1 Scenario at the outset

The starting point of this study was a scene that, recurring many times, went as follows:

> In Leh, capital "city" of Ladakh, where I have a modest residence, I sit with two of my Ladakhi collaborators, Sonam Norboo Spurkhapa and Tsultim Kubet, on the terrace in front of the house. We all have a 200-300 page text on their knees. The texts are transcriptions, copied word-for-word from audio tape recordings of either shamanic séances or conversations with shamans, shamanic assistants, relatives of shamans, or people acquainted with shamanism. The texts are in the Ladakhi language and written in Tibetan script.

> Our task is to translate these texts. Out of the three of us, Tsultim can best read the Tibetan script. He is competent at English. I can also read the Tibetan script but cannot speak or understand much Ladakhi. But I am the most familiar with the contents of the transcripts because I always wrote extensive protocol notes of the sessions or conversations to which they refer. Sonam Norboo cannot easily read Tibetan script, and must focus on the transliteration (conversion into Latin script); but he speaks perfect English. At least one of these two collaborators was present during all sessions or conversations we are now trying to understand and translate.

Tsultim reads out. Very stagnantly. Sonam reads out the transliteration – more stagnantly still. They both read it once again out loud. They read it out again (a third time): still very laboriously. Sonam begins a long speech in English – indirect speech, by no means a translation: "He says that ... and then he says that..." "No", Tsultim cuts him off, "that's not right, he DOESN'T say that..." And I say "Sonam, that can't be right, because I remember that conversation very well and look, I have my original protocol notes..."

So, we all return to the text. Again laboured, loud parallel reading by Tsultim and Sonam... Now Tsultim has an "idea" as to what might have been said here, and it goes as follows: "So, the shaman says that..." "No", Sonam interrupts him, "look at this passage, what he's actually saying is..." And Sonam reads out turgidly, and the two of them start arguing in Ladakhi about what the shaman supposedly said ...

And so they continue endlessly. I draw a halt to the discussion, we are not getting anywhere. The two native speakers don't agree about what was said. And so we refer back to more basic work: firstly, we mark the places in our text where words are separated (Tibetan script separates syllables, not words – thus each sentence is made up of a long row of syllables...). With this task completed, the text does at least become a little easier to read. We then try to produce a word-for-word translation – very painstakingly – one has to be patient. Once again, I summarise all the information we can extract from my original protocol notes – and we poise ourselves for a fresh attempt at translating – again with some hefty disagreement between the two Ladakhi speakers...

This scene portrays the extreme difficulties encountered when working on transcribed Ladakhi texts. (I had the same experience with my other two transcription collaborators). In the following paragraphs, I would like to show firstly why I work with such texts at all ("speaking anthropology") and secondly what it is about the Ladakhi language ("ecliptic coding") that makes cultural anthropological research of the "speaking" variant so challenging.

1.2 Silent and speaking anthropology

I coined this term 12 years ago with a critical intent (RÖSING 1988/1995): There is a wealth of ethnography in which no one except the author speaks: *he* describes, *he* clarifies, *he* interprets, *he* erects great pinnacles of thought, *he* theorises, *he* generalises. The persons under research never get to speak for themselves. This is what I term (somewhat polemically) SILENT anthropology – although there is ONE person speaking, without interruption.

This one person, who commentates uninterrupted and alone, is, in cultural anthropological research, the most unimportant speaker. It is far more important that the so-called "researchees" should have the opportunity to give their account, in their own words, so that THEY describe, explain, clarify, theorise and generalise. What they say must be carefully documented (using a tape recorder) and it must be transcribed in full so that the dynamics of a conversation can also be reconstructed for critical analysis. And in the researcher's report these native accounts should be quoted in minute detail – that is SPEAKING anthropology.

Speaking anthropology is more than a particular method of approach preferred by a researcher. It is also an ethical and an epistemological approach. In the words of Ivo STRECKER (1990):

> Ethnology must, I believe, release itself from certain practices – those practices which since Malinowski characterise its empiricism in a particular way. In the first quarter of the 20th century, Bronislaw Malinowski brought ethnological field research to its apparent perfect form. From now on, field research was no longer a random gathering of facts without a theory, but instead consisted of intensive, theory-directed, and very consciously selective par-

ticipant observation. Selective observation was followed by selective description. Since Malinowski, the empirically working ethnologist, – that is the ethnographer – does not document all empirical data, but only those which would be of use to him in the development of his argument or to prove a theory.

... according to this method the ethnographer "illustrates" only his theoretical point of view. It is as though he is the sole administrator of all the knowledge on the society he is analysing. Incessantly, he disproves and reaffirms himself and no-one knows which data he has, and which he does not have.

One might think that this approach is only an intra-scientific scandal. But unfortunately, this approach does also include a sizeable portion of disdain vis-à-vis the persons who are being investigated... If the ethnologist appears and acquires knowledge, which is only of value to himself and within a very specific scientific community, then where does that leave the person under investigation? In such a case, would we not view it as "crass scientific colonialism"? (p.611)

Against this selective approach, full of disdain regarding the persons and matters investigated, Ivo Strecker puts forward, amongst other things, the following maxims: firstly, the requirement for the ethnologist to try to understand in the first instance the IDIO-SYNCRASIES of a foreign culture, and secondly that DOCUMEN-TATION, i.e. careful data description, is indeed given much greater prominence. I adhere to these two maxims in my own research without fail:

I work on the assumption that what I study is going to be more pluralistic and disunified, contradictory and complicated, more involved and certainly more difficult to penetrate than it appears at first sight. It is not my language, nor my ordering systems and theories that are important; it is much more important that the people of a foreign culture have their own say, in their own language and their own way of thinking.

Furthermore, I work on the understanding that even when I have lived and worked a long time in a foreign culture – in this case in Tibetan culture – I will NEVER have understood it fully: would I ever claim to understand everything even in my OWN culture? With this basic attitude the diverse aspects and levels of a foreign culture, not forgetting its contradictions and taciturn elements – and with this I would say its wealth and its REALITY – come into focus much more readily.

Working on these premises, however, does lead to a number of impracticalities for research. It certainly will not suffice to simply look into what I see in shamanic séances, make a few notes, dress it up in my own words and add a theory to fit and then offer it to the reader. I always need the spoken word, the explanation and the understanding of the shaman himself – and moreover not only in my own language, but in the shaman's native tongue. It is essential for me to learn his language and let him speak for himself, in his OWN language, not mine. Therefore, my Ladakhi tape recordings have to be transcribed, and I must document and listen to the voice of the shaman speaking Ladakhi long *before* making any attempt at interpretation. Only by doing this are validity checks ensured; only by doing this can one allow for all the complexities of a foreign culture.

Taking into consideration the principles above, one can immediately appreciate the importance of having comprehensive tape-recorded documentation of all data gathered and also the necessity of comprehensive transcription.

In reconstructing a shamanic séance, elucidating ambivalent data, making sense out of apparently controversial standpoints, the analysis of the tape-recordings plays an important role.

At a séance attended by possibly more than a dozen people, many of whom may, of course, be speaking at the same time, with numerous disturbances and background noises (coughing, children crying, my tape recorder being jostled in its confined space etc) and with the many activities, the comings and goings of the performers and also the shaman's trance – the complete transcription or note-taking of such a séance is a really stressful task, and likewise my controlling the transcripts by listening to the tape again and again. But it has always been worthwhile in the end.

For, with tape recordings and transcripts, not only is the language documented, but also a great amount of additional information is transferred in the course of the healing séance: atmosphere, everyday conversations, values, sequences of events.

An additional, very important function of a comprehensive transcription is of course that it is a highly effective means of co-ordinating observational data (the proceedings of the ritual), on the one hand, and the language, above all the prayers, on the other. In my written notes, I have not only noted what one could SEE, but also what one could HEAR – I even set little signals by clearing my throat. The transcripts do also include very precisely such events as "child screams", "dog barks"; "bout of coughing" and my indicating throat clearing. And by referring to my written note "cleared throat twice" and the corresponding note in the transcript, I am able to synchronise with great precision a particular ritual event with particular lines in the prayer that the shaman was saying.

Systematic checks of the transcriptions from the tape recordings are also an essential corrective procedure to counteract hasty conclusions or interpretations of supposedly unambiguous situations. The texts provide a wealth of information on how the protagonist perceives things HIMSELF.

The comprehensive recording and subsequent transcription as well as the constant playing back and checking of the transcriptions is, moreover, critical for the reconstruction of the research process. Mistakes, dead-ends, detours, misunderstandings, the influence of moods, etc are unsparingly exposed. I can recognise the stupidity of my own questions and the polite response of the person to whom I am talking, who nevertheless endeavours to answer them. From the proceedings of a conversation I can reconstruct precisely the point at which a misunderstanding arose, and how, as a result of this, absurd results emerge. I can also recognise the occasionally persistent suggestive questions of my research collaborator, Sonam Norboo. Frustration, disbelief and impatience on my part, and the attempt of the partner in conversation to present himself as knowledgeable and wise – all this is revealed with great clarity in the analysis of a fully transcribed text of the conversations. By following this procedure, one can effectively sort the wheat from the chaff.

1.3 The present methodological approach in the context of the development of the field

How is this methodological approach embedded in the context of the development of cultural anthropology? The years after Malinowski, during which the subject of ethnology had been comfortably slotted into the category of "true science" without being questioned, have now gone. An epistemological, ideological, postmodernist fundamental critique has swept the discipline according to which ethnology is little more than subjectivity, poetry and politics (CLIFFORD & MARCUS 1986).

The fundamental critique has released a self-destructive MALAISE in the field – but it has also brought forth a countermovement, a new understanding of ethnology which is emerging from the storm of radical "deconstruction" (e.g. D'ANDRADE 1995; BOWLIN & STROMBERG 1997; KUPER 1994; LINDHOLM 1995, 1997; REYNA 1994; SPIRO 1996).

The fundamental critique was useful and it was successful (for an account of this development see KOHL 1993; GOTTOWIK 1997). The new portrait of ethnology can be summarised with reference to three key features (KOHL 1993; CLIFFORD 1986):

(1) Ethnology has become SELF-REFLEXIVE. Today no researcher can afford to practise ethnology without including searching, critical reflection and documentation of his own subjectivity.

(2) Ethnology has become CONTEXTUALISED. Such categories as "the Nuer", "the Navaho", etc no longer exist. The discourse is specified (CLIFFORD 1986): Who speaks where, when, with whom,

about what, and under which personal, institutional and political circumstances? This contextualisation effectively removes the illusion of a cultural consensus among the persons being studied ethnologically. There is dissent in all cultures. As a result, no description can ever be complete. Ethnology is becoming multifocal; the researcher is moving away from the centre and the descriptions and accounts are becoming polyphonic.

(3) Where subjectivity has to be critically reflected again and again and cannot be entirely ruled out, matters of power can infiltrate. A new ethnology has become aware of the ETHICAL dimension and reflects its political and ideological basis as well as its political and ideological consequences. The field has assumed responsibility; there is no longer mere writing "about" the others, the results are being exposed to the testing judgement of those it "describes" (GOTTOWIK 1997).

With all this, the ethnological undertaking has become much more modest, and, at the same time, also far more complex. Its hitherto more ahistorically and statically-described subject – foreign cultures – has changed its appearance. Culture is "contested, temporal and emergent" (CLIFFORD 1986). Grand theories are no longer *en vogue*. Contradictions are not unreasonable. Change is a fundamental element. Culture and description of culture assumes the character of a dynamic, ongoing process. The self-paralysis of the field has been constructively overcome. Nobody doubts the existence of subjectivity, power and interest. In his book *Fear and Method in the Behavioural Sciences*, according to DEVEREUX (1973), the problem is not subjectivity itself, i. e. transference and countertransference – on the contrary, they are themselves excellent data – but ignoring subjectivity and avoiding their systematic analysis.

Both, unquestioned belief in science and "mind numbing scepticism" (BOWLIN & STROMBERG 1997) are now equally obsolete. Bowlin and Stromberg recommend an attitude which they call NOA: natural ontological attitude. This means allowing the person and subject matters to speak for themselves, without theorising, and putting them into context with other observations, searching inexhaustively for further evidence and counter-evidence alike, and always being open to revision and amendment – in other words, to practise epistemic humility, as they call it.

To this approach, one would have to add D'ANDRADE's (1995, 1997) plea for ethical modesty in which a "moral" position is presented not PRIOR to the data but WITH them.

What is the place of "speaking anthropology" in this greater context of the development of the field of cultural anthropology or ethnology? What I term "speaking anthropology" means putting aside the researcher and his theories – it means a radical de-centering, de-focussing of the ethnologist – and it is a method of allowing polyphony to emerge and contradictions to have a legitimate place. The fact that something is not only "discovered" but at the same time also formed and "constructed" (and so, to a certain degree, not only "found" but also "invented" and "created" for the culture) is not ignored. This becomes quite plain in the dialogues with the persons being researched: after their initial astonishment regarding the results of the so-called "ethnological eye" (which de-familiarises the familiar and thus sees things anew) they become co-researchers (RÖSING 2001).

2. ECLIPTIC CODES

A code represents something more encompassing than itself. Words are codes for meaning. Languages vary greatly according to the degree of redundancy within their codes. When, in German, the personal pronoun "du" (you) is used with the appropriately conjugated verb, it becomes redundant: both indicate the second person singular.

In the Tibetan-Burmese language of Ladakh, when counting numbers beyond *nyi shu* (two-ten = twenty) another syllable specifically for "twenty" is introduced (*rtsa*) before the counting continues – so there is also redundancy. With *nyi shu rtsa nyis* we immediately know from two constituents that this particular number belongs to the 20- series.

This example (specific suffixes also exist in Ladakhi from thirty to ninety) is indeed one of the very few examples of redundant codes in Ladakhi. In most other respects this language is overtly hostile to redundancy – it is redundancy-abstinent. I call this characteristic "ecliptic"[1] which is a descriptive term without value.

In order to demonstrate the formidable problems, ecliptic language codes can present within speaking anthropology, I must firstly introduce the Ladakhi language (Section 2.1 to 2.3), and the family of languages it belongs to and outline its key features with respect to speech codes as well as in script and orthography.

By providing this background the problems portrayed in the scenario at the outset, described at the start of this appendix, will be clarified in a systematic manner (2.4). In the final section, I shall then show how one can at least partially solve the problem of ecliptic codes in the context of "speaking anthropology".

2.1 The Tibetan-Burman language family

Ladakhi belongs to the Tibetan-Burman language family (EGEROD 1974; HALE 1982; MASPERO 1952; MILLER 1969; SHAFER 1957, 1963, 1966-1973). This includes a great variety of languages from Tibet in the north to Burma in the south; from Baltistan in the west to the Chinese provinces of Sechuan and Yünnan in the east (GRIERSON 1909 / 1967a, Volume III, Part 1).

The Tibetan-Burman languages are monosyllabic. The monosyllabic units are never modified. They always remain unchanged and are linked together as unchanged units. Monosyllabic particles take over the role of grammatical modification.

---

1 Greek: eliminated, disappeared. Eclipse of the sun and lunar eclipse are used in the same sense.

These monosyllabic units are not easily identified as particular categories of words: the same syllable can be substantive, adjective or verb. Nevertheless a particular word order within a sentence is observed – subject, object, verb – which makes it easier to identify the word category.

The vocabulary is very rich – one reason being that, for different variants of objects there are often also different words. The Tibetan-Burman language Lushei, for example, includes nine different words for "ant" and twenty words for "basket" (GRIERSON 1909/ 1967a, Vol. III Part 1). Generic words that summarise different variants ("all ants") scarcely exist, and rarer still are abstract words.

Substantives have no gender. The gender of a living being is indicated by an additional syllable. Substantives do not have plurals either. The plural must be expressed by using "many" or "all". Substantives can be declined (there is no distinction between nominative and accusative, but these can be differentiated by word order) by adding suffixes, but these are identical for singular and plural.

A further feature of substantives is that the subject of a transitive verb is written in the ergative case, i.e. is characterised by the agent. "The man reads the book" must therefore be expressed as "The man through him read book".

A particular feature of these languages is that they do not have real verbs. The verb is more like a substantive. Verbs do not vary according to person, number or gender; i.e. they are neither conjugated nor pluralized. I, you, he, she, it, we, they go – is all one word. And if one wants to express WHO it is, WHO is "going", it can only be achieved by saying "my go".

Also verb tenses (present, past, future) can only be expressed in many of these languages by using additional words – in Ladakhi, for example, *nge sil tshar* "my/study/complete": I (had) studied.

2.2 Ladakhi linguistics

Whilst it is true that Tibetan-Burman languages have phonetic similarities, there are also any number of differences. The phonetic system specific to Tibetan and to Ladakhi is extremely complicated insofar as there are many monosyllabic words with several combinations of (sometimes silent) consonants at the start of a word. According to GRIERSON (1909/1967b), this is a result of the merging of different monosyllabic words. In the variant of the Tibetan language spoken in central Tibet these relics of consonants are left out, and the meaning lost as a result of this is expressed in the intonation instead.

I am mentioning this because the variant of Ladakhi spoken in Changthang is similar to that of central Tibet – while the other Ladakhi variants retain the system of combining consonants and do NOT have changes of voice and intonation to clarify meaning. Even in 1909/1967a (Vol. III, Part 1) GRIERSON – and before him FRANCKE (1904) – lamented that the language of Rupshu (Changthang) had up to then scarcely been investigated – and this is true even into the new millennium; I am not aware of a single linguistic article on the Changthang dialect.

Also, overall Ladakhi linguistics – in contrast to Tibetan – is very undeveloped, which is to be regretted, for both these languages are so different that understanding between the two is not at all easy. Nevertheless, next to the old[2], there are also a few new Ladakhi dictionaries[3], some books on grammar[4], an article on Ladakhi dialectology[5] and at least one serious teaching book (KOSHAL 1982)[6].

---

2 JÄSCHKE 1881/1992, SANDBERG 1894/1999 Part III.
3 NORBERG-HODGE & PALDAN 1991; HAMID 1998.
4 FRANCKE 1901/1979; GRIERSON 1909/1967a, KOSHAL 1979.
5 See HOSHI & TSERING 1978.
6 See also KOSHAL 1976; NORMAN 1994.

Linguistic studies on specific aspects of the Ladakhi language are likewise rare. Of the few that exist[7], there is one of particular note: Bettina ZEISLER (1999) studied the increasing influence of English and Urdu in Ladakhi with the ongoing process of modernisation and the many encounters with foreigners, and cites some grotesque passages from political texts in which heavily corrupted English words threaten to invade Ladakhi, substituting the Ladakhi word with a parallel, corrupted English word: "*Modern times madlap sipa nang tyuris Ladakse economy la mangpo change sostok...*"

Zeisler shows that words have by no means been borrowed only for technical or sundry new terms for which there was no word in Ladakhi; for radio they say *raidi*, instead of the charming Ladakhi word, *lungs thin* (air-message); an aeroplane is today called *jaz* (Urdu: jahaz) instead of the Ladakhi word, *nam du* (skyship).

The same applies to everyday terms too, such as time (one speaks of *tem* instead of *tus* or *long*, native Ladakhi words), *happy* instead of *kit po*, one speaks of *rastrant* (restaurant) instead of *za khang*, etc.

One can predict that in the process of so-called modernisation, another unique and special feature of Ladakhi will be lost, although it does still exist today and must be carefully cherished and protected. This uniqueness of Tibetan and also Ladakhi does not make the language any easier to learn. It is the existence of two partly parallel languages, an honorific language and an informal, non-honorific language. Ladakhi's honorific language was described as early as the 19th century by FRANCKE (1898), and nearly a century later in more depth and also socio-linguistically by KOSHAL (1987).

In other languages, too, there are honorific words. German may serve as an example: there is "Sie" (formal YOU) instead of "Du"

7 DENWOOD 1980, 1995; FRANCKE 1898, 1903, 1904; GHOSH 1999; JASCHKE 1865; KOSHAL 1987; MILLER 1956; NAMGYAL 1995; ROERICH 1931; TSEWANG 1985; ZEISLER 1999.

(informal YOU – like old English "thou"), the address "Eure Majestät" (Your Majesty), and the *pluralis majestatis* etc., but this is nothing in comparison with Ladakhi, where there are either additional honorific words or additional syllables for many substantives, verbs and of course pronouns for the second and third person. Even the word "because" has an honorific and a non-honorific variant.

Honorific Ladakhi language is particularly rich in substantives. There is for all parts of the body a parallel vocabulary – from hair and vertex, to ear, tooth, eyebrow and finger[8] and likewise all imaginable things that one owns – from hat to trousers and horse to dog.[9]

Even feelings, motives and values have different words[10] depending on whether the speaker is of high social standing or an ordinary citizen. Similarly, love, joy and sorrow, as well as anger and temptation...

As regards verbs there are often parallel words especially for the everyday realm.[11] If I ask a person of high standing "Where are you going?" I must use another word for "go" (*skyot*) as I must when I answer an identical question asked by him (in that case I use *cha* for "go"). Sit, make, come, eat, drink, speak – even to give

---

8   The normal everyday word comes first and the honorific word second: Head: *mgo/u*; heart: *snying/thugs*; eye: *mig/chan*; eyebrow: *mit sma/chan spu*; face: *rdong/zhal dong*; ear: *nam chhag/snyan*; nose: *sna/shang*; tooth: *so/tshems*; mouth: *kha/zhal*; hand: *lak pa/chhags*; foot: *rkang pa/zhabs*, etc.

9   Hat: *tibi/dbu zwa* (FRANCKE 1898), trousers: *snam ya/phyag rten* (FRANCKE 1898); dress: *nam bza/na bza* (FRANCKE 1898); shoe: *pabu/zhab lam*; dog: *khyi/dogs khyi* (FRANCKE 1898); horse: *rta/chibi* (FRANCKE 1898); beer: *chhang/skyems*; bread: *tagi/don kyir*.

10 Anger: *sro, tho/thugs gyal, thugs sro*; soul: *sog/thugs yid*; patience: *zodpa/thugs zod* (FRANCKE 1898); love: *byams pa/byams thugs* (FRANCKE 1898), joy: *thad pa/thugs thad* (FRANCKE 1898); pain: *zurmo/snying zug;* temptation: *nyams sadpa/thugs sadpa* (FRANCKE 1898).

11 To make: *cho/dzad*; to go: *cha/skyot*; to give: *thang/sal*; to speak: *zer/mol*; to eat: *zha/don*; to drink: *thung/skyog thabs*; to give birth *skye/khrun* (FRANCKE 1898); to die: *shi/tongs*; to sit: *dug/zhugo*.

birth and to die are expressed differently depending on the status of the partner addressed in conversation.

In Ladakhi, there are various construction principles for this parallel language (for a comprehensive overview see KOSHAL 1987). There are often completely independent words. Sometimes special honorific syllables are added to the standard everyday word. In particular, the latter occurs in connection with verbs (see below) and in the description of feelings, motives and values, where often *thugs* – the honorific word for heart/sense – precedes the normal word: *sro* is MY anger (normal speech); *thugs sro* is yours (in case you are of higher status) – yours is, in a manner of speaking, an anger that "comes from the heart"!

Where there are no honorific words for verbs one can "honorise" the verb by adding *dzad*. Studying/reading is *sil* – but only if it is me or a subordinate person; not when a respected colleague is doing it. His studying or reading is *sil dzad*. But these words must be linked together with phonetic elegance, which does make learning the language altogether more challenging. This phonetic linkage consists of the insertion of a pure phonetic syllable that involves repetition of the end consonant (if present) plus a vocal "a" – thus one has the honorific reading: *sil la dzad*. "Shut" is *kyon*, so, honorifically, "shut" is: *kyon na dzad*. "Open" is *phe*, and thus honorifically: *phe a dzad*, etc.

Besides this, there is yet another word – *le* – the use of which converts all words and expressions into an honorific variant. I can ask a younger person: who are you, *su inog*? If it is someone older than me I would ask: *su inog le*?

Who are these higher status persons for the benefit of whom one must still learn this parallel language in Ladakhi? They are the foreigners, the elderly, the aristocrats, all members of the Buddhist clergy and everyone for whom one wishes to show respect (e.g. officials, shamans, the military etc., and formerly also one's parents and elderly relatives). Above all, however, it is for the benefit of the upper classes. Ladakh today is still a strictly class-governed society (KOSHAL 1987) in which this particular use of language must be carefully observed – down to the smallest detail – depending on whether communication is addressed to one's superiors, one's equals and one's inferiors. Is your little finger hurting? This would be expressed in completely different ways depending on whether you were speaking "up" to a person, or "down" to him: for "little finger" and "pain" have specific honorific words.

For some words in Ladakhi, there are even three categories: honorific, non-honorific and "derogatory". An example: a king's unconsciousness is *sku rgal*; my unconsciousness is *tsha rgyal*, and a beggar's is *mun*. Whole sentences can sound completely different when expressed in the three variations:

Have you eaten?

Questioning a superior: *Don tang dons sa?*
Questioning an equal: *Khar ji zos sa?*
Questioning an inferior: *Tot nak sngos sa?*

He's gone home.

Speaking up to a person: *Zims khang nga skyot pin.*
Speaking to an equal: *Khang pa a song pin.*
Speaking down to a person: *Rong khang nga khyams pin.*[12]

2.3 Tibetan script and orthographic difficulties

The Ladakhi language uses Tibetan script. According to Tibetan historical writings (PALDAN 1990), the Tibetan script was devised in about 632 A.D by Thonmisambhota, based on the Indian Gupta script. (For the origins of Tibetan script see, e.g. LAUFER 1918, NARKYID 1983). At that time the minister, Thonmisambhota, was sent to Kashmir by his king to learn the art of writing and grammar for the purpose of translating the Buddhist texts from the Indian languages.

12 Both examples are taken from KOSHAL (1987). p156.

Two Tibetan scripts were devised – one *dbu chan*, i.e. "with top lines", the printed script with a clear upper line; and *dbu med* – without an upper line – this is handwriting or fast writing (see illustrations).

མདང་འདི་རིང་འཛིག་རྗེན་གྱི་ཕྱོགས་ཚང་མ་ནས་ལ་དུགས་སི་ཤེས་ རིག་སོ་སོ་དང་། ལམ་ལུགས་སྤྱལ་ཀུན་ལ་ལྷར་ཡོང་ང་ནོག་ ལ་དུགས་པོ་ ཤེས་རིག་ཕྱུག་པོ་དང་ལམ་ལུགས་སྤྱལ་བཟང་པོ་ཀུན་ནེ་བང་མཛོད་ཅིག་ཡིན་ ནོག་ ག་ཀུན་མི་རབས་ནས་མི་རབས་ལ་ཡར་རྒྱས་ཆའི་ཡོངས། འི་ཀུན་ སྟོར་བྱས་པོ་མཆེར་གའི་དཔེ་ར་ཞིག་ཡིན་ནོག་ ང་དང་ཀུན་ལ་མདང་འདི་ རིང་ངེ་ནུག་ནྲུག་པེད་པེད་ཀུན་ལ་མགོ་འཁོར་ཏེ་མ་ལུས་ས་བདེན་པའི་ཡར་ རྒྱས་པོ་ཆེ་ཡིན་ཏུ་གོ་དགོས་ཡིན་ནོག་ ང་དང་རང་ཎེ་ཤེས་རིག་དང་ཁྲིམས་

Dbu chan: Extract from MELONG (Ladahki newspaper)

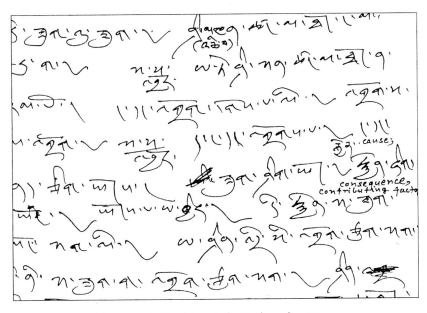

Dbu-med: Tsultim Kubet's handwriting

The Tibetan alphabet has 30 letters. The vowel "a" is inherent in every letter. The letter "k", for example, indicates "ka". If the "k" is combined with another vowel, one of the four vowel symbols (e,i,o,u) must be added to the letter.

In addition, a number of letters are formed by "melting" together two single ones. However, Ladakhi orthography is difficult not only because of these additional letters. It is extraordinarily difficult above all because of the numerous silent letters for which there are no apparent rules. There is an abundance of words that are pronounced in exactly the same way. Their varying meanings in spoken language are identifiable exclusively by the context and in the written language through the orthography – that is, by the addition or removal of diverse silent letters, e.g.:

Pronunciation	Orthography	Meaning
ngos	ངོས / ngos	surface, side
	དངོས / dngos	reality, real
do	མདོ / mdo	Sutra
	རྒོ / rgo	wheat
	འགྲོ / agro	(suffix to verb) perhaps
	སྒྲོ / sgro	quill
la	གླ / gla	salary, fee
	ལ / la	pass
	ལྷ / lha	god
lo	ལོ / lo	year
	ལྷོ / lho	South
go	མགོ / mgo	head
	འགོ / ago	origin, source
dom	དོམ / dom	bear
	འདོམ / adom	arm span (= approx. 6 ft)
	སྡོམ / sdom	total, entire

2.4 Difficulties in working with Ladakhi transcriptions

Against the background of this linguistic characteristics of the Ladakhi language and its Tibetan script, I can now elucidate the problem which I described in the introductory scenes. Whosoever works on the basis of "speaking anthropology" will never be spared the chore of learning in great depth the language of the culture being studied. I have tried to illustrate that Ladakhi is not at all easy in this respect – primarily because of the tendency for the language to have very little redundant (duplicated) vocabulary and because of its parallel language and the orthography. I would like to explore more deeply the following four characteristics of Ladakhi in connection and the problem they present for transcription work:

(1) The syllabic script and homonymy of syllables;
(2) Multiplicity of polyphonic homonyms;
(3) The great number of silent letters and alternative ways of writing; and
(4) Ecliptic codes.

(1) The syllabic script and homonymy of syllables

In the sample of *dbu-chan* script shown above, it can be seen that in Tibetan script it is not words but syllables that are separated from each other. As mentioned, sentences are not structured but they are from a completely homogenous sequence of syllables.

Where one word begins and where one ends is not always easy to recognise, firstly because in Ladakhi there are a great number of homonymic syllables (identical syllables that have different meanings) and secondly because many of these ambiguous syllables can be:

– a free-standing, monosyllabic word
– the first syllable of a compound word

- the middle syllable of a compound word
- the last syllable of a compound word, or
- not an independent syllable at all

which, because of the lack of divisions between words in the sentence, cannot be immediately identified. I would like to illustrate this complication with two examples: *nang* and *gang*.

a) *Nang*

First of all, the single syllable *nang* is an independent word. This word has various meanings. It can be a substantive or a preposition. As a substantive it means "room" or "house", and as a preposition it means "and", "with" or "in / within"

Nang can, however, also be the first syllable of a word comprising several syllables, e.g. *nang med la* "suddenly", *nang wa* "caution", *nang tshang* "family", *nang dig cho ches* "settle a dispute", *nang par* "the year after next".

Nang may also be a middle syllable, e.g. in *bab nang stun cha ches* "to suit the conditions" or *phi nang log cha ches* "to turn"; or as a final syllable, e.g. *chi yin nang* "despite".

The greatest ambiguity with *nang* however is to be found *not* within the context of a simple syllable but as a PHONETICALLY EXTENDED syllable. The suffix *ang*, which is attached to words, has two different meanings:

- attached to verbs it creates a polite request
- attached to verbs, substantives and adjectives it means "also".

One of the most important phonetic rules of combinations of syllables in Ladakhi is that one must firstly double the end consonant of a word to which one will attach a suffix beginning with a vocal (of which *ang* is an example), An example: *Yon tan* means culture. Combined with *ang*, ("also") results in: *yon tan nang*. *Kun*, "damage" with *ang*, becomes *kun nang*. *Sdan* "cushion" with *ang* becomes *sdan nang*, and the same with all other words which end with n and will be used with "also": a proliferation of *nang*.

b) Gang

Gang is another example of homonymy and therefore ambivalence of a syllable that, combined with the syllablic writing, impedes the speed at which one can decypher a text.

Gang is an independent monosyllabic word and means "draw". *Gang* is also a unit of measure when quantifying fluids (approximately one cupful). *Gang*, however, according to the phonetic rule treated under *nang*, can mean "also" belonging to a word ending with "g". It can also express a friendly imperative when combined with a verb ending with "g".

(2) Multiplicity of polyphonic synonyms

Since there is an abundance of suffixes starting with a vowel and an abundance of words ending in a consonant, the phonetic rule mentioned above (doubling the end consonant of a word preceding a suffix that starts with a vowel) leads to an impressive multiplicity of polyphonic (differently sounding) but synonymous (of same meaning) syllables.

Tog, mog, rog, log, shog, ngog, dog, nog, pog, etc. are identical in meaning: It all means *og* (a verb suffix indicating the evidence base of a statement) – similar to *nang, sang, lang, pang, ngang*, etc. explained above, except that each word in this latter group can have two meanings, since *ang* is ambivalent. In the list below, *ngang, mang, bang, dang, rang* – are all variants meaning "also":

> *khang* (house) + *ang* (also) becomes *khang ngang*
> *nye lam* (abbreviation) + *ang* becomes *nye lam mang*
> *nyob nyob* (lazy, stupid) + *ang becomes nyob bang*
> *nyid* (sleep) + *ang* becomes *nyud dang*
> *don kyir* (bread, formal) + *ang* becomes *kyir rang.*

These examples could easily be extended and it is quite apparent that Ladakhi words can be rather ambiguous – not a trace of re-dundancy! In addition to this, many of these homonymic syllables are sometimes also independent words or alternatively part of a compound word, i.e. they are homonymic as well as hetero-nymic.

(3) The great number of silent letters and alternative ways of writing

As a result of the proliferation of silent letters – for which there are no Ladakhi grammatical rules for guidance in usage – the ortho-graphy occasionally becomes phenomenally challenging.

"Joy" or "delight" in Ladakhi is *ga de*. But it is never written simply *ga de*, as it is spoken, but is enriched with diverse silent letters before and after: *dgaa bde*. Another example: a king or a lord in Ladakhi is *nga dag*: This could be written using four letters (*nga* is one letter). In Ladakhi, however, seven letters are used: *mngaa bdag*: a silent *m* is placed at the start, a silent "a" at the end of the first syllable, and a silent *b* at the start of the second sylla-ble.

Unfortunately, with the combinations of consonants there is also a minefield of irregularities in pronunciation which makes the transcription of spoken texts very difficult. The double letters overwriting each other, (e.g.) *snga* – can be pronounced *snga*, or *nga* or *snya* or *nya* (HAMID 1998 p. 7). A further example: In *gchig* the first "g" is silent. Sometimes, however, the "g" placed at the front is pronounced like an "l": e.g. as in *gchin*, pronounced *lchin* (idem p. 73).

From the pronunciation of a word in Ladakhi, then, one can by no means be certain how it will be spelt. The letter pronounced as "t" is a particularly difficult case in point when it comes to spell-ing. The "t" sound can be represented by the letter "t", but also by rk, rg, rd, rb, rp. For "k" there are 18 different ways it can be writ-ten, for "kh" 9 ways, and for "g" 21 ways; and only in a minority of cases are differently written words actually pronounced differently too. With this "enrichment" process an additional, silent letter is very soon inserted before or after a spoken letter, or is put on top of it, or below, partly melting to one letter. It is also not uncommon to add silent letters in front, at the end, and below...

(4) Ecliptic codes

The greatest problem when working on Ladakhi transcriptions, however, involves the redundancy-abstinent Ladakhi verb. As I mentioned, the verb is in fact like a substantive. Exactly *who* (i.e. the subject) is doing the activity – making, going, eating, etc, is not specified in the language. We do not know who is speaking (I, you, he, she?) nor how many are speaking (I, we, they?) nor the gender of the speaker (he, she?). As an illustration of what kind of sentences result from these rules, please note the following examples:

> *Gonpa tap ste to tsam song kak.*
> Monastery. Founded. Year. How much. Go. Was.
>
> Rin po che *sngan me pod ne zhus khan yin nok.*
> Rinpoche. Previous. From Tibet. Brought. Is.
>
> *Khong* La ma *nang jal te spe ra tangs.*
> He. Lama. With. Visited. Language. Give.

In everyday conversational language where context, facial expression, gesture and intonations come into play, identification of the actor is possible thanks to non-verbal signs. However, if this additional information is not available, as is the case when one works with transcribed texts – then the job of establishing who evidently was saying or doing or omitting something, becomes difficult – and certainly this is the case for a native Ladakhi-speaker too. My transcript work with my Ladakhi collaborators is littered with examples of this type.

Where the language does not provide for precision of meaning, the doors are wide open to imagination and fabrication. There was one occasion at a time when I was still less familiar with Ladakhi, when my Ladakhi collaborators thought they had understood a key passage of a text (the woman shaman spoke of a broken vessel) and based on THIS understanding we translated the next 10 pages of the text – until on page 11 we read that a pretty vessel was standing on the table perfectly intact. That did not tally. We returned to the key passage. Written there it said *"ma"*. *Ma* can mean "very" (very, badly broken!); however it can also mean "not", i.e. not broken. The vase was not "badly" broken, it was "not" broken, it was intact. It was also nothing symbolic – the vessel of life, as my collaborators fabricated, but just a silly tea cup ...

In translating from Ladakhi into other languages, one cannot avoid adding text in order to render this impressively minimalist "stenographic speech" comprehensible to a foreign speaker. One must of course be very wary when expanding the text (to include conjugation, particles etc), not to create additional or incorrect meanings. This can only be avoided if, on the first and basic level, one translates the text single word for single word: "Monk. Monastery. Be. (I/you/he/she/it/we/they). Speak.", and only then, taking into account the complete context, should one carefully decipher step by step who is speaking. Otherwise some gross misunderstandings can arise. Rigid adhesion to this task prior to attempting a flowing translation of Ladakhi stenographic speech ("stenospeak") is essential for accurate translation. One day the subject of some transcription work of mine was the lessons of an *onpo* on love magic. The effect of that love magic was translated as follows by two of my (male) transcription collaborators (who evidently wanted to spare me the true meaning): "And then the people immediately become favourably inclined towards the person." "Then" "incline" (the Ladakhi word also means to lie down), "immediately" – this was in the text, but whether the "inclining" (or, as mentioned, lying down on the bed) was referring to me, you, or anyone else, and whether it is a person, man or woman, is NOT explicit in Ladakhi, and the passage can equally mean "Then the woman will immediately lie down (on the bed) for you." And this is precisely what the *onpo* had meant. This was confirmed not only by the ensuing text but also – during that teaching – by all our screeches of laughter, which the tape recorder captured and which I played to these considerate collaborators as proof.

3. WORK IN DIALOGUE

All of these characteristics of the Ladakhi language substantially complicate research studies according to the approach of "speaking anthropology". In the first place it is, without question, difficult to learn the language. More tricky still is learning to write (and therefore read) it – not because of the Tibetan script, which one can master quickly and easily, but because of the absence of rules in the complex orthography – which of course even local mother tongue transcription collaborators do not always fully command.

However, if words with several meanings, only distinguishable in the orthography, are incorrectly transcribed from sound to text, then an incorrect interpretation – which unfortunately is precipitated by the redundancy-abstinence of the language – can quickly creep in.

If, as a foreign researcher working with the texts, one is suspicious of something not being quite right and wishes to check the words in the dictionary, one can be assured that the many possible ways of writing these words all sounding the same (see the many written variations of t, k, kh, g) will keep the researcher busy for quite some time, checking on all possible variants offered in the dictionary.

If one adds to these problems the burden of the syllabic script (where does a word begin? Where does it end?) – as a result of which not too many native Ladakhis are able to read a text flu-

ently – the homonymy of syllables as well as the widespread polyphony of synonyms (words meaning the same but pronounced
differently) then one can certainly see why Ladakhi transcription
work is not only painstaking and tedious but riddled with pitfalls
when it comes to translating.

All these difficulties can, however, be overcome. Nevertheless,
it does not alter the fact that for my Ladakhi transcription work I
require ten times the amount of time compared with, for example,
my transcription work in relation to my Andean research (in
Quechua language).

I soon realised that I cannot tackle the transcription work in
Ladakhi so precisely as I can in Quechua. This is partly because of
the linguistic reasons described above – but also because of an ex-
tra-linguistic reason (see below).

In Quechua, I have one main transcription collaborator and I
check his transferral from voice to text word by word, and likewise his translation. Any aspects remaining unclear will be clarified on my next field trip by the speaker himself, the Andean
Quechua-speaking medicine man, the ritualist, or ritual expert.

In Ladakhi, however, there is not one single transcription collaborator or translator who can fully come to grips with a text
completely unaided. I alone as supervisor of voice-to-text transcription am not sufficient – not only because my command of
Ladakhi falls way short of my command of Quechua, but mainly
because of the many linguistic and orthographic problems discussed.

Working with my Ladakhi collaborators, I have finally devised
an elaborate procedure involving many stages, in which the
DIALOGUE plays a very important role.

The first stage – preparing a transcript text in Tibetan script – is
certainly a very helpful first step since this transcription is highly
time-consuming. My collaborator, Thinley Gyurmet, has always
worked excellently. However, he was not present for any of the
research work, and for him to attempt translating material on a
subject that he knows of only indirectly through the brief information I have given him, is NOT possible.

The second stage of my work on the text must proceed with those collaborators who were present at the particular séance or conversation being transcribed. We listen once again – text in hand – to the tape recording, and, referring to my protocols, I once more remind us all, as usual, of the ritual process and the context of the séance. Thus the transcription will be checked against the tape.

The third stage is the obligatory word division and word for word translation. As I have shown, this step – if one wishes to ensure the accuracy of a translation – is absolutely essential. What happens at this stage is guaranteed to make one despair: "Shamans. Come. Inside. Shut." (to which a suffix is added which means "without having seen it oneself") – and this kind of "nonsense" for hundreds of pages ...

The fourth stage has always involved intensive dialogue. Sonam Norboo, Tsultim and I pore over the Tibetan text and the "staccato-speak" (word for word translation) and we ask – what was said here? The possibility of misunderstanding ecliptic codes is, however, so great, that at every attempt at translation one must tirelessly be on one's guard and maintain a stance of rigorous scepticism. However, my collaborators are often irritated by this procedure. Sonam Norboo is highly educated, quick and imaginative in thinking. In our discussions, he always throws a few balls into the air at once. Tsultim, on the other hand, is more careful and with it also much more precise. Like me, he will not entertain imaginative speculation without substance to back it up. And then we discuss: Did he say A? Did he say B? What the Ladakhi collaborator brings with him in a very exciting way into these discussions is additional culturally relevant information. Tsultim: "I'm convinced the shaman spoke of ARROW". Sonam Norboo: "How come then?" "I was there when my daughter, who has received a shamanic calling, had the *lha* god and the *de* daemon separated – and on that occasion we used arrows and they look like X had just described – and so he is not talking about twigs but ARROWS." And then I can ask: "Tsultim, tell me more about the separation of *lha* and *de* – what was it like on that occasion?" And I put the tape recorder on. And as a result, all three of us understand more, and, having learned a great deal about arrows – we return to the grindstone and continue with the Ladakhi transcription.

This to my mind is dialogical anthropology[13] in the best sense. Dialogue implies not equality – we three had completely different roles, duties and areas of expertise in connection with this work. But it is dialogue in the sense of a lively conversation.

The most fruitful aspect of this form of dialogical anthropology (as a means of constructing the text through which speaking anthropology becomes possible) is given when one can resolve anything that is unclear directly with the speaker himself – this was a natural step in my Andean research with the Quechua people of the Apolobamba-Cordillere of Bolivia. Nevertheless, one can use it only to a very limited extent if one has set out to study the shamans in Tibetan culture: the Tibetan shamans heal under trance – i.e. possession by a god, and they are amnesic with respect to all they did and said in trance. Here, this is not only the language but the SUBJECT MATTER itself which makes the task so phenomenally difficult. But I hope to have shown in the present book that there are solutions even to this problem.

13 See CLIFFORD (1983), DAMMANN (1991), DWYER (1977, 1982), EMERSON & POLLNER (1992), FELD (1987), JAUSS (1982), KÖGLER (1989/1990), KOHL (1998), MICHRINA & RICHARDS (1996), TEDLOCK (1986, 1987, 1993), TEDLOCK & MANNHEIM (1995).

APPENDIX D

Jarkko Niemi

Musical transcription of some verses from the great shamanic song [1]

The Great Shamanic Song of Paldan Lhamo. Music transcribed by Jarkko Niemi.

1 Cross-headed notes stand for the approximate beats of a pellet-rum *da ma ru*, played by the performer. (He also plays a jingle bell *dril bu*, not shown in this transription.)

The performer continues to play the *da ma ru* with this kind of rhythmic motive together with his singing, until he pauses the *da ma ru* (see the sixth line in the transcription).

The capital letters (A, B, C) refer to the division of the main motivic groups in the melody. (See also: Figure 2.)

Figure 1.

The melody is based on the anhemitonic pentatonic mode of the "La" type (La-do-re-mi-sol).

This mode corresponds to the Yü-mode of the ancient Chinese anhemitonic pentatonic system, basing both to theoretical working of the natural harmonic scale and to the theory of series of natural intervals of the fifths.

The possible connection of the mode in Lhamo's song to the Chinese Yü is not dealt here from the perspective of modal analysis.

However, closer examination of the modal functions of the tones reveal the straightforward correspondence of the main tones to the natural harmonics (see their ordinal numbers under the notes). The tones here that have only an approximate correspondence to the harmonic system (the lower g instead of the 5th harmonic f# in this tonality and the upper g instead of the 11th harmonic high g# in this tonality) appear to be almost exclusively passing tones. They do not appear in metrically emphasized places in the melody and hence their actual pitch levels are more likely to vary.

The actual pitch level of the vocal part in the recording (the lower a' → g#'-a') is connected to the approximate pitch level of the *da ma ru.*

Note that not according to the conventional system, the actual pitches sound an octave lower than what is written here.

Figure 2.

The descending overall modal shape of the melody. It is noteworthy that the descension is organized by the third anhemitonic degree (d), which can be hence considered as the dominant tone of the mode.

All in all, the transcription was organized in a panoptical layout, which may help the reader to discern the corresponding melodic events between the motivic groups (A, B and C). This analytical layout was made also with the aim to suggest something of the correspondence of the song text to the metrical structure of the melody.

Space not permitting here, let it be merely suggested that while the groups A and B are more exclamatory and melismatic by their nature, the more syllabic motivic group C suggests to a kind of metrical system, in which, at least a part is formed by a four-stress metric foot pattern (each foot containing mostly two syllables).

Jarkko Niemi (Ph.D.),
Department of Music Anthropology,
University of Tampere,
Finland

CITED LITERATURE

AHMED, M. (1990), *Village Oracles and Healing with Special Reference to Ladakh;* Oxford: Institute of Cultural and Social Anthropology, Unpublished Manuscript.

AHMED, M. (1996), *"We are Warp and Weft": Nomadic Pastoralism and the Tradition of Weaving in Rupshu (Eastern Ladakh);* Oxford: University Press.

AHMED, M. (1999), The salt trade: Rupshu's annual trek to Tso Kar; In: BEEK, M. van; BERTELSEN, K. B.; PEDERSEN, P. (Eds.), *Ladakh – Culture, History, and Development between Himalaya and Karakoram;* Aarhus: Aarhus University Press, 32-48.

AHMED-SHIRALI, K.; SAIN, N. (1994), Self-image and sexuality of Kinnauri polyandrous indigenous women; *Journal of the Indian Academy of Applied Psychology,* 20/1: 87-96.

ALTMANN, A.; RABOUAN, J.-B. (1999), Woll-Lust aus dem Himalaya; *Fokus,* 49: 129-138.

AL-WARDI, A. (1972), *Soziologie des Nomadentums: Studie über die iraqische Gesellschaft;* Neuwied: Luchterhand.

ANDERSON, J. N. (1973), Ecological anthropology and anthropological ecology; In: HONIGMANN, J. J. (Ed.), *Handbook of Social and Cultural Anthropology;* Chicago: Rand McNally, 179-239.

ANDRADE, R. d' (1995), Objectivity and militancy: A debate. Moral models in anthropology; *Current Anthropology,* 26/3: 399-408.

ANDRADE, R. d' (1997), *The Development of Cognitive Anthropology;* Cambridge: Cambridge University Press.

ASAD, T. (1979), Equality in nomadic social systems? Notes towards the dissolution of an anthropological category; In: L'ÉQUIPE ÉCOLOGIE ET ANTHROPOLOGIE DES SOCIÉTÉS PASTORALES (Ed.), *Pastoral Production and Society. Proceedings of the International Meeting on Nomadic Pastoralism, Paris 1-3 Dec. 1976;* Cambridge/Ma.: Cambridge University Press, 419-428.

BACON, E. E. (1954), Types of pastoral nomadism in Central and Southwest Asia; *Southwestern Journal of Anthropology,* 10/1: 44-68.

BARFIELD, T. J. (Ed.) (1993a), *The Nomadic Alternative;* Englewood Cliffs/NJ: Prentice Hall.

BARFIELD, T. J. (1993b), The yak breeders: High altitude pastoralism in Tibet; In: BARFIELD, T. J. (Ed.), *The Nomadic Alternative;* Englewood Cliffs/NJ: Prentice Hall, 180-201.

BAUMAN, Z. (1996), From pilgrim to tourist – or a short history of identity; In: HALL, S.; GAY, P. du (Eds.), *Questions of Cultural Identity;* London: Sage Publications, 18-36.

BEALL, C. M.; GOLDSTEIN, M. C. (1981), Tibetan fraternal polyandry: A test of sociobiological theory; *American Anthropologist,* 83/1: 5-12.

BERREMAN, G. D. (1960), *Himalayan Polyandry: A Comparative Study;* Berkeley: University of California Press.

BERREMAN, G. D. (1962), Pahari polyandry: A comparison; *American Anthropologist,* 64: 60-75.

BERREMAN, G. D. (1968), Pahari polyandry: A comparison; In: BOHANNAN, P.; MIDDLETON, J. (Eds.), *Marriage, Family and Residence;* New York: Natural History Press, 147-167.

BERREMAN, G. D. (1975), Himalayan polyandry and the domestic cycle; *American Ethnologist,* 77/2: 127-138.

BERREMAN, G. D. (1978), Ecology, demography and domestic strategies in the Western Himalayas; *Journal of Anthropological Research,* 34/3: 326-368.

BERREMAN, G. D. (1980), Polyandry: Exotic custom vs. analytic concept; *Journal of Comparative Family Studies,* 11/3: 377-383.

BHASIN, V. (1996), *Transhumants of Himalayas. Changpas of Ladakh, Gaddis of Himachal Pradesh and Bhutias of Sikkim;* Delhi: Kamla-Raj Enterprises.

BHATT, G. S. (1991), *Women and Polyandry in Rawain Jaunpar;* Jaipur/ New Delhi: Rawat Publications.

BHATT, G. S. (1997), Anthropology, women, and polyandry; *The Eastern Anthropolgist,* 50/3-4: 433-443.

BHATTACHARJI, C. (1994), Der Tsomoriri See. Zerstörung durch Zivilisationseinflüße; *Südasien,* 14/3: 32-33.

BHATTACHARJI, R. D. (1993), Back to Rupshu; *Himalayan Journal,* 50: 123-143.

BONNEMAIRE, J. (1976), Le yak domestique et son hybridation; *Ethnozootechnie,* 15: 46-77.

BOWLIN, J. R.; STROMBERG, P.G. (1997), Representation and reality in the study of culture; *American Anthropologist,* 99/1: 123-134.

BRAIDOTTI, R. (1999), Response to Dick Pels (Reply to the Article "Privileged Nomads: On the strangeness of intellectuals and the intellectuality of strangers" by Dick Pels.); *Theory Culture & Society,* 16/1: 87-93.

BRAUEN, M. (1980), Ladakh – Menschen und Kunst hinter dem Himalaya; *Du – Die Kunstzeitschrift,* 1: 16-64.

BRAUEN, M. (1982), Volksglauben; In: MÜLLER, C. C.; RAUNIG, W. (Eds.), *Der Weg zum Dach der Welt;* Innsbruck: Pinguin Verlag; Frankfurt/Main: Umschau-Verlag, 244-274.

CASSIDY, M. L.; LEE, G. R. (1989), A study of polyandry: A critique and synthesis; *Journal of Comparative Family Studies,* 20/1: 1-11.

CHANDRA, R. (1972), The notion of paternity among the polyandrous Kanet of Kinnaur, Himachal Pradesh; *Bulletin of the Anthropological Survey India,* 21/1 & 2: 80-87.

CHANDRA, R. (1973), Types and forms of marriage in a Kinnaur village; *Man in India,* 53/2: 176-187.

CHANDRA, R. (1987), Polyandry in the north-western Himalayas: Some changing trends; In: RAHA, M. K.; COOMAR, P. C. (Eds.), *Polyandry in India;* Delhi: Gyan Publishing House, 130-154.

CLARKE, G. E. (1988), China's reforms of Tibet, and their effects on pastoralism; *Kailash,* 14/1-2: 63-131.

CLARKE, G. E. (1992), Aspects of the social organisation of Tibetan pastoral communities; In: IHARA, S.; YAMAGUCHI, Z. (Eds.), *Tibetan Studies. Proceedings of the 5th Seminar of the International Association for Tibetan Studies, Narita 1989; Vol 2: Language, History and Culture;* Narita: Naritasan Shinshoji, 393-411.

CLARKE, G. E. (Ed.) (1998), *Development, Society and Environment in Tibet;* Wien: Verlag der Österreichischen Akademie der Wissenschaften.

CLIFFORD, J. (1983), Power and dialogue in ethnography: Marcel Griaule's initiation; In: STOCKING, G. W. (Ed.), *Observers Observed;* Madison: University of Wisconsin Press, 121-156.

CLIFFORD, J. (1986), The topological realism of Michel Leiris; *Sulfur,* 15: 4-125.

CLIFFORD, J.; MARCUS, G. E. (Eds.) (1986), *Writing Culture: The Poetics and Politics of Ethnography* (A School of American Research Advanced Seminar, Santa Fé, NM., April 1984); Berkeley/Los Angeles: University of California Press.

COX, T. (1987), Tibetan nomads before the Chinese invasion; *Himalayan Research Bulletin*, 7/2-3: 11-12.

COX, T. (1991), Pre-Chinese invasion political relations between Tibet's monastic state and Changtang (Byang thang) nomads: A response to Goldstein; *Himalayan Research Bulletin*, 11/1-3: 151-152.

CROOK, J. H. (1994), Explaining Tibetan polyandry: Socio-cultural, demographic and biological perspectives; In: CROOK, J. H.; OSMASTON, A. H. (Eds.), *Himalayan Buddhist Villages: Environment, Resources, Society and Religious Life in Zanskar, Ladakh*; Delhi: Motilal Banardidas, 735-786.

CROOK, J. H.; CROOK, S. J. (1988), Tibetan polyandry: Problems of adaptation and fitness; In: BETZIG, L.; BORGERHOFF MULDER, M.; TURKE, P. (Eds.), *Human Reproductive Behaviour – A Darwinian Perspective;* Cambridge: Cambridge University Press, 97-114.

CROOK, J. H.; SHAKYA, T. (1994), Six Families of Leh; In: CROOK, J. H.; OSMASTON, H. A. (Eds.), *Himalayan Buddhist Villages. Environment, Resources, Society and Religious Life in Zanskar, Ladakh*; Delhi: Motilal Banardidas, 701-734.

DAMMANN, R. (1991), *Die dialogische Praxis der Feldforschung; Der ethnographische Blick als Paradigma der Erkenntnisgewinnung;* Frankfurt am Main: Campus Verlag.

DAY, S. (1989), *Embodying Spirits: Village Oracles and Possession Ritual in Ladakh, North-India* (Doktorarbeit an der London School of Economics and Political Science); London: London University.

DAY, S. (1990), Ordering spirits: The initiation of village oracles in Ladakh; In: ICKE-SCHWALBE, L.; MEIER, G. (Eds.), *Wissenschaftsgeschichte und gegenwärtige Forschung in Nordwest-Indien* (Internationales Kolloqium 9. – 13.3.1987 in Herrnhut); Dresden: Staatliches Museum für Völkerkunde in Dresden, 206-222.

DENWOOD, P. (1980), Linguistic studies in Ladakh; In: ARIS, M.; AUNG SAN SUU KYI (Eds.), *Tibetan Studies in Honour of Hugh Richardson* (Proceedings of the International Seminar on Tibetan Studies, Oxford 1979); Warminster: Aris & Phillips, 93-96.

DENWOOD, P. (1995), The Tibetanisation of Ladakh: The linguistic evidence; In: OSMASTON, H.; DENWOOD, P. (Eds.), *Recent Research in Ladakh 4 and 5. Proceedings of the Fourth and Fifth International Colloquia on Ladakh;* Delhi: Motilal Banarsidass, 281-287.

DEVEREUX, G. (1973), *Angst und Methode in den Verhaltenswissenschaften;* München: Hanser-Verlag.

DOLLFUS, P. (1996), Maîtres du sol et dieux du territoire au Ladakh; *Etudes Rurales,* 143-144: 27-44.

DOLLFUS, P. (1999), Mountain deities among the nomadic communities of Kharnak (Eastern Ladakh); In: BEEK, M.; BERTELSEN, K. B.; PEDERSEN, P. (Eds.), *Ladakh – Culture, History, and Development between Himalaya and Karakoram;* Aarhus: Aarhus University Press, 92-118.

DOWNS, J. F.; EKVALL, R. B. (1965), Animals and social types in the exploitation of the Tibetan Plateau; In: LEEDS, A.; VAYDA, A. P. (Eds.), *Man, Culture and Animals. The Role of Animals in Human Ecological Adjustments;* Washington/DC: American Association for the Advancement of Science, 169-184.

DUNCAN, M. H. (1933), Eastern Tibetan nomads; *China Journal,* 19: 68-75.

DWYER, K. (1977), On the dialogic of fieldwork; *Dialectical Anthropology,* 2: 143-151.

DWYER, K. (1982), *Morroccan Dialogues; Anthropology in Question;* Baltimore: John Hopkins University Press.

DYSON-HUDSON, R.; DYSON-HUDSON, N. (1980), Nomadic pastoralism; *Annual Review of Anthropology,* 9: 15-61.

DYSON-HUDSON, R.; SMITH, E. A. (1978), Human territoriality: An ecological re-assessment; *American Anthropologist,* 80: 21-41.

EBBINGHOUSE, D.; WINSTEN, M. (1982a), Tibetan dZi beads, Pt. I; *Ornament,* 5/3: 19-27, 53.

EBBINGHOUSE, D.; WINSTEN, M. (1982b), Tibetan dZi beads, Pt. II; *Ornament,* 5/4: 36-39.

EGEROD, S. C. (1974), Sino-tibetan languages; *Encyclopedia Britannica,* 16: 796-806.

EKVALL, R. B. (1939), *Cultural Relations on the Kansu-Tibetan Border;* Chicago: University of Chicago Press.

EKVALL, R. B. (1961), The nomadic pattern of living among Tibetans as preparation for war; *American Anthropologist,* 63/3: 1250-1263.

EKVALL, R. B. (1964a), *Religious Observances in Tibet: Patterns and Function;* Chicago/London: The University of Chicago Press.

EKVALL, R. B. (1964b), Law and individual among Tibetan nomads; *American Anthropologist,* 66: 1110-11115.

EKVALL, R. B. (1964c), Peace and war among the Tibetan nomads; *American Anthropologist*, 66: 1119-1148.

EKVALL, R. B. (1968/1983), *Fields on the Hoof: Nexus of Tibetan Nomadic Pastoralism* (Case Studies in Cultural Anthropology), Prospect Heights/Ill: Waveland Press.

EKVALL, R. B. (1974), Tibetan nomadic pastoralists: Environments, personality and ethos; *Proceedings of the American Philosophical Society*, 118/6: 519-537.

EMERSON, R. M.; POLLNER, M. (1992), Difference and dialogue: Members' readings of ethnographic texts; In: HOLSTEIN, J. A.; MILLER, G. (Eds.), *Perspectives on Social Problem: A Research Annual;* Greenwich: JAI Press, 79-98.

EPSTEIN, H. (1974), Yak and chauri; *World Animal Review*, 9: 9-12.

EVERDING, K.-H. (1993), *Tibet; Lamaistische Klosterkulturen, nomadische Lebensformen und bäuerlicher Alltag auf dem Dach der Welt;* Köln: DuMont.

FAEGRE, T. (1979), *Tents: Architecture of the Nomads;* London: John Murray.

FAHLÉN, S. (2000), *A Woman With Several Husbands Is Like a Blooming Flower: The Decline of Polyandry as an Indicator of Social Change in Ladakh;* Uppsala: Uppsala University Press.

FEILBERG, C. G. (1944), *La Tente Noire: Contribution Ethnographique à l'Histoire Culturelle des Nomades;* Kopenhagen: Nationalmuseum.

FELD, S. (1987), Dialogic editing: Interpreting how Kaluli read sound and sentiment; *Cultural Anthropology*, 2: 190-210.

FERNANDEZ, R. L. (1981), Comments on Tibetan polyandry: A test of sociobiological theory; *American Anthropologist*, 83: 896-897.

FÖLLMI, O.; FÖLLMI, D. (1999), *Les Bergers de L'Hiver;* Pampelune: Editions de la Martinière.

FRAKE, C. O. (1962), Cultural ecology and ethnography; *American Anthropologist*, 64/1: 53-59.

FRANCKE, A. H. (1898), Die Respektssprache im Ladaker tibetischen Dialekt; *Zeitschrift der Deutsch-Morgenländischen Gesellschaft*, 52: 275-281.

FRANCKE, A. H. (1901/1979), *Ladakhi and Tibetan Grammar;* Delhi: Seema Publications.

FRANCKE, A. H. (1903), Kleine Beiträge zur Phonetik und Grammatik des Tibetischen; *Zeitschrift der Deutsch-Morgenländischen Gesellschaft*, 57: 285-298.

FRANCKE, A. H. (1904), A language map of West Tibet with notes; *The Journal of Asiatic Society of Bengal*, 7/Part I/4: 362-367.

FRANCKE, A. H. (1929/1979), *Ladakhi and Tibetan Grammar*; Berlin: de Gruyter / Delhi: Seema Publications.

FRANK, W. A. (1983), Protocol of a spontaneous paranormal healing in Ladakh; In: KANTOWSKY, D.; SANDER, R. (Eds.), *Recent Research on Ladakh*; München/Köln/London: Weltforum Verlag, 135-137.

GALATY, J. G.; JOHNSON, D. L. (1990), *The World of Pastoralism: Herding Systems in Comparative Perspective*; New York/London: The Guilford Press.

GALVIN, K. A. (1996), Nomadism; In: LEVINSON, D.; EMBER, M. (Eds.), *Encyclopedia of Cultural Anthropology*; New York: Henry Holt and Company, 859-863.

GELEK (1998), The Washu Serthar: A Nomadic Community of Eastern Tibet; In: CLARKE, G. E. (Ed.), *Development, Society, and Environment in Tibet*; Wien: Verlag der Österreichischen Akademie der Wissenschaften, 47-58.

GHOSH, A. (1999), Tibetan literary language and Ladakhi speech: A continuity; In: BEEK, M van; BERTELSEN, K. B.; PEDERSEN, P. (Eds.), *Ladakh – Culture, History, and Development Between Himalaya and Karakorum* (Recent Research on Ladakh; 8), Aarhus: Aarhus University Press, 125-130.

GINAT, J.; KHAZANOV, A. M. (Eds.) (1998), *Changing Nomads in a Changing World*; Portland/OR: Sussex Academic Press.

GOLDSCHMIDT, W. (1971), Independence as an element in pastoral social systems; *Anthropological Quarterly*, 44/3: 132-142

GOLDSCHMIDT, W. (1979), General model for pastoral social systems; In: L'EQUIPE ÉCOLOGIE ET ANTHROPOLOGIE DES SOCIÉTÉS PASTORALES (Ed.), *Pastoral Production and Society. Proceedings of the International Meeting on Nomadic Pastoralism, Paris, 1-3 Dec. 1976*; Cambridge/MA: Cambridge University Press, 15-27.

GOLDSTEIN, M. C. (1971), Stratification, polyandry and family structure in Central Tibet; *Southwestern Journal of Anthropology*, 27/1: 64-74.

GOLDSTEIN, M. C. (1976), Fraternal polyandry and fertility in a High Himalayan valley in Northwest Nepal; *Human Ecology*, 4/3: 223-233.

GOLDSTEIN, M. C. (1977), Population, social structure and strategic behavior: An essay of polyandry, fertility and change in Limi Panchayat; *Contributions to Nepalese Studies*, 4/2: 47-62.

GOLDSTEIN, M. C. (1978), Pahari and Tibetan polyandry revisited; *Ethnology*, 17/3: 325-337.

GOLDSTEIN, M. C. (1981), High-altitude Tibetan populations in the remote Himalayas: Social transformation and its demographic, economic and ecological consequences; *Mountain Research and Development*, 1/1: 5-18.

GOLDSTEIN, M. C. (1988), On the political organization of nomadic pastoralists in Western Tibet: A rejoinder to Cox; *The Himalayan Research Bulletin*, 8/3: 15-17.

GOLDSTEIN, M. C. (1992), Nomadic pastoralists and the traditional political economy – a rejoinder to Cox; *The Himalayan Research Bulletin*, 12/1-2: 54-62.

GOLDSTEIN, M. C.; BEALL, C.M. (1986), Studying nomads on the Tibetan plateau; *China Exchange News*, 14/4: 2-7.

GOLDSTEIN, M. C.; BEALL, C. M. (1987), Anthropological fieldwork in Tibet studying nomadic pastoralism on the Changtang; *The Himalayan Research Bulletin*, 7/1: 1-4.

GOLDSTEIN, M. C.; BEALL, C. M. (1989a), The remote world of Tibet's nomads; *National Geographic*, 176/6: 752-781.

GOLDSTEIN, M. C.; BEALL, C. M. (1989b), The impact of China's reform policy on the nomads of Western Tibet; *Asian Survey*, 29/6: 619-641.

GOLDSTEIN, M. C.; BEALL, C. M. (1990), *Nomads of Western Tibet: The Survival of a Way of Life*; Berkeley: University of California Press. (German: *Die Nomaden Westtibets: Der Überlebenskampf der tibetischen Hirtennomaden*; Nürnberg: DA-Verlag – Das Andere, 1991.)

GOLDSTEIN, M. C.; BEALL, C. M. (1991), China's birth control policy in the Tibet Autonomous Region; *Asian Survey*, 31/3: 285-303.

GOLDSTEIN, M. C.; BEALL, C. M. (1994), *The Changing World of Mongolia's Nomads*; Berkeley: University of California Press.

GOLDSTEIN, M. C.; BEALL, C. M.; CINCOTTA, R. P. (1990), Traditional nomadic pastoralism and ecological conservation on Tibet's northern plateau; *National Geographic Research*, 6/2: 139-156.

GOLDSTEIN, M. C.; KELLY, T. L. (1987), When brothers share a wife; *Natural History*, 3, 39-49.

GOLDSTEIN, M. C.; TSARONG, P. (1987), De-encapsulation and change in Ladakh; In: RAHA, M. K. (Ed.) *The Himalayan Heritage;* New Delhi: Gyan Publishing House, 443-455.

GOLOMB, E. (1995), Oracles in Ladakh: A personal experience; In: ADLER, L. L.; MUKHERJI, B. R. (Eds.), *Spirit Versus Scalpel. Traditional Healing and Modern Psychotherapy;* Westport/CT: Bergin & Garvey/Greenwood Publishing Group, 59-75.

GOTTOWIK, V. (1997), *Konstruktionen des Anderen. Clifford Geertz und die Krise der ethnographischen Repräsentation;* Berlin: Dietrich Reimer.

GRIERSON, G. A. (Ed.) (1909/1967a), *Linguistic Survey of India* (Vol. III, Part I); Delhi: Motilal Banarsidass.

GRIERSON, G. A. (1909/1967b), Ladakhi; In: GRIERSON, G. A. (Ed.), *Linguistic Survey of India* (Vol. III, Part I); Delhi: Motilal Banarsidass, 51-68.

GUILLET, D. W. (1983), Toward a cultural ecology of mountains: The Central Andes and the Himalayas compared; *Current Anthropology*, 24/5: 561-574.

GUPTA, J. (1985), Himalayan polygyandry: Bondage among women in Jaunsar Bawar; In: PATNAIK, U.; DINGWANEY, M. (Eds.), *Chains of Servitude. Bondage and Slavery in India;* Madras: Sangam Books, 258-281.

GUTSCHOW, K. (1997), A study of "wind disorder" or madness in Zangskar, India; In: DODIN, T.; RÄTHER, H. (Eds.), *Recent Research in Ladakh 7* (Ulmer Kulturanthropologische Schriften; 8); Ulm: Kulturanthropologische Schriften, 177-202.

HADDIX, K. A. (1998), *Marital Strategies in a Polyandrous Tibetan Community in Northwest Nepal;* Davis: University of California.

HALE, A. (1982), *Research on Tibeto-Burman Languages* (Trends in Linguistic, State-of-the-Art Report; 14); Berlin/New York/Amsterdam: Mouton Publishers.

HAMID, A. (1998), *Ladakhi – English – Urdu Dictionary with an English-Ladakhi Index;* Leh/Ladakh: Melong Publications.

HEBER, A. R.; HEBER, K. M. (1903/1976), *In Himalayan Tibet and Ladakh: A Description of Its Cheery Folk, Their Ways and Religion, of the Rigours of Climate and Beauties of the Country, Its Fauna and Flora*; Delhi: Ess Ess Publications.

HERMANNS, M. (1949), *Die Nomaden von Tibet; Die soziologischen und wirtschaftlichen Grundlagen der Hirtenkulturen in A mdo und von Innerasien. Ursprung und Entwicklung der Viehzucht*; Wien: Verlag Herold.

HERMANNS, M. (1953), Polyandrie in Tibet; *Anthropos*, 48: 637-641.

HERMANNS, M. (1956), *Mythen und Mysterien, Magie und Religion der Tibeter*; Köln: Pick Verlag.

HERMANNS, M. (1959), *Die Familie der A mdo-Tibeter*; Freiburg: Verlag Karl Alber.

HOFFMANN, T. (1998), Über die Nomaden; *Acta Ethnographica Hungarica*, 43/3-4: 399-444.

HOSHI, M.; TSERING, T. (1978), *Zanskar Vocabulary: A Tibetan Dialect Spoken in Kashmir* (Monumenta Serindica; 4); Tokyo: Institute for the Study of Languages and Culture of Asia and Africa.

HUC, R.-E. (1931), *Souvenirs of a Journey through Tartary, Tibet and China during the Years 1844, 1845 and 1846*; Beijing: Lazarist Press.

JAHODA, C. (1994), *Heiratsmuster ausgewählter Gesellschaften Tibetischer Kultur und Sprache, mit besonderer Berücksichtigung der Polyandrie und Prinz Peters Forschungsbeitrag* (Diplom-Arbeit); Wien: Universität Wien.

JÄSCHKE, H. A. (1865), Note on the pronunciation of the Tibetan language; *Journal of the Asiatic Society of Bengal*, 34: 91-100.

JÄSCHKE, H. A. (1881/1992), *Tibetan-English Dictionary. With Special Reference to the Prevailing Dialects to which is Added an English-Tibetan Vocabulary*; Delhi: Motilal Banarsidass Publishers.

JAUSS, H. R. (1982), Zum Problem des dialogischen Verstehens; In: LACHMANN, R. (Ed.), *Dialogizität*; München: Wilhelm Fink Verlag, 11-24.

JINA, P. S. (1990), Pasture ecology of Leh, Ladakh; In: ICKE-SCHWALBE, L.; MEIER, G. (Eds.) *Wissenschaftsgeschichte und gegenwärtige Forschungen in Nordwest-Indien*; Dresden: Staatliches Museum für Völkerkunde, 171-181.

JINA, P. S. (1995), *High Pasturelands of Ladakh Himalaya*; New Delhi: Indus Publishing Company.

JINA, P. S. (1999), The Chang Pa of the Ladakh Himalayas: Some observations of their economy and environment; *Nomadic Peoples*, (N. S.), 3/1: 94-105.

JONES, S. (1996), *Tibetan Nomads. Environment, Pastoral Economy and Material Culture*; London: Thames and Hudson.

KALWEIT, H. (1987), *Urheiler, Medizinleute und Schamanen*; München: Kösel.

KAPLANIAN, P. (1981), *Les Ladakhi du Cachemire. Montagnards du Tibet Occidental*; Paris: Hachette.

KAPLANIAN, P. (1984), Le chamanisme au Ladakh; *Nouvelle Revue Tibétaine*, 8: 55-63.

KAPLANIAN, P. (1985), Une séance de la Lhamo de Sabu; In: DENDALETCHE, C.; KAPLANIAN, P. (Eds.), *Ladakh, Himalaya Occidental: Ethnologie, Ecologie* (Acta Biologica Montana, 5); Pau: Centre Pyrénéen de Biologie et Anthropologie des Montagnes, 135-147.

KAPLANIAN, P. (1995), L'homme dans le monde surnaturel Ladakhi; In: OSMASTON, H.; DENWOD, P. (Eds.), *Recent Research on Ladakh 4 and 5, Proceedings of the Fourth and Fifth International Colloquium on Ladakh*; Delhi: Motilal Banarsidass Publishers, 101-108.

KAPLANIAN, P.; RAAB, G.; RABOUAN, J.-B. (1992), *Ladakh. De la Transe à l'Extase*; Paris: Editions Peuples du Monde.

KAWAKITA, J. (1966-1967), Structure of polyandry among the Bhotiyas in the Himalayas; *Japanese Journal of Ethnology*, 31: 11-27.

KHAZANOV, A. M. (1998), Pastoralists in the contemporary world: The problem of survival; In: GINAT, J.; KHAZANOV, A.M. (Eds.) *Changing Nomads in a Changing World*; Portland/OR: Sussex Academic Press, 7-23.

KÖGLER, H.-H. (1989/1990), Gadamer und die Ethnologie. Wege und Irrwege des Versuchs, ethnologisches Fremdverstehen als Dialog zu begreifen; *Anthroblatt – Fachzeitschrift der Universität Frankfurt*, 7: 16-23.

KOHL, K.-H. (1993), *Ethnologie – Die Wissenschaft vom kulturell Fremden: Eine Einführung*; München: C. H. Beck.

KOHL, K.-H. (1998), Against dialogue; *Paideuma*, 44: 51-58.

KOSHAL, S. (1976), *Ladakhi Phonetic Reader* (CIIL Phonetic Reader Series; 18); Mysore: Central Institute of Indian Languages.

KOSHAL, S. (1978), *Conflicting Phonological Patterns: A Study in the Adaptation of English Loan Words in Hindi;* Chandigarh: Bahri Publications.

KOSHAL, S. (1979), *Ladakhi Grammar;* Delhi: Motilal Banarsidass.

KOSHAL, S. (1982), *Conversational Ladakhi;* Delhi: Motilal Banarsidass.

KOSHAL, S. (1987), Honorific systems of the Ladakhi language; *Multilingua,* 6/2: 149-168.

KRAUSE, I. (1991), *Besessenheitsphänomene in Tibet und Ladakh;* Bonn: Philosophische Fakultät der Rheinischen Friedrich-Wilhelms-Universität (Unveröffentlichte Magisterarbeit).

KRESSING, F. (1997), Candidates for a theory of shamanism: A systematic survey of recent research results from Eurasia and Native America; *Shaman,* 5/2: 115-141.

KRESSING, F.; RÖSING, I. (2001a), Licht und Schatten über Ladakh: Subjektive Fremdheitserfahrung in einer Region des indischen Himalaya; Unveröffentlichter Materialbericht.

KRESSING, F.; RÖSING I. (2001b), Schamanenproliferation in Ladakh; Unveröffentlichter Materialbericht.

KUHN, A. S. (1988), *Heiler und ihre Patienten auf dem Dach der Welt. Ladakh aus Ethnomedizinischer Sicht* (Medizin in Entwicklungsländern, Bd. 25); Frankfurt: Peter Lang.

KUPER, A. (1994), Einheimische Ethnographie, politische Korrektheit und das Projekt einer kosmopolitischen Anthropologie; *Anthropos,* 89/4-6: 529-541.

KUSSMAUL, F. (1952/53), Frühe Nomadenkulturen in Innerasien. Einige Bemerkungen zu Hermanns: Die Nomaden von Tibet; *Tribus: Jahrbuch des Lindenmuseums Stuttgart,* 2/3: 305-360.

LAUFER, B. (1918), Origin of Tibetan writing; *Journal of the American Oriental Society,* 38: 34-46.

LE CALLOC'H, B. (1987), Un phénomène de géographie humaine: la polyandrie. Le Ladakh au temps d'Alexandre Csoma de Körös (1822-1826); *Acta Geographica,* 3: 2-19.

LEACH, E. R. (1955), Polyandry: Inheritance and definition of marriage with particular reference to Sinhalese customary law; *Man,* 55: 182-186.

LEVINE, N. E. (1977), *The Nyinba: Population and Social Structure in a Polyandrous Society* (Ph. D. diss.); University of Rochester/Department of Anthropology.

LEVINE, N. E. (1980), Nyinba polyandry and the allocation of paternity; *Journal of Comparative Family Studies*, 11/3: 283-298.

LEVINE, N. E. (1988), *The Dynamics of Polyandry. Kinship, Domesticity and Population on the Tibetan Border*; Chicago: University of Chicago Press.

LEVINE, N. E. (1998), From nomads to ranchers: Managing pasture among ethnic Tibetans in Sichuan; In: CLARKE, G. E. (Ed.), *Development, Society and Environment in Tibet*; Wien: Verlag der Österreichischen Akademie der Wissenschaften, 69-76.

LEVINE, N. E.; SANGREE, W. H. (1980), Conclusion: Asian and African systems of polyandry; *Journal of Comparative Family Studies*, 11/3: 385-410.

LEVINE, N. E.; SILK, J. B. (1997), Why polyandry fails – Sources of instability in polyandrous marriages; *Current Anthropology*, 38/3: 375-398.

LINDHOLM, C. (1995), The new Middle Eastern ethnography; *Journal of the Royal Anthropological Institute* (N. S.), 1: 1-16.

LINDHOLM, C. (1997), Logical and moral dilemmas of postmodernism; *Journal of the Royal Anthropological Institute*, 3/4: 747-760.

LIU, R. K. (1980), Identification: Tzi beads; *Ornament*, 4/4: 56-58.

MA LIHUA (1993), Shamanic belief among nomads in northern Tibet; In: RAMBLE, C.; BRAUEN, M. (Eds.), *Proceedings of the International Seminar on the Anthropology of Tibet and the Himalaya, Sep. 21-28, 1990 at the Ethnographic Museum of the University of Zürich*; Zürich: Völkerkundemuseum der Universität Zürich, 193-197.

MAFFESOLI, M. (1997), *Le Mystère de la Conjonction*; Paris: Fata Morgana.

MAJUMDAR, D. N. (1954-1955), Demographic structure in a polyandrous village; *Eastern Anthropologist*, 8: 161-172.

MAJUMDAR, D. N. (1960-1963), *Himalayan Polyandry: Structure, Function and Cultural Change – A Field Study of Jaunsar-Bawar*; Bombay: Asia Publishing House.

MAJUMDAR, D. N.; ANAND, S. K. (1956-1957), The functioning of school system in a polyandrous society – in Jaunsar Bawar, Dehra Dun District, U.P.; *Eastern Anthropologist*, 10: 182-210.

MANDERSCHEID, A. (1998), Life and economic patterns of nomads on the Eastern Tibet plateau: Brog Pa and Sa Ma Brog in Dzam Thang; In:

CLARKE, G. E. (Ed.) *Development, Society and Environment in Tibet;* Wien: Verlag der Österreichischen Akademie der Wissenschaften, 59-67.

MANDERSCHEID, A. (1999a), *Lebens- und Wirtschaftsformen von Nomaden im Osten des Tibetischen Hochlandes;* Berlin: Dietrich Reimer Verlag.

MANDERSCHEID, A. (1999b), Mobilität zwischen saisonalen Aktionsräumen: Eine Fallstudie zu nomadischen Gruppen im Osten des tibetischen Hochplateau; In: JANZEN, J. (Ed.), *Räumliche Mobilität und Existenzsicherung: Fred Scholz zum 60. Geburtstag;* Berlin: Dietrich Reimer Verlag, 132-151.

MANN, R. S. (1978a), Ladakhi polyandry reinterpreted; *Indian Anthropologist,* 8/1: 17-30.

MANN, R. S. (1978b), Eco-system and society in Ladakh; *Journal of Social Research,* 21: 60-76.

MANN, R. S. (1985), The Ladakhis: A cultural ecological perspective; In: VIDYARTHI, L. P.; JHA, M. (Eds.), *Ecology, Economy and Religion in Himalaya;* Delhi: Orient Publications, 3-16.

MANN, R. S. (1990), Culture and ecology in Ladakh; *Man in India,* 70/3: 217-277.

MASPERO, H. (1952), Langues de l'Asie du Sud-Est; In: MEILLET, A.; COHEN, M. (Eds.), *Les Langues du Monde;* Paris: Centre National de Recherches Scientifique, 525-644.

MERKLE, R. (2000), Nomadism: A socio-ecological mode of culture, *Proceedings of the Third International Congress on Yak, Lhasa, Tibetan Autonomous Region People's Republic of China, September 4-9, 2000;* Manuscript, 7 pages.

MICHRINA, B. P.; RICHARDS, C. A. (1996), *Person to Person. Fieldwork, Dialogue, and the Hermeneutic Method;* Albany: State University of New York Press.

MILLER, R. A. (1956), Segmental diachronic phonology of a Ladakh (Tibetan) dialect; *Zeitschrift der Deutsch-Morgenländischen Gesellschaft,* 106: 345-362.

MILLER, R. A. (1969), The Tibetan-Burman languages of South Asia; In: EMENEAU, M. B.; FERGUSON, C. A. (Eds.), *Linguistics in South Asia;* The Hague: Mouton, 431-449.

MILTON, K. (1997), Ecologies: Anthropology, culture and the environment; *International Social Science Journal,* 49/4: 477-495.

MORAN, E. F. (2000, 2. ed.), *Human Adaptability – An Introduction to Ecological Anthropology;* Boulder: Westview Press.

MÜLLER, F.-V. (1994), Ländliche Entwicklung in der Mongolei: Wandel der mobilen Tierhaltung durch Privatisierung; *Die Erde*, 124/4: 213-222.

NAMGYAL, C. (1995), Ladakhi language; In: OSMASTON, H.; TSERING, N. (Eds.), *Recent Research on Ladakh 6;* Delhi: Motilal Banarsidass, 351-568.

NANDI, S. B. (1977), Status of women in polyandrous society; *Man in India*, 57/2: 137-151.

NARKYID, N. (1983), The origin of the Tibetan script; In: STEINKELLNER, E.; TAUSCHER, H. (Eds.), *Contributions on Tibetan Language, History, and Culture: Proceedings of the Csoma de Körös Symposium held at Velm-Vienna, Austria, 13-19 September 1981, 1* (Wiener Studien zur Tibetologie und Buddhismuskunde; 10); Wien: Arbeitskreis für Tibetische und Buddhistische Studien, 207-220.

NEBESKY-WOJKOWITZ, R. (1952), Prehistoric beads from Tibet; *Man*, September: 131-132.

NEWELL, W. H. (1994), Review of: GOLDSTEIN, M. C.; BEALL, C. M., *Nomads of Western Tibet: The Survival of a Way of Life.* Berkeley: University of California Press, 1990; In: *Australian Journal of Chinese Affairs*, 32: 208-209.

NORBERG-HODGE, H.; PALDAN, G. T. (Eds.) (1991), *Ladakhi-English, English-Ladakhi Dictionary;* Delhi: Jayyed Press.

NORMAN, R. (1994), *Getting Started in Ladakhi;* Ladakh: Melong Publications.

PALDAN, T. (1990), The language and literature of Ladakh: An overview; In: RUSTOMJI, N. K.; RAMBLE, C. (Eds.), *Himalayan Environment and Culture: Analysis and Prospect;* Shimla: Indian Institute of Advanced Study, 256-262.

PANT, R.; RAWAT, D. S.; SAMAL, P. K. (1997), The changing scenario of polyandry culture: A case study in Central Himalaya; *Man in India*, 77/4: 345-353.

PARMAR, Y. S. (1975), *Polyandry in the Himalayas;* Delhi: Vikas Publishing House.

PATAI, R. (1951), Nomadism: Middle Eastern and Central Asian; *Southwestern Journal of Anthropology*, 7: 401-414.

PELS, D. (1999), Privileged nomads: On the strangeness of intellectuals and the intellectuality of strangers; *Theory Culture & Society*, 16/1: 63-86.

PETER PRINCE OF GREECE AND DENMARK, H. R. H. (1948), Tibetan, Toda, and Tiya polyandry, a report on field investigations; *Transactions of the New York Academy of Sciences*, 10/6: 210-225.

PETER PRINCE OF GREECE AND DENMARK, H. R. H. (1955a), Polyandry and the kinship group; *Man, 55:* 179-181.

PETER PRINCE OF GREECE AND DENMARK, H. R. H. (1955b), The polyandry of Tibet; In: *Actes du IV°. Congrès International des Sciences Anthropologiques et Ethnologiques, Vienne, 1952; Vol. 2,* 176-184.

PETER PRINCE OF GREECE AND DENMARK, H. R. H. (1963), *A Study of Polyandry;* The Hague: Mouton & Co.

PETER PRINCE OF GREECE AND DENMARK , H. R. H. (1965), The Tibetan family; In: NIMKOFF, M. F. (Ed.), *Comparative Family Systems;* Boston: Houghton Mifflin Co., 192-208.

PETER PRINCE OF GREECE AND DENMARK , H. R. H. (1974/75), Zor – A western Tibetan ceremonial goat sacrifice; *Folk,* 16/17: 309-312.

PETER PRINCE OF GREECE AND DENMARK, H. R. H. (1980), Comments on the social and cultural implications of variant systems of polyandrous alliances; *Journal of Comparative Family Studies,* 11/3: 371-375.

PETERS, L. G.; PRICE-WILLIAMS, D. (1980), Towards an experiential analysis of shamanism; *American Ethnologist,* 7/3: 397-418.

PHYLACTOU, M. (1989), *Household Organisation and Marriage in Ladakh, Indian Himalaya;* London: University of London – London School of Economics.

PITTARD, E. (1900), A propos de la polyandrie chez les Tibétains; *Bulletin de la Société Neuchâteloise de Géographie,* 12: 302-305.

PLANHOL, X. de (1979), Saturation et sécurité: Sur l'organisation des sociétés de pasteurs nomades; In: L'EQUIPE ÉCOLOGIE ET ANTHROPOLOGIE DES SOCIETES PASTORALES (Ed.), *Pastoral Production and Society. Proceedings of the International Meeting on Nomadic Pastoralism, Paris, 1-3 Dec. 1976;* Cambridge/MA: Cambridge University Press, 29-42.

POHLHAUSEN, H. (1954), *Das Wanderhirtentum und seine Vorstufen: Eine ethnographisch-geographische Studie zur Entwicklung der Eingeborenenwirtschaft;* Braunschweig: Limbach.

Polyandrie (1980), *Journal of Comparative Family Studies*, Special Issue, 11/3).

QUIERS, P.-J. (1998), Les nomades des déserts du Tibet; *Combat Nature*, 122: 50-52.

RABOUAN, J-B. (2001), *Ladakh: A Journey to the Kingdom of Pashmina*; France: Cheminements Editions.

RAHA, M. K. (1991), Polyandry in India: Retrospect and Prospect; *Man in India*, 71/1: 163-181.

RAHA, M. K.; COOMAR, P. C. (1987), Polyandry in a High Himalayan society: Persistence and change; In: RAHA, M. K.; COOMAR, P. C. (Eds.), *Polyandry in India*; Delhi: Gyan Publishing House, 62-129.

RÄTHER, H.; RÖSING, I. (2001), Die Rolle der ladakhischen Rinpoches; Unveröffentlichter Kurzbericht.

REYNA, S. (1994), Literary anthropology and the case against science; *Man* (N. S.), 29: 55-582.

RIZVI, B. R. (1987), Class formation and conflict in a polyandrous village of Himachal Pradesh; In: RAHA, M. K. (Ed.), *The Himalayan Heritage*; New Delhi: Gyan Publishing House, 413-426.

RIZVI, J. (1996), *Ladakh: Crossroads of High Asia*; Delhi: Oxford University Press.

RIZVI, J. (1999), The trade in Pashm and its impact on Ladakh's history; In: BEEK, M.; BERTELSEN, K.B.; PEDERSEN, P. (Eds.), *Ladakh – Culture, History, and Development between Himalaya and Karakoram*; Aarhus: Aarhus University Press, 317-338.

ROERICH, G. N. de (1931), Modern Tibetan phonetic with special reference to the dialect of Central Tibet; *Journal of the Royal Asiatic Society of Bengal*, 27/2: 285-312.

RÖSING, I. (1988/1995), *Dreifaltigkeit und Orte der Kraft: Die Weiße Heilung. Nächtliche Heilungsrituale in den Hochanden Boliviens*; Mundo Ankari Band 2, Buch I und Buch II; Nördlingen: Greno, 1. Aufl. 1988/Frankfurt: Zweitausendeins; 3. Aufl. 1995.

RÖSING, I. (1997), The hidden psychology of ritual healing: A bridge to the transcultural transfer of traditional healing methods with special references to Tibetan medicine; In: ASCHOFF, J.; RÖSING, I. (Eds.), *Tibetan Medicine. "East meets West – West meets East"*; Proceedings of the International Symposium, University of Ulm/Germany, 19/20th July 1996; Ulm: Fabri Verlag, 111-124.

RÖSING, I. (2001), *Religion, Ritual und Alltag in den Anden; Die zehn Geschlechter von Amarete, Bolivien; Zweiter* ANKARI-*Zyklus;* MUNDO ANKARI Band 6; Berlin: Reimer Verlag.

RÖSING, I. (2002a), Frakturen der Liebe; Rituelle Heilungen – ein transkultureller Vergleich zwischen den Schamanen im Himalaya und den Medizinmännern in den Anden; Manuskript.

RÖSING, I. (2002b), Seelenverlust – Krankheitskonzepte und Heilungsanlaß in fremden Kulturen und bei uns; Manuskript.

SAKSENA, R. N. (1962), *Social Economy of a Polyandrous People;* Bombay: Asia Publishing House.

SALZMAN, P. C. (1979), Inequality and oppression in nomadic society; In: L'EQUIPE ÉCOLOGIE ET ANTHROPOLOGIE DES SOCIÉTÉS PASTORALES *(Ed.), Pastoral Production and Society. Proceedings of the International Meeting on Nomadic Pastoralism, Paris 1-3, Dez. 1976;* Cambridge/MA: Cambridge University Press, 429-446.

SALZMAN, P. C. (1980), Is „nomadism" a useful concept? *Nomadic Peoples,* 6: 1-7.

SAMAL, P. K.; CHAUHAN, M. S.; FERNANDO, R. (1996), The functioning and eco-cultural significance of marriage types among the Jaunsaries in Central Himalaya; *Man in India,* 76/3: 199-214.

SAMAL, P. K.; FARBER, C.; FAROOQUEE, N. A. et al. (1996), Polyandry in a Central Himalayan community: An eco-cultural analysis; *Man in India,* 76/1: 51-65.

SANDBERG, G. (1894/1999), *Handbook of Colloquial Tibetan. A Practical Guide to the Language of Central Tibet;* New Delhi: Asian Educational Services.

SARKAR, N. (1973), The so-called polyandry among the Gallongs; *Man in India,* 53/2: 128-134.

SCHALLER, G. B. (1993), Tibet's remote Chang Tang; *National Geographic,* 184: 62-87.

SCHALLER, G. B. (1997), *Tibet's Hidden Wilderness: Wildlife and Nomads of the Chang Tang Reserve;* New York: Harry N. Abrams Inc. Publishers.

SCHENK, A. (1990), Tranceverhalten der Orakelheiler in Ladakh; In: ICKE-SCHWALBE, L.; MEIER, G. (Eds.), *Wissenschaftsgeschichte und gegenwärtige Forschung in Nordwest-Indien* (Internationales Kolloquium 9. – 13.3.1987 in Herrnhut); Dresden: Staatliches Museum für Völkerkunde in Dresden, 234-243.

SCHENK, A. (1993), Inducing trance: On the training of Ladakhi oracle healers; In: RAMBLE, C.; BRAUEN, M. (Eds.), *Proceedings of the International Seminar on the Anthropology of Tibet and the Himalaya, September 21-28, 1990 at the Ethnographic Museum of the University of Zürich* (Ethnologische Schriften, ESZ 12); Zürich: Völkerkundemuseum der Universität Zürich, 331-342.

SCHENK, A. (1994), *Schamanen auf dem Dach der Welt: Trance, Heilung und Initiation in Kleintibet;* Graz: Akademische Druck- und Verlagsanstalt.

SCHENK, A. (1996), Trance als Therapie: Die Bewußtseinstransformation bei den Schamanen Kleintibets; In: QUEKELBERGHE, R. van, EIGNER, D. (Eds.), *Trance, Besessenheit, Therapie – Heilrituale und Psychotherapie* (Jahrbuch für Transkulturelle Medizin und Psychotherapie 1994); Berlin: VWB – Verlag für Wissenschaft und Bildung.

SCHLENKER, H. (1975/1983), *Tibeter (Zentralasien, Ladakh): Ausbildung einer Orakelpriesterin;* Göttingen: Institut für den Wissenschaftlichen Film.

SCHOLZ, F. (Ed.) (1991), *Nomaden: Mobile Tierhaltung. Zur gegenwärtigen Lage von Nomaden und zu den Problemen und Chancen mobiler Tierhaltung;* Berlin: Das Arabische Buch.

SCHOLZ, F. (1992), *Nomadismus;* Berlin: Das Arabische Buch.

SCHOLZ, F. (1994), Nomadismus – Mobile Tierhaltung. Formen, Niedergang und Perspektiven einer traditionsreichen Lebens- und Wirtschaftsweise; *Geographische Rundschau*, 2/46: 72-78.

SCHOLZ, F. (1995), *Nomadismus. Theorie und Wandel einer soziologischen Kulturweise* (Erdkundliches Wissen, 118); Stuttgart: Steiner Verlag.

SCHULER, S. (1978), Notes on marriage and the status of women in Baragaon; *Kailash*, 6/2: 141-152.

SCHULER, S. R. (1983), *Fraternal Polyandry and Single Women: A Study of Marriage, Social Stratification and Property in Chumik, a Tibetan Society of the Nepalese Himalaya;* Cambridge: Harvard University Press.

SCHULER, S. R. (1987), *The Other Side of Polyandry: Property, Stratification, and Nonmarriage in the Nepal Himalayas* (Women in Cross-Cultural Perspective Series); Boulder: Westview Press.

SHAFER, R. (1957), *Bibliography of Sino-Tibetan Languages, Part I*; Wiesbaden: Otto Harrassowitz Verlag.

SHAFER, R. (1963), *Bibliography of Sino-Tibetan Languages, Part II*; Wiesbaden: Otto Harrassowitz Verlag.

SHAFER, R. (1966-1973), *Introduction to Sino-Tibetan*; Wiesbaden: Otto Harrassowitz Verlag.

SHARMA, D. D. (1987), Kinship organization of the polyandrous Lahulas; In: RAHA, M. K. (Ed.), *The Himalayan Heritage*; Delhi: Gyan Publishing House, 387-412.

SISHAUDHIA, V. K. (1987), Polyandry in a Cis-Himalayan community; In: RAHA, M. K.; COOMAR, P. C. (Eds.), *Polyandry in India*; Delhi: Gyan Publishing House, 220-232.

SMITH, E. A. (1998), Is Tibetan polyandry adaptive? Methodological and metatheoretical analyses; *Human Nature*, 9/3: 225-261.

SPIRO, M. E. (1996), Postmodernism, anthropology, subjectivity, and science: A modernist critique; *Comparative Studies in Society and History*, 38/4: 759-780.

SPOONER, B. (1971), Towards an generative model of nomadism; *Anthropological Quarterly*, 44/3: 198-210.

SPOONER, B. (1973), *The Cultural Ecology of Pastoral Nomads*; Reading/Mass.: Addison Wesley Publisher.

STEIN, R. A. (1972), *Tibetan Civilization*; Stanford: Stanford University Press.

STEWARD, J. (1968), Cultural ecology; In: SILLS, D.L. (Ed.), *International Encyclopedia of the Social Sciences, 4*; New York: The Macmillan Company & The Free Press, 337-344.

STRECKER, I. (1990), Forschung und Freundschaft; In: KOHL, K.-H.; MUSZINSKI, H.; STRECKER, I. (Eds.), *Die Vielfalt der Kultur. Ethnologische Aspekte von Verwandtschaft, Kunst und Weltauffassung*; Berlin: Dietrich Reimer Verlag, 606-613.

STULPNAGEL, C. R. (1955), Polyandry in the Himalayas; *The Indian Antiquary*, 7: 132-135.

TEDLOCK, D. (1986), The analogical tradition and the emergence of a dialogical anthropology; *Journal of Anthropological Research*, 43/3: 387-400.

TEDLOCK, D. (1987), Questions concerning dialogical anthropology; *Journal of Anthropological Research*, 43/4: 325-337.

TEDLOCK, D. (1993), Fragen zur dialogischen Anthropologie; In: BERG, E.; FUCHS, M. (Eds.), *Kultur, soziale Praxis, Text. Die Krise der ethnographischen Repräsentation;* Frankfurt: Suhrkamp Verlag, 269-287.

TEDLOCK, D.; MANNHEIM. B. (Eds.) (1995*), The Dialogic Emergence of Culture;* Champaign/Urbana: University of Illinois Press.

TOPGYAL, T.; TOPGYAL, T. et al. (1998), The lifestyle of nomads; *The Tibet Journal,* 23/3: 34-49.

TOWNSEND, J. B. (1997), Shamanism; In: GLAZIER, S. D. (Ed.), *Anthropology of Religion. A Handbook;* Westport/CT: Greenwood Press, 429-469.

TREVITHICK, A. (1997), On a panhuman preference for monandry: Is polyandry an exception? *Journal of Comparative Family Studies,* 28/3: 154-181.

TSEWANG, L. (1985), Problem of Ladakhi language and its solution; In: PALJOR, T.; TRIPATHI, S. R. S.; DORJE, S. S. (Eds.), *Ladakh Men Bauddh Vidyaun Ka Atihasik Evam Darshanik Sandarbh* (Ladakh-Prabha; 3); Leh, Ladakh: Kendriya Bauddha Vidya Sansthan, 37-42.

UJFALVY, C. E. (1884), Über das Vorkommen der Polyandrie bei den Völkerschaften im westlichen Himalaja; *Deutsche Rundschau für Geographie und Statistik,* 6: 14-20.

VAJDA, L. (1968), *Untersuchungen zur Geschichte der Hirtenkulturen* (Veröffentlichungen des Osteuropa-Institutes München, 31); Wiesbaden: Otto Harrassowitz.

VOLF, P. (1994), *Seger åt Gudarna. Rituell Bestatthet hos Ladakhier* (Victory to the Gods. Ritual Possession among Ladakhis); Stockholm: Allmqvist & Wiksell International.

YAMADA, T. (1991/1993), Spirit possession and shamanism among the Ladakhi in Tibet; In: HOPPAL, M.; HOWARD, K. D. (Eds.), *Shamans and Cultures. Regional Aspects of Shamanism;* Budapest: Akadémiai Kiadó, 214-222.

ZEISLER, B. (1999), Borrowed language: Passive assimilation or active incorporation of modern concepts; In: BEEK, M. van; BERTELSEN, K. B.; PEDERSEN, P. (Eds.), *Ladakh – Culture, History, and Development Between Himalaya and Karakoram* (Recent Research on Ladakh; 8); Aarhus: Aarhus University Press, 389-401.